the *painted* pink dress

A Daughter's Story of Family, Betrayal, and Her Search for the Truth

Minu Cash

SANDRA JONAS
PUBLISHING

Sandra Jonas Publishing House
PO Box 20892
Boulder, CO 80308
sandrajonaspublishing.com

Printed in the United States of America
29 28 27 26 25 24   1 2 3 4 5 6 7 8 9

Book and cover design by Sandra Jonas

Publisher's Cataloging-in-Publication Data
Names: Cash, Minu, 1958–, author.
Title: The Painted Pink Dress : A Daughter's Story of Family, Betrayal, and Her
    Search for the Truth / Minu Cash.
Description: Boulder, CO : Sandra Jonas Publishing, 2024.
Identifiers: LCCN 2024937800 | ISBN 9781954861183 (hardcover) | ISBN
    9781954861190 (paperback)
Subjects: LCSH: Cash, Minu, 1958– | Hispanic American women — Biography.
    | Mexican American families — Arizona. | Identity (Psychology). |
    Avondale (Ariz.) — Biography. | LCGFT: Autobiographies. | BISAC:
    BIOGRAPHY & AUTOBIOGRAPHY / Personal Memoirs.
Classification: E184.M5 .C374 | DDC 305.4886
LC record available at http://lccn.loc.gov/2024937800

Photography credits: page 249, Chad Ufheil; all other photographs are from the
author's private collection.

*To Jeremy, my son, though you are no longer
with us, your presence is felt in every word of this book.
Your love for reading and writing continues to guide me,
and I know you are watching over me and beaming.*

*To Jacqueline, my beautiful daughter, your wisdom and
support have been my anchor through every twist and turn.
You have brought light and warmth to my darkest days,
and I am endlessly grateful for your love.*

*To Ernesto Jr., my son I did not give birth to,
but recognize as my own. Thank you for always
being there for me. I am proud of you and
the great man you have become.*

My mother and father, Mariá and Julio Becerra, 1948.

Left to right: my sisters Irma and Dolores, me, my sister Esméralda,
and my brother Julio. 1962.

Author's Note

This is a story told through my eyes and heart. I have summarized years into sentences, compressed or omitted relationships and interactions, and condensed details. Names and identifying details for some individuals have been changed to protect their privacy.

While this memoir offers an intimate glimpse into my life, it is but one perspective. Each life is like an article of clothing—perhaps, in this instance, a pink dress—woven from countless threads of experience, emotion, and memory.

It is my hope that readers will approach these pages with openness and understanding, recognizing the beauty found in the uniqueness of everyone's journey.

PART ONE

My third birthday party. July 16, 1961.
Back row, left to right: my father (Julio Sr.), me, and my brother Julio.
Front row, left to right: my sisters Irma, Dolores, and Esméralda.

1

he day was hot, so hot that even the trees were looking for shade. The swamp cooler in our small one-story home blew warm air into the living room.

Cashion was a decent Arizona neighborhood then. Green, yellow, and brown houses with manicured dirt lawns lined the streets. Primarily white folks made up the quiet area, keeping to themselves on the weekdays and washing their shiny Chevy Corvairs in their driveways on the weekends. We were one of only a few Mexican families living there.

My father appeared from the kitchen. "The cake will be ready soon," he said, tapping his foot to the rhythm of the 1950s Spanish music playing on the radio. "We have to celebrate my *güera*."

That was Apá's nickname for me, Spanish slang for "pale-skinned" or "white girl." It always made me feel special.

Julio, my four-year-old brother, moaned. "Why does Minu get a cake for her birthday?" He, my three older sisters, and I crowded around our small square table, finishing my birthday meal: red chile, rice, beans, and my favorite treat, *nopalitos*.

"Because she's spoiled, that's why," Esméralda said, rolling her eyes. "Admit it. She's the favorite."

Dolores laughed. Irma, the oldest of my siblings and eleven at the time, ignored the banter and cleared the table for dessert, always the dutiful child.

"None of that," Amá said, leaning across the table to gather the rest of the plates. She straightened back up and cupped her round belly in her tight orange dress. She was pregnant with David then. "She gets a cake because she turns three years old today."

Julio crossed his arms over his chest. "I didn't get no cake when I turned three."

"I didn't either," Esméralda said. "This is her third birthday party, and the rest of us haven't had any."

"*Callate, cabrónes*," Apá barked from the kitchen. "Shut up, you little shits."

They both kept quiet. We all knew not to challenge Apá.

But maybe I *was* spoiled. Amá never gave my brother and sisters presents, but that day, she had given me a polka-dot red dress with a sewn-in black belt that she bought from a local department store. Most of our clothes came from church clothing drives or thrift stores, or Amá sewed them from scratch. In front of the mirror earlier that day, I spun like a ballet dancer with my arms arched above my head, letting the dress twirl around me.

Just then, Apá appeared from the kitchen with a round cake smothered in silvery frosting. His broad white smile gleamed behind three flickering candles. "*Estas son las mañanitas . . .*" he sang in his low, harmonious voice.

Amá chimed in, and my siblings mumbled along, their cheeks resting on their palms, unimpressed. "*Feliz cumpleaños*, Minu."

I stood on the chair, laughing and clapping. Apá placed the cake on the table before me—I could already taste the sweet, rich bite on my tongue.

From across the room, Amá took a photo with a bulky Polaroid camera. Her face lit up with a beaming smile, the kind that crinkled her eyes and the sides of her nose.

I filled my lungs with air and blew out each candle, watching the smoke drift into the air. My siblings applauded, knowing they'd be gobbling down cake soon.

"That's my Güera," Apá said.

2

*P*ots and pans rustled in the kitchen, and a beam of light snuck through the crack of the door. I rubbed the sleep from my eyes and wiggled my toes to force myself awake. The bedroom was stuffy and smelled like dirty socks.

Apá had turned the swamp cooler off the night before, complaining again about the electric bill, so we were forced to swelter in the August heat. Through the window, the stars in the night sky shone brightly. As I sat up in my cot, sweat trickled down my back, soaking through my shirt. My parents' unmade bed in the corner was empty. They had already started their day.

"*Vamos, hermano,*" I whispered to Julio, sleeping in his bed across the room. "Time to wake up." He grumbled but didn't budge.

I walked into the kitchen with squinted eyes. Amá hummed as she stood over the steamy stove frying tortillas, meat, and chilies, my favorite smell. She wore khaki pants and a faded cream long sleeve shirt—her usual attire when working the fields.

"Wake up your brother and sisters, *mija,*" she said, keeping her attention on the pan.

I was always the first one up, so now that I was three, it was my job to rally my siblings. But I didn't move, mesmerized by Amá's cooking. Apá leaned against the kitchen counter in his leather-soled boots and cowboy hat tipped to the side, puffing on his first cigarette of the day.

"You heard your ma, Güera. Get 'em up. We're leaving in fifteen."

Another Saturday in the Becerra household, and it was time to go to work, because that's what little girls and boys did.

My siblings and I rode in the bed of Apá's rusted blue Chevy pickup, our bodies swaying with the bumps in the road. The moon illuminated the silhouettes of the cacti around us. Dolores, Esméralda, and Julio rested their heads on their arms and tried to sleep. In the front cab, Apá and Amá stared straight ahead.

I peeked over the truck bed to see the large wooden sign. "Anderson Clayton Cotton Farm," Irma told me when I'd asked her once what it said. Stretching ahead for miles were rows of long, frothy cotton plants. It looked as if a cloud had fallen from the sky and shattered across the cracked desert dirt.

As the sun appeared over the horizon, Apá parked the truck next to a giant barn that stored the plucked cotton. The foreman raised his hand in a friendly wave and approached us with a stack of long, dingy burlap sacks. "Good morning, *señor*." He tipped his cowboy hat. "Nice to see you bright and early. Looks like you brought the entire crew with you."

Apá shook his hand. "*Sí*. We'll be here picking all day."

With heavy eyelids, my siblings and I leaped over the side of the truck, each landing with a loud thump. Dozens of other Mexican workers began arriving at the farm to join us.

The foreman handed out the sacks. "Great. I'll let the boss know. He'll be happy to hear the cotton is gettin' off them fields. Payment is same as usual. A dollar twenty-five a pound."

"You hear that, *hijos*?" Apá said. "A dollar and a quarter for every pound of cotton. We're gonna pick every boll out there today. One hundred pounds filled by noon. I can feel it."

Julio moaned. "A hundred pounds?"

Esméralda muttered a swear word under her breath.

"You heard me. *¡Vamonos!*" Apá's voice soared across the rows as if to wake up the cotton.

Irma and Dolores strolled out to the field without a grumble or a complaint. They'd both been doing this since they were four or five and were used to it. Esméralda and Julio joined them, all of them spreading out evenly like a chain gang.

I tagged behind Amá through the field. She stopped when patches of blossoming puffs surrounded us, and I held out the long sack as she tossed in the white bolls. Amá taught me that the cotton was ripe for picking when the branches grew long and the fluffy white fibers began to bud out.

I reached out to grab one of the bolls.

"No, no, you're still too young to pick, *mija*," Amá said. "*No te apuras.* Your day will come."

We walked row after row, and she picked boll after boll after boll. When Amá wasn't looking, I pulled a handful of cotton out of the sack and wadded it into a ball. Like carrying a soft baby rabbit.

Late July through November in the Southwest were typically the ideal months for cotton harvesting. Most every day, or every chance we had—or Apá had—we'd spend in the fields plucking away. One tortuous minute after another. November through February, we would freeze our rears off picking green onions and carrots, and then March through June, we'd pick yellow onions. Apá told us we had no choice but to *sigue recogiendo*, keep pickin', if we wanted food for dinner and lights in the house.

To make the time go faster, my siblings and I would search for valuable rocks in the field, hoping one day we'd find a piece of gold and never have to pick another cotton boll again. We chased tumbleweeds through the fields and tried to catch lizards and scorpions. We'd torment the scorpions by poking them with sticks, their red pincers snapping in the air during battle. We were too young and dumb to fear them, but lucky enough not to get stung.

Sometimes fights would break out. We'd throw clumps of dirt and dust at one another until Apá screamed at us from across the field. "*¡Deja de ser estúpido y vuelve al trabajo!*" (Stop being stupid and get back to work!)

That Saturday with Amá, we trudged through the field as the scorching sun rose in the sky. When it hung directly overheard, the foreman rang a large gold bell.

"*Hora de comer*!" Amá yelled. Lunchtime. The workers dropped their bags and raced in from the fields for a break. My siblings and I camped out under a mimosa tree, eating the chorizo burritos Amá had made earlier that morning. We scarfed down each bite with hardly a chew, and as parched as the Sonoran Desert itself, we washed the food down with warm flat water from the farm spigot.

"Eat up and get back out there," Apá said with a stern face. "I don't see three hundred pounds of cotton plucked yet."

After a twenty-minute break and our bellies were full, we returned to the fields. By this time, I was so tired I could barely move. I hung onto the half-filled sack as Amá dragged it across the dirt. She picked more cotton and dumped it into the sack, repeating the motion over and over and over. The afternoon crawled by like a desert tortoise, sluggish and dawdling. The temperature roasted our skin and overheated our insides, while the dry dirt sizzled around us. Julio and I took turns in the smelly outhouse. It was hotter than an oven in the cramped box, but we'd do anything to escape the sun.

Just when I thought I'd fall over, Apá called us in from the fields. Though suffering from cracked lips and dehydration, we gathered the last bit of energy we had and ran to the warehouse. The relief of surviving yet another eleven-hour day in the fields made us forget the pain.

The foreman emptied the cotton sacks one by one into a large metal bin in the warehouse. Apá's eyes narrowed as the scale's red marker increased with each dump.

"Y'all done good. Sixty-two pounds for the day," the foreman said, handing Apá a wad of cash.

Apá tightened his mouth. "Well, that ain't no one hundred pounds, but it'll do for today."

As we were about to pile into the truck to head home, Julio and I gave one another a mischievous look. We knew what the other person was thinking.

"Can we today, mister?" we both asked the foreman. "Can we? Can we? Can we?'

He chuckled. "You better ask your pop."

Julio and I looked at Apá. "Please? Please, oh please."

Apá rolled his eyes. "Fine, but make it quick."

Julio and I both squealed with excitement. I followed my brother as he climbed the ladder to a wooden board that overlooked a bin of cotton. Julio leapt into the air, belly flopping on the pile of white fluff. I jumped in after him, the soft, cushiony fuzz catching me. We rolled around, laughing and laughing.

"I wish I could sleep here every night," I said. "This is way better than my bed at home." I turned onto my back and made a snow angel—or a *cotton* angel.

"A million times better! Who needs a swimming pool when you have a giant bucket of cotton!" Julio lay still for a moment, his hands behind his head, staring at the warehouse ceiling. Pieces of the blue sky showed through the boarded roof.

"Do you think clouds feel like this?" I asked.

"Yes, Güera, I bet they do!"

Apá and Amá left the field with a day's pay, while we kids left with swollen fingers and thick dirt caked on our faces. Under all that dirt, my siblings had shiny bronzed skin, perfectly kissed by the sun, but I was as pink as a ham. My sisters teased me on the drive back. "*Ella está quemada.*" (She's burned.)

The next day, we'd have to go back. By Monday, I wouldn't be able to touch my skin. It helped when Irma put me in the bathtub and filled it with cool water. But nothing kept the blisters away.

I stood out next to my family. They all had stocky builds, round faces, and tan skin to match their dark hair. They looked the same—like Mexicans. I was bony and scrawny and had a square face with high cheekbones, but it was my fair skin and curly light brown hair that turned people's heads. When family members or neighbors asked where on earth I had come from, Amá had a ready response: "She looks like her grandmother."

Amá's mother, Abuelita Ángela, had the revered Spaniard gene. Her brown skin was lighter, but it still wasn't as light as mine. On the bedroom wall was an old black-and-white photograph of Abuelita standing in front of their farm in Mexico. Her squinty face, squared jawline, thin hair, and crooked teeth stared back at me.

"But, Amá, why is my skin whiter than everyone else's?" I would ask, holding out my arms to show her my skin as if she'd forgotten. "Why don't I look like my sisters? Why don't they look like Abuelita? Why am I different?"

"Minu, I've told you this so many times," she'd snap. "You get your looks from *tu abuelita*. Now quit asking."

3

Through the dusty living room window, I watched Amá hang the damp laundry on the crooked clothesline. Her small eyes squinted from the sun, and her long hair blew in the desert breeze. Ruby red lipstick lined her lips, and she wore her all-white uniform from her job at the local laundromat.

How did she do laundry all day at work, and then come home and do *more*? But Amá never complained. When she wasn't working the fields or at the laundromat, she worked at the local tortilla factory part-time, occasionally bringing home packages of leftover tortillas we used for our taco dinners. She'd never let us go hungry.

On the other hand, my father, Julio Sr., never hung on to a job. He went from working odd jobs on irrigations farms to searching near and far for metal to scrap at the local dump. Once, he disappeared for weeks claiming he'd been looking for pay in California. Whenever he started a new job, it wouldn't be long before he'd come home announcing they had fired him. He would storm into the house and pace through the kitchen, his chest puffed out like he was getting ready for a fight.

"I didn't want to work for those *cabrónes* anyway." He'd slam his fist on the counter.

Standing in the corner, Amá would purse her lips, cross her arms, and shake her head. As frustrated as she was by Apá's inability to keep a job, she stayed clear of him when he released his anger.

According to my mother, she grew up in a small adobe house in San Guillermo, Chihuahua, Mexico. Her father, Abuelito Rosalio, was a cowboy who served in the Mexican Civil War at seventeen years old. During the war, he joined forces with the Mexican Revolutionary General Francisco "Pancho" Villa. Villa and his group of Mexican civilians fought to combat the Mexican President Porfirio Díaz and commander of the División del Norte, in the Constitutionalist Army. After realizing Pancho's banditry and intentions weren't for the people of Mexico, Abuelito Rosalio abandoned Pancho's troops. He stowed away his guns and stabled his horses to settle down with Abuelita Ángela.

Together they raised chickens, pigs, three sons, and a daughter—the lovely and free-spirited Mariá, my mother. When the farm grew too big for my grandparents to manage on their own, the four children left school to help. Amá dropped out just before the sixth grade.

As she grew older and entered her late teenage years, Amá spent most of her time dancing and singing at dance halls. She became a popular act in the area, often traveling from one radio station to the next to sing in contests. She'd hoped to become a full-time singer one day and travel around Mexico on tour and live a fancy life. But her lucky break never came.

Amá was eighteen and Apá was twenty when they met at a dance hall. Apá said he knew he'd marry Amá from the minute they danced the tango that night. From the start of the romance, Abuelito Rosalio disapproved of Apá, cautioning his only daughter that this man was too vulgar and rough around the edges to make her happy. Even with Abuelito's warning, they married a year later—*un Mexicano Romeo y Julieta*.

Not long after their wedding, while living in Consuelo, Amá gave birth to their firstborn son, Luis. But just before his first birthday, he died unexpectedly of the flu. Apá never talked about him and made it clear we weren't supposed to bring him up. Amá only broached baby Luis to us kids when we found a picture of him stored away in a drawer. He was dressed in a blue jumpsuit with a big smile. She mentioned that after he died, she started noticing Apá's dark moods. Drinking more, he started losing his jobs, and his temper grew short.

A year later, Irma was born.

"She's the good one," Apá would say when talking about sweet Irma. She looked like his mini twin with her dark eyes and wide smile.

As she grew older, she became the model child, carefully crafted by Amá. She'd give the younger siblings baths and know when to take ground beef out of the freezer without Amá having to ask. Soon after Irma turned two, Dolores, the hardy sister of the bunch, was born. She was the tallest of us siblings, with a sweet face and a dime-sized beauty mark just below her nose that showed she was special.

Striving to build better lives for themselves and their young daughters, my parents moved their family of four to Juárez, Mexico, a border town on the Rio Grande opposite El Paso, Texas. Apá landed a job at a local cannery, and from there, my parents' eagerness to procreate surpassed their meager budget.

Amá wanted her next child to be born an American citizen, so she walked over the border into the state of Texas to give birth to the feisty Esméralda, who brought sass into the family. She'd take over a conversation teasing and spitting sarcasm, and of the Becerra girls, she'd have the thickest and most luscious hair, hanging like a silk blanket down her back.

After four years of living in Juarez, Apá lost his job when an aggressive argument with his manager broke out. Undeterred, he saw this as an opportunity to move farther west, where he expected better employment possibilities. With just hope in my father's pocket, he packed up the family and headed to Arizona, ending up in the small town of Laveen. He found a job as a cotton picker on the Anderson Clayton Cotton Farm and Amá sold her homemade chili to the workers.

Her pregnancy streak continued with Julio Jr. She, my father, and my sisters lived in a trailer on the farm property, renting from the owner for a low cost. Uncle Chalio, eighteen years old at the time, traveled from Mexico on a work visa to live with them. He picked cotton too, eventually becoming the owner's chauffeur.

It was early 1958 when Amá, twenty-seven and pregnant with me, had somehow saved enough money to buy a house. She moved our family of six—soon to be seven—into the Cashion neighborhood and into the house that would shape the Becerra family.

4

I dreaded Christmas. Each year I'd make a Christmas list of toys I wanted: puzzles, books, a drum set, a tetherball to play with in the yard. I'd address the letter to Santa Claus, seal it in a white envelope, and slide it into the Letters to the North Pole mailbox. But every Christmas morning, I'd wake up disappointed when Santa had skipped our house once again.

"Should've worked harder in those fields. Then maybe Santa would have stopped by," Apá would say as we watched the neighbor kids race down the street on their fancy scooters and shiny-new bikes.

The week before Christmas 1963, when I was five, Amá, my sisters, and I strolled through the A. J. Bayless Plaza. Dazzling red and green lights flashed and flickered around us. Jolly Christmas music played while busy shoppers hustled from store to store with their arms lined with bags like a closet rack. We walked empty-handed. We didn't buy any clothes or items, only marveling at the rhinestone handbags with matching wallets and sparkly dresses on display. My sisters and I knew our parents could barely afford the electric bill, not to mention Christmas gifts, so we never asked for anything.

As we approached the center of the corridor, I saw a replica North Pole display. A tall Christmas tree topped with a silver star soared high while children and their mothers snaked in a line around the crowded area. A helper elf decked out in her festive vest escorted the next lucky kid in line down a long red carpet. As I craned my neck to get a better view, I spotted him. There, sitting in a tall red chair, was the head honcho of Christmas himself.

"Amá, can I see Santa? Oh, *por favor, por favor*—" I said, tugging her arm.

"No, *mija*. That line is far too long."

"*Por favor.* I just want to talk to him."

She finally agreed, and she and my sisters waited at a nearby bench as I made my way to the end of the line. I didn't take my eyes off him. His bushy white beard overlapped with his fluffy red suit that covered his round belly. I hardly blinked, watching each kid take a turn sitting on his lap. They all smiled when they told him what electric race car model or Barbie they wanted this Christmas. The mothers would proudly snap a photo. Santa would do his "ho, ho, ho" bit, and they'd be off on their way, not a doubt in the world Santa and his reindeer would deliver gifts under their tree on Christmas Eve.

As I drew closer to the front, I thought about what I wanted to say to him. Now was my chance, and I wouldn't waste my breath this holiday asking for another tetherball.

When it was finally my turn, his helper elf led me down the long carpet to Mr. Kris Kringle and hoisted me onto his lap. Small bubbles of sweat glistened on his forehead, and he smelled of sweat mixed with too much aftershave.

"Well, hello, young lady," Santa said. His voice was muffled by his bushy beard. "What would you like for Christmas?"

I could have answered his question, telling him once again of the toys I wanted for Christmas. But instead, this time, I would take control of the conversation and ask him a question.

"Santa, do you visit everyone in the world?"

"Why yes, young lady." He chuckled. "My nine strong reindeer fly my magical sleigh. Ho, ho, ho."

Most kids would have swooned at this, but not me. The old guy was lying. I looked down at his curly white beard and patted it with my hand. I started to say something, then stopped.

"What is it, little miss? Why the long face this close to Christmas?"

Before I could stop the words from escaping my mouth, I blurted out, "You never come to our house, you fucker."

Santa's jaw dropped. One of the sweat bubbles dripped down the side of his nose to his tangled beard. I kept going. "I know we don't have a chimney, but you could still get into our house if you tried. Apá keeps the back door unlocked."

"Now, young la—"

Before he could finish his words, I leapt off his lap.

"Hey, you! You get back here!"

I didn't look back. I sprinted out of that fake North Pole's gate as fast as my legs could take me. I weaved in and out of shoppers and their bags until I reached the bench where Amá and my sisters were sitting. I bent over, resting my palms on my knees to catch my breath.

"How'd it go?" Esméralda asked. "You tell him 'bout that tetherball you wanted?"

I shook my head. "Not this time. I had other things to talk to him about."

"Well, don't be disappointed if you don't get it, Minu," Dolores said. "Santa seems to stay away from our house."

"What do I always tell you girls?" Amá said. "Who needs gifts? Mexicans unwrap their tamales on Christmas Day."

The next day, just before dark, the desert night turned cold when the sun sank behind the Estrella Mountain range. Purple streaks spread across the sky while a few stars took their place. Julio and I sat in the front yard admiring the Christmas trees glimmering through the front windows of the Cashion residences. Red and green, white and gold, silver and blue, each tree with a unique theme.

Julio tilted his head to the side as if deep in thought. "Maybe Santa doesn't come to our house because we don't have a Christmas tree."

Every year, when we asked Apá if we could get a tree, he told us no. It was a waste of time and money, he said, and the tree would just end up in the trash.

"Well, maybe we should ask him one more time," I said.

"*You* can ask." Julio blew into his hands to get warm. Our shirts were too thin to keep out the chill.

"Fine, but at least come with me."

We found Apá in the backyard with a cigarette rammed into the crevasse of his mouth while constructing a barbed-wire fence for the chicken shack. He was always starting new projects while doing another, rarely finishing any of them, but we all hoped he'd see this one through to stop the chickens from roaming all over the yard.

"Damn filthy, rotten, *cabrónes*!" he'd yell at the dirty chickens as they bawked around him.

"Apá," I said. He didn't look up from the piece of wire. Julio stood behind me, staring at the ground. "Can we get a Christmas tree this year?"

He looked at me, then at Julio, and shrugged. "Sure."

Julio perked up. "Really? You mean it?"

"*Está bien*, but it ain't gonna be in the house. It's gotta stay outside."

Julio and I both nodded, our smiles stretching from ear to ear. We were getting our first Christmas tree, and we were happier than the neighbor kids riding their fancy scooters on Christmas morning.

Later that week, Apá brought home a three-foot stubby pine tree, just a bit taller than me. The branches were scraggly, the pine needles were skimpy, and the trunk was no thicker than a pencil, but we didn't care. Apá dug a hole in the front yard with his rusty shovel and wedged the tree into it.

Once the tree stood sturdy, Apá handed us a bucket of old, chipped Christmas ornaments he had bought at the thrift store. Sorting through them, we set aside the ones that still had a sparkle and hung them on the tree. Just like the neighbor's Christmas decorations, we wanted ours to twinkle. Then we wrapped a knotty auburn garland from branch to branch.

"Santa is going to love this tree," I said, hanging a cracked gold bulb near the top. "I can feel it! Best one in the neighborhood!"

Across the street, the nosy Mrs. Sanchez peeked through her living room curtains to get a better view of the circus taking place in our yard.

Julio stepped back to take a good look at our masterpiece. "There's no way Santa will miss our house this year."

On Christmas Eve night, Julio and I kept waking up to look out the window. I wanted to see the bright red dot flying through the sky, leading the rest of the reindeer, and Santa's magical sleigh.

"Why aren't we seeing him?" Julio whispered so softly, making sure not to wake my parents sleeping on the other end of the room.

"Santa has to make his rounds around the entire world tonight. He probably hasn't even made it to our country yet," I whispered back.

The next morning, Julio and I jumped out of bed and raced to the scrimpy tree in the yard. No gifts. No tetherball. Santa skipped us once again. The only things we unwrapped that Christmas were Amá's tamales.

5

The mornings in the Becerra household were anything but calm. The hum of the clipper as Apá trimmed his facial hair. The hiss of hairspray before Amá's long day at the laundromat. The shouts of my sisters as they fought over the bathroom mirror. Julio mostly kept to himself but didn't hesitate to start an argument if he didn't have the space to brush his teeth.

Most days, while my siblings were off at school, I went with Amá to the laundromat, helping her fold sheets and uniforms for some commercial bigwig company. But one day, I woke up and didn't want to go. I wanted to go to school instead.

So I plotted a scheme to sneak onto that big yellow bus my sisters and Julio took to that magical place. All I needed was a book—that would make me look like a student. With Apá's Bible from his nightstand tucked under my arm, I followed my siblings out the front door, down the driveway, and to that big yellow school bus.

The doors cranked open, and I climbed up, making it as far as the bus aisle when the driver called out, "Hey, you. Yeah, you! You can't be on here!"

I raised the Bible in the air. "Yes, I can. Here's my book. I have my book right here!"

The driver scoffed and then honked the horn until Amá finally came flying from the house to retrieve me.

"A book, Amá! That's all I needed to get on the big yellow school bus!"

"¡Estupida tu!" Amá said over and over, dragging me back to the house by my ear. "First grade, Minu. You're going to have to wait for first grade."

There was a knock at the door. Esméralda and Julio ran to the front window to see who it was.

"Minu! Your dad is here!" they all yelled through the house.

"Güera, tell your papa we have nothing for him this week," Apá said from the sofa. My siblings broke out in laughter. Even Amá laughed from the kitchen.

Another knock.

I opened the door to reveal a tall, lanky forty- or fifty-something-year-old man dressed in his white uniform with a plastic laundry basket leaning on his hip. His wavy brown hair flowed from his white cap and his skin was pink—the same color as mine.

"Good evening, Miss Minu," he said with a tip of his cap. "Do you have anything in need of cleaning on this fine day?" He grinned, the corners of his mouth reaching up to his rosy cheeks. He did sort of look like me. More than my own parents. He even had the cat-like eyes I had—the kind that pointed up in the corners.

Every Friday, he'd park his van at the end of our street and go from house to house. We never gave him anything, but he stopped by just the same.

"We're all set today, mister," I said with a smile. "My mama has been working extra hours at the laundromat and all our laundry is either washed, drying, or folded and ready to be put away. But thank you for asking."

He nodded once and tipped his hat again. "Always a pleasure seeing you, Miss Minu." Then he turned back toward the street.

When I shut the front door, giggles filled the house. Apá called from the living room, "Did you give your papa a hug when he left?"

Julio laughed. "That was your dad. Why didn't you go home with him?"

"Shut up!" I finally yelled.

It was the most unfunny joke I'd ever heard.

It was another hot day. The swamp cooler hummed on full blast, and table fans blew warm air throughout the house. Amá cooked in the kitchen, making the usual tortilla, rice, and beans for dinner. Even at six years old, I did a lot of the chores, spending the morning dusting each room to get rid of the spiderwebs and sweeping under the dining room table as Apá sat there smoking. Next, I'd help Amá out by doing a load of laundry myself. Besides, if I was going to work at the laundromat like she did when I grew up, it was best I learned now.

We kept the Maytag electric washing machine in the bathroom. Amá had already started a load of dirty clothes, filling the white enamel tub with water, pouring in the soap, and tossing in an armful of shirts, pants, and socks (we usually wore clothes repetitively until they stunk).

I hadn't used the machine before but had watched Amá complete several loads of wash with it. It seemed easy, although I'd have to do this chore secretly. If either she or Apá saw me using the machine alone, they would get mad. But once they saw the clean clothes, they'd forget to be angry.

I locked the bathroom door and climbed onto the toilet seat to get a better view into the tub. I swished the clothes around the water, watching the dirt and dust detach from the garments, turning the soapy water a muddy brown.

Next, just as I'd seen Amá do, I scooped a white sock out of the water and stuck it through the wringer's two rolling pins assembled above the toilet. When I pulled the lever, the machine awoke and snarled. As the sock glided into the wringer, the machine yanked my left hand along with it.

I tugged my arm back to my body, but the wringer heaved my hand further into its grasp, pulling my skin and bones with it. My forearm slipped through the tight pins, lifting me off the toilet seat and hanging from the rollers. The pressure heavy on my hand forced a blood-curdling scream from my mouth that filled the house.

"Amá, help me!"

A blaze of heat shot through my arm, and I smelled the scent of burning flesh. I screamed again. I jerked my arm, but the peeling of my skin made me lose my breath. The doorknob jiggled and pounding came from the other side. Apá's voice shook through the door.

"Minu? *¿Qué estás haciendo?* Open up!"

"Apá, my arm's stuck! Make it stop! Make it stop!"

A thump against the door, then a loud bang. Apá barged into the bathroom, thrashing the door against the wall.

"What the fu—!" He pushed past me and reached around the back of the washer to unplug it. "What were you thinking? *¡Cabróna, estúpida!*"

I retracted my arm from the wringer, revealing ripped skin on my hand and forearm. Blood gushed out and tears poured down my cheeks.

Amá ran into the room. "What have you done?"

I held up my left arm. "I was just trying to help."

"Head to the truck," Amá said frantically. "We're taking you to the hospital."

I had never been to the doctor in my life, not even for checkups.

"No, María! We can't afford that!" Apá yelled.

"Julio, look at her arm!" Amá's cried, her voice shaking. "We'll go to the county hospital."

Within minutes, the three of us were speeding in the station wagon down Buckeye Road. Amá had wrapped my arm in a towel, now soaked with blood. I lay in the back seat, the excruciating pain pounding through my arm and up to my shoulder. I almost threw up.

When we arrived at the hospital, I was taken back immediately for an examination. Everything was white—the floors, the walls, the lights, and the ceilings—even the nurses and doctors wore white. It was so clean and bright. Dried tears on my face, I sat on the exam chair in the center of the room. The doctor and his nurse had stopped the bleeding and mended the hanging tissue with several bandages.

"Well, Miss Minu, you've had quite the accident," the doctor said calmly. "You're lucky your father unplugged the machine when he did or the damage could have been much worse. You could have lost your arm."

I examined my arm, trying to imagine what it would feel like if it wasn't there. I wiggled my fingers to make sure one hadn't slipped off without me noticing.

Across the room, my parents stayed quiet since they barely understood a word the doctor said. They sat in the stiff plastic chairs, their faces blank as if they were hiding their annoyance. I translated to them what the doctor was saying, tongue-tied, still shaking inside. The strong smell of rubbing alcohol didn't help.

"There'll be a bruise, and most likely a scar will surface afterward," the doctor said, lifting my arm into a sling.

No big deal. I'd put aloe vera oil on it, something Amá had taught us. Along with soothing my sunburn, it seemed to heal any injury. Plus, I wasn't afraid of some stupid scar. If anything, it would remind me of the battle I once won with an electric washer.

On the way home, Amá and Apá threw jokes around the car.

"Good thing she didn't stick her other arm in the wringer," Amá said, chuckling. "An unarmed child. Can you imagine?"

"She wouldn't be able to pick the fields, María." Apá laughed. He looked in the rearview mirror, making eye contact with me in the back. "Why don't you *think* next time, *pendeja*."

I didn't do laundry for a long time after that. Maybe I wasn't cut out to be a laundry professional like Amá after all.

6

Finally, it was my first day of school! I dressed myself in a red plaid skirt and a white ruffled shirt Amá had made for me. I'd been dreaming of this for such a long time. Today I'd finally have the chance to learn, make friends, read fancy books, and be just like my older sisters.

On that morning, the house was calm, something that almost never happened. In the bathroom, Amá tamed my swirls with Brylcreem, a styling cream for men. She slathered it through my hair with the tips of her fingers. My hair always looked more collected and primed afterward. I stretched onto my tippy toes to meet my reflection in the bathroom mirror. A scrawny, pale girl looked back at me. I grinned at her, practicing my first-day smile until I had it perfected.

"You look pretty," Amá said, wetting her fingertips and patting my hair to level the flyaway strands.

I wrinkled my nose. "Not as pretty as you."

My mother was gorgeous. She usually wore her dark hair twisted and pinned on the sides, and her face was free of makeup except for her red lipstick. She had perfectly aligned eyebrows, a narrow nose, and eyes the shade of wet desert soil, rich and glossy. Her ears were even perfect. They were small and always decorated with shiny gold hoop earrings.

"Amá, I want your ears," I said, moving my hair to reveal my slightly protruding ones. "I hate that mine stick out."

"How can you say that? My ears are flat like a fish." She caught her reflection in the mirror and tugged on her earlobes. "Do you want ears like a fish, *el pescado*?"

I sucked in my cheeks and moved my lips up and down, making a fish face. Amá laughed.

As I walked into the living room in my thoughtfully planned first-day-of-school attire, Apá smiled his wide, cheery grin. "And what do we have here? A beauty." He applauded and hollered as if I'd won an award. "It's my Güera's first day of school," he said in a sweet singsong.

He grabbed my hands and twirled me to the tempo of the faint *norteña* music playing from the kitchen radio. I giggled shyly. I loved his happy moods. He twirled me again, and I let my skirt drift with the movement. The Mexican dancing gene had skipped me. I danced with two left feet compared to Apá's smooth and graceful moves, but at that moment, he didn't care, and neither did I.

"You've come so far, Güera," he said as we swayed back and forth. "Look how small you used to be." He pointed to the photograph of me as a toddler hanging on the otherwise blank living room wall. Small brown curls framed my face, and I wore a plush pink dress and shoes with high laced socks. Rather than smiling in the photograph, I looked confused, as if I were staring at something foreign.

Although I didn't think much of it at the time, I was the only Becerra child to have a professional photograph taken. I smiled at the little girl across the room. Apá twirled me around once more.

Littleton Elementary was bigger than I expected. Students of every shape, size, and skin color flowed through the hallways like a steady stream of chaos. The bell rang, and I stumbled into what I hoped was the right first-grade classroom. I sat in the back row and neatly organized my folder, notebook, and pencil across the wooden desk. They were all hand-me-downs from Dolores. Two windows overlooked the dusty playground with a twirly slide, high chain-linked swings, and monkey bars I couldn't wait to try.

Chatty kids congregated in circles, talking about the fun summer activities they attended during their time off. I couldn't help but feel a twinge of envy. Horseback riding? Guitar lessons? Dance classes? It was all foreign to me, except for my brief stint at a low-income summer camp.

My parents didn't see the value in hobbies or extracurricular activities. To them, the most important thing was making money to support the family. So while the other kids were off having fun, my brothers, sisters, and I were toiling in the fields under the hot Arizona sun, our childhood slipping away with each passing day.

My first-grade teacher, Mrs. Stillwall, a pudgy older woman with bright turquoise jewelry on her ears, neck, and wrists, politely ordered the class to take their seats. As she called out each name, my stomach grew tighter. I dreaded this part.

My name always called attention, and not in a good way. People would often ask if it was my real name. Yes, I would say. Then they'd ask me to repeat it or spell it for them. Sometimes, they'd ask if it was Mexican. Yes, I'd say, confused by their question. I was one hundred percent Mexican—although Amá told me Minu was French and the name of a character she saw in a 1950s movie. "I didn't know what else to name you," she'd say whenever I asked her about it. "You should be proud to have such a unique name."

"Alejandro."

"Carmen."

"Rodrigo."

Several other students took turns standing up and introducing themselves to the class.

"Me. Nu," Mrs. Stillwall called.

I stood and flashed a smile. Thirty pairs of eyes gawked at me. As expected, the name caused a raucous as waves of laughter filled the room.

"Men—new?" a boy student echoed from the front row. "What kind of name is that?"

"Like *menudo*? The Spanish soup?" another student chipped in.

"Sounds Chinese," another student called out. The class laughed louder.

"Class," Mrs. Stillwall said.

My cheeks burned as I sat down in my seat and wiped my sweaty palms on my skirt.

And then someone blurted out over the giggles, "Well, I like that name."

The chirp came from a tall, hefty dark-haired boy sitting in the row ahead of me. He looked more like a fifth-grader.

He turned around with a cheeky grin. "Don't let them bother you," he whispered, reaching his hand out for a shake. "The name's Sixto."

Sixto and I became fast friends. At recess that afternoon, we slid down the twirly slide, swung so high on the swings we thought we'd hit the trees, and swayed from the monkey bars until our palms burned with blisters.

"Minu's got a boyfriend," Julio teased as he walked by with a group of his second-grade friends.

"Can it, Julio!" I yelled, giving him a don't-even-think-about-it look.

I wasn't ready for boys.

My parents weren't the slightest bit curious about my education. They refused to learn English, so they didn't attend the PTA meetings or help with homework, and they never asked to see my grades. I signed my own report cards and field trip slips. I even opted myself out of school vaccinations.

"Nope, Minu doesn't need this," I'd say to myself as I scribbled my mother's name on the dotted line.

The world of school was different than I imagined. When it came to the learning part, math and science were my favorite subjects. Addition equations were fun and learning about stratus and cirrus clouds in Earth Science was fascinating, but I struggled the most with English.

Sometimes Mrs. Stillwall made us read passages aloud to the rest of the class—my worst nightmare. As a native Spanish speaker, I couldn't keep the languages straight. Whenever I'd stumble over my English words, my face got hot with embarrassment and the other students giggled. Eventually, I'd give up and finish the sentence in Spanish.

"Ahem. We speak English in this classroom, young lady," Mrs. Stillwall would say slowly and dramatically as if that would help. "We'll use only English words in this school," "You'll stand in the corner if that happens again."

I stood in the corner many times that year.

Mrs. Stillwall also got mad when I couldn't pronounce my Rs or wrote my letters backward.

"Start over, Minu," she'd say. "And do it right this time."

On paper, I'd write "day" instead of "bay," or "Agril" instead of "April" or "85" instead of "58." Sometimes, I'd write a word, and it would come out backward. I'd write and erase again and again, trying to get the jumbled letters right in my head. I would practically hyperventilate through each assignment, smudging the lined paper with pencil lead and covering it with pink eraser shavings. It didn't take long for the other students to catch on and start calling me dumb or *estúpida*.

The only thing that helped was memorization. I practiced with anything I could get my hands on: Apá's Bible, my sisters' comic books, worksheets from school. Reading at a snail's pace, I would put my finger under every word and study the shape of each letter. I'd continue into the late hours of the night. Since Apá turned the house lights off at eight, I would use a flashlight under my blanket.

Even with all the time I put into learning, it was easy to fall behind during the ripe vegetable seasons. Instead of homework, our afternoons were filled with picking and plucking and stuffing burlap sacks. Working the fields and paying the mortgage took priority over school—my parents' minds were entirely occupied with making ends meet. Like Amá, Apá quit school at an early age to earn money for the family household.

But those were the olden days, I told myself. That would never happen to me.

Reading and writing were hard enough, but making friends was impossible. Sixto was nice and all, but I wanted girls to play with at the monkey bars. But they didn't seem to like me very much. In their tight-knit circles with their backs to the world, they gossiped, laughed, and flipped their hair, moving in synchronized unison.

When I asked if I could play Red Rover or Double Dutch with them at recess, it was usually Jolene, the leader of the bratty pack, who delivered the ruling.

"We don't have room. Too bad so sad," she'd say.

Jolene was the daughter of one of the rich farmers in the area—possibly one of the farms where my family picked and plucked to make a buck. She always wore the prettiest and most stylish dresses, the kinds of dresses I'd eye in the department stores but knew Amá couldn't afford. My sisters and I practically shared a rack of clothes.

One day at recess, while swinging across the monkey bars, I heard Jolene call out from across the playground, "See Minu's dress, everyone?"

I focused on grasping the metal bar and then swinging to the next.

"That dress used to be mine," she said. "I put that *exact* white and brown dress in the school clothing drive last month. It was too out of date for me." She let out a wicked laugh. "Now look at who's wearing it."

Her bratty pack snickered, anticipating my answer to her taunting. On my next sway, I maneuvered my momentum and leaped into the air to land right in front of Miss Jolene. She flinched as I stared straight into her ice-cold blue eyes.

"This *is* your dress, Jolene. But you know what?" I tilted my head with the utmost pride and confidence. "Too bad it looks better on me."

Jolene gasped in disgust. So did the other girls.

I walked off toward the twirly slide. Like Apá would say about someone like Jolene, I didn't have time to waste on such *pinche cabrónas* during recess.

7

*A*pá and I often went to the dump looking for cans, iron, aluminum, metal, and other pieces of material he could sell for money. The landfill sat at the base of a rounded mountain in a desolate area. The stench of rotten garbage hung in the air, forcing Apá and me to cover our noses with our forearms or we'd dry heave.

Roadrunners, jack rabbits, and quail scurried across the dirt as we sifted through the piles of debris, hoping to find something worth a buck. Apá took on the heavier items, ripped couches, blown-out tires, and rusted appliances, chucking them to the side. I stretched into the dumpster, digging through the trash bags, moving around banana peels, Styrofoam cups, musty coffee grinds, and other household garbage, hunting for a diamond in the rough that would whisper, "Take me home."

One Saturday, as I pushed aside a pair of grubby rubber-soled shoes, I found an eyelash curler. Rust spots dotted the handle and clamp, but it still looked usable. I'd seen Esméralda use one like it before she snuck out of the house with the neighbor boy. She clamped it around her long lashes and pressed tightly, giving them a slight upward curl that made her look lovely.

Perhaps if I gave the contraption a try, my lashes would curl so long they'd touch my eyebrows. Dolores told me that makeup and beauty tools made women attractive, and when a woman felt attractive, she had confidence. Maybe this eyelash curler would fix my looks, something I thought about all the time. It'd be my treasure for the day—although

I'd have to sneak it. Apá was strict with my sisters and me when it came anything related to womanhood. We couldn't shave our legs or have boyfriends, and he said wearing makeup was slutty. Although my sisters applied eye makeup and bubblegum-flavored lip gloss the minute they were far enough from the house, they would wipe it off before walking through the front door later that evening.

I glanced at Apá, who hurled a broken rocking chair out of his way. While he was distracted, I quickly slipped the eyelash curler into my right jeans pocket. It bulged in my pants, but I covered it with my palm so he wouldn't see.

After rifling through grease-soaked napkins, leftover apple cores, cat food cans, half-filled milk cartons, and other rubbish, Apá stood up and wiped his filthy hands on his faded jeans. "C'mon, Güera. There ain't *caca* in this dump today. Gonna have to work the fields all week so we can afford the electric bill since you damned kids keep turning the swamp cooler on at night."

On the way home, I sat in the passenger seat of the pickup, thinking only of the eyelash curler in my pocket. I couldn't wait to try it.

In the reflection of the side mirror, I stared at the short dull lashes that surrounded my eyes. I peeked over at Apá driving. He looked deep in thought, listening to the old AM radio chattering about, yet again, another drought season.

"*La mierda,*" Apá mumbled under his breath. Bullshit.

I turned toward the window so he couldn't see me pulling the curler from my pocket. I slowly lifted it up to my right eye, placed the clamp around the lash, and squeezed the handle tight. A sharp pinching pain shot through my eyelid. My piercing scream filled the truck. "Aye! Aye!"

Apá jumped out of his daze. "What the fuck! *¡Pinche, cabróna!*"

I put my hand over my eye and examined the curler with my other. No wonder it had hurt—the rubber pads on the clamp were missing.

"*¡Estúpida!*" Apá yelled. He jerked the truck over to the side of the road and jolted it into park. A cloud of dust rose into the air.

He slapped my hand away from my face and looked closely at me. "You pulled your goddamn eyelashes out." He grabbed the curler from me and inspected it. "Where did you get this piece of shit?"

"I found it at the dump!" I cried. "Dolores does it to her eyelashes all the time."

"Not anymore, I'll be sure of that." He chucked the curler out the window and then smacked me on the back of my head, knocking my chin into my chest. He skirted back onto the road and sped all the way home.

As far back as I can remember, I wanted to look like my sisters. Every day, I prayed to turn brown like them and the rest of my family, but it never happened. I'd wake up hating my pasty skin. All I needed was a few sunburns to darken my skin for good, or so I thought.

One cloudless afternoon, when the steaming sun was at its peak, I sat in an old camping chair in the backyard. Sweat bubbled up and dripped down the sides of my cheeks. The sun took hold of me, but I gripped the armchairs and crinkled my forehead, telling myself just a bit longer.

When my skin started tingling, I peeled the back of my legs from the chair and sprinted into the house, ready to see my progress in the bathroom mirror, expecting to see the glistening tan my siblings flaunted after a day spent under the sun. Instead, my scorched face stared back at me as crisp as an overcooked tortilla. For the next week and a half, I spent my mornings and nights covering myself with aloe vera gel to put out the fire on my skin. The suntanning plan was a failure.

Next, I tried matching my sisters' pin-straight hair. When Amá carefully slathered my head with Brylcreem, my ringlets seemed to disappear. So one day, when she was busy in the kitchen, I locked the bathroom door and squeezed out a clump of the cream from the big red tube. I lathered it on top of my frizzy head and drenched the rest of my hair, piece by piece, clump by clump. Starting at my scalp, I combed each strand. For sure, this would be the magic potion to keep my curls from reappearing.

After I finished, I shook my head to test out my new hairdo, but my hair didn't budge. It was as stiff as straw—stuck in place as if the strands had been glued together. It took me a week to wash out all the cream.

No one in my family noticed.

8

My eighth birthday came and went. No cake, no gifts, no party. All of that had stopped after I turned three. My siblings and parents wished me a happy birthday, and Amá made my favorite dish: *nopalitos* with red chile rice and beans. But that was it.

By now the Becerra household had grown from eight to eleven with the births of my three younger brothers. They were all born in three consecutive years. Danny, four years old, was a perfect mix of my mother's side of the family with his shiny auburn hair, yet his broad smile looked just like Apá's. Ruben was three, had big dark eyes, and battled a slight stutter when he spoke. And Sammy, two years old, was a happy baby yet as fragile as a newborn bird—we'd eventually toughen him up.

David, now five, and Julio, nine, butted heads. Their rivalry was on an evolutionary course, David trying to overpower and Julio determined to stay dominant. Irma was about to graduate from high school while Dolores was about to quit—she said school wasn't for her. And Esméralda was a boy-crazed middle schooler on the hunt for her next make-out.

Through the constant chaos and disorder, the only thing consistent in our lives was going to church on Sundays. I liked God. I pictured him as a man with a long brown beard dressed in a white robe watching people from the clouds. During the church services, I bowed my head in prayer and tightly folded my hands in my lap.

I'd tell God about us picking cotton and onions in the fields and the hundreds of bags I filled for Apá. In my politest words, I asked for things like new clothes, for my sisters to stop fighting, or for him to bless Amá since she worked so hard to put food on the table. I also asked for forgiveness when I was mean, like when I called David *estúpido*. I thought for sure I'd be sentenced to hell.

"Apá, I'd like to get baptized," I said one evening at dinner. We huddled around the small wooden table, eating Amá's homemade green chile burritos with rice and beans.

Apá's face lit up and his hands shot into the air as if they would touch the heavens themselves. "Aha! That's what I like to see, Güera. You're always thinking ahead. Next Sunday, I'm signing you up."

Before my brothers and I were born, my parents and sisters were practicing Catholics. That was until Irma, at only eight years old and tight as a drum in her Christian faith, attended a Baptist church down the road. She got herself baptized, and eventually, my parents trusted their firstborn's instinct and followed suit by joining the congregation.

Ever since then, Sundays in the Becerra household were dedicated to church. As a family, we attended both the morning and evening church services. Just before the sermon began, Miss Hernandez, the Sunday school teacher who whistled through her nose when she breathed, dismissed the students and gathered us in a small classroom. She read us stories about Jesus healing the blind or turning water into wine. My favorite story was when he raised Lazareth from the dead. Jesus was like some amazing magician.

When the Bible mentioned heaven, I pictured an enchanted paradise with waterfalls, colorful rainbows, and happy people sitting around laughing, playing Lotería, and sipping on tequila (like my parents did). If being baptized guaranteed me a golden ticket to this afterlife, count me in. The cookies and red Kool-Aid served after church were an added bonus.

Sundays were Apá's happiest hours too. He held his wide smile all day, singing each hymn in his deep voice, and nodding his head along with Pastor Gonzalez's sermons. He still kept a tight ship with us, though. If any of us fell asleep during the service or got caught whispering or fighting with one another, he would give us a tight pinch. When we arrived home after the evening service, my siblings and I would spread across the living room floor while Apá sat cross-legged on the sofa with his Bible in his lap. He'd read from the books of Luke, John, or Job, emphasizing his favorite parts and talking in a mighty voice when Jesus spoke.

Sundays were my favorite day.

On the day of my baptism, I wore a white lace dress Amá had sewn from a pile of unused material scraps she found behind a garment factory. She steamed the wrinkles from the cloth, lathered the Brylcreem through my hair, and buckled my shiny black shoes she bought for me for fifty cents at the thrift store. She leaned back, studied me for a moment, and smiled with satisfaction. "You look lovely, *mija*."

She led me from the bathroom to the living room where she twirled me in front of Apá. "Well, Papi? What do you think?"

"Ah, look at my beautiful Güera." He flashed his cheery grin. He was dressed in the button-up shirt and khaki dress pants he wore only on holidays or special occasions.

"You look *precioso*, Minu," Irma said, bouncing little Sammy on her hip.

"*Muy hermosa*," Dolores chipped in.

Between the fancy white gown and the googly-eyed attention, I was certain this was what a wedding day felt like.

Esméralda laughed. "Sure, *bonita*. But you'll look like a wet dog in about an hour." Julio laughed too.

The eleven of us crammed into the station wagon, a car that sat in the driveway unless we were going to church. Growing up, we never had car seats, so little Sammy sat on Irma's lap, and Ruben sat with Dolores. We also didn't have air conditioning, so we rode with the windows down to keep the interior from feeling like a burning hot sauna. My siblings and I avoided the seat directly behind Apá since he spat his loogies out the window. They'd wisp through the air and hit the kid behind his seat smack-dab in the face. Luckily, Julio got the loogie seat that day. He dodged the flying spit the entire ride to the church.

My stomach heaved as we pulled into the parking lot. People from the congregation flooded into the front doors: men dressed in their

Sunday slacks and women in their fanciest dresses with their church bulletins and Bibles in hand.

"Are you ready, Güera?" Apá asked as he parked the station wagon. He swiveled to look at me in the back seat. A smile pressed under his pencil-thin mustache.

I nodded.

"I'm proud of you, ya know?" he said.

I nodded again.

We entered the church through the tall oak French doors. A piano played softly in the background, entwining with the chatter. Columns of wooden pews stretched to the end of the church where the altar stood.

Pastor Gonzalez greeted my family, shaking Apá's hand with a polite grin. "*Buenos días, familia Becerra*. Ah, look who we have here." He crunched down to my eye level, his frayed Bible tucked under his arm. "One of our obedient believers. I'm so happy you've decided to join God's community, Miss Minu. If you're ready, you can head to the classroom."

Apá nudged me forward. "Go ahead, *mija*. We'll be watching."

I smiled stiffly and weaved in and out of the congregation members to the Sunday school room where Miss Hernandez greeted me. She handed me what looked like a folded white sheet and told me to change into it quickly. I recognized a few familiar students: a quiet girl in the corner and some rambunctious boys. They were all dressed in floor-length boxy white gowns that zipped in the front. I threw the gown over my dress and joined the others.

The faint sound of a graceful church hymn caught our attention, cueing us it was time. Nerves buzzed like bees in the pit of my stomach. Miss Hernandez told us to form a line at the hefty wood door leading to the altar. I was first.

The church song dwindled, and the closing of songbooks and muffled voices came from the pews. I leaned forward to see my family stretched across one of the front rows. Apá sat at the end, bright-eyed, his neck craned high to get a better view of the altar. I didn't notice my hand resting on the door hinges, when one of the boys in line bumped the door, ricocheting it forward and smashing my middle finger.

"Aye!" I yelped. "Aye! Aye! Aye!" I bit my lip not to cry or, even worse, scream, and tucked my hand in between my knees, rocking back and forth.

"Oh, no. Are you okay, *cariño*?" Miss Hernandez asked.

I inspected the damage and saw my finger and nail were already turning purple. I let the tears fall. A sob followed naturally, and in seconds, I was bawling.

Miss Hernandez shushed me. "You must stop crying, Minu. The ceremony will begin soon."

Just then, Pastor Gonzalez called out for the first student to come forth to receive the Holy Spirit. My finger throbbed, but I'd made it this far—I had to get baptized. Today was the day, and no bruised finger would stop me. I stumbled onto the altar with a flushed face and tears gushing down my cheeks.

"And what do we have here? Look at this one," Pastor Gonzalez called out to the congregation as I made my way to the white marble tub where he stood. "She's so happy to be saved by our dear Lord and Savior, she is shedding tears!"

The church erupted with laughter.

I approached the tub filled with water and gasped for air between sobs. Pastor Gonzalez took my hand, and I stepped into the bath, letting the water hit my feet, calves, and thighs.

"So happy to see your passion for Christ, Minu," Pastor Gonzalez said. "We don't see many students get so emotional over the sacrament of baptism. The Lord has truly touched you."

He put a hand on my back and the other on my forehead, and after saying some words about forgiving my sins, he tipped me in the water completely. Coldness blanketed my body and for a second, I forgot about my throbbing finger. When he lifted me back up, applause filled the church.

I stepped out of the tub and sprinted off the altar. Tears of pain—and maybe even joy that I was officially baptized—streamed down my cheeks.

9

A couple of weeks later, Apá found a job installing irrigation systems in field ditches in Waddell, twenty miles from Cashion. The job came with a house to stay in rent-free, so the eleven of us packed up both the truck and the station wagon for my parents' idea of a retreat. We all thought it would be a nice getaway before school started the following month.

The Waddell farmhouse was even smaller and dilapidated than our Cashion house. It had two small bedrooms just big enough for a bed, one bathroom with a rusted toilet, and tall white walls that made the space feel claustrophobic and stifling. The swamp cooler spat out lukewarm air, giving our foreheads a constant glisten. We left the windows open, but there was no breeze, only the smell of the cattle lingering.

I didn't understand why we lived in a cruddier place than our own house, but Irma explained that Apá had finally found work that paid well. She told me we had to make sure everything went okay at the farmhouse so Apá could keep this job, or it was back to the fields for us. I didn't argue with that. Plus, I liked being surrounded by wildflowers and rich brown fields that looked as if they stretched to the ends of the earth. And it was nice being away from the Cashion neighborhood— the nearest house was a mile down the road.

Since we kids didn't have to work the fields, my brothers and I made forts, hunted for scorpions, played countless games of hide-and-seek, and climbed the mesquite trees to their highest branches. My sisters stayed inside, helping Amá in the kitchen. Sometimes, Esméralda came out to play with my brothers and me, but she'd eventually grow bored and call our games childish and disappear back inside the old rickety house.

The irrigation job annoyed Apá. He'd come back to the house agitated after the twelve-hour shifts. With each passing day, he became more like a coiled rattlesnake ready to strike anything that crossed him.

We'd been living on the dusty old Waddell farm for a week and a half when Apá came in yelling one evening. "Those damn *pendejos*! I could run this farm better than these rotten farmers!" Covered in sweat and dirt, he stomped around the kitchen. Julio taught me that Apá's footsteps mirrored his mood. Through his scuffs or stomps, we knew whether he was feeling drained or itching for a fight. Tonight, his footsteps told us someone might get hurt.

The rest of us squeezed around the small wooden paint-chipped dining room table, eating Amá's homemade tortillas, beans, and rice. We sat in silence, fearful even a blink might trigger him. The only sound was the kitchen faucet's constant dripping.

And then Julio went into the kitchen for a glass of water. All at once Apá unleashed on him. I didn't hear what he said to my brother, but he took hold of Julio's shirt and pushed him into the cupboards.

"What! What'd I do?" Julio asked, his voice terrified.

Julio backed into the corner, curling himself into a ball against the cabinet. Apá hovered over him, undid his belt from his torn jeans, and thrashed it onto Julio.

"Please, I'm sorry," Julio cried. "I won't do it again, whatever it was. I promise."

Amá and the rest of us at the table sat still. We stared at the chipped glass plates in front of us that held our half-eaten dinner.

Apá whisked Julio from the corner and dragged him through the door and into the backyard. We all shot up from the table and followed the commotion outside. The sun was fading below the horizon, and golden streaks formed across the sky.

Apá threw Julio against one of the mesquite trees that stood in the middle of the yard. A long, rusty metal chain—possibly from a family's dog who stayed in the farmhouse before us—lay on the ground nearby.

"Put your back to the tree," Apá spat out, his eyes bulging from his head.

Julio turned his back to the trunk, his eyes wide with fear. Apá began wrapping the metal chain around Julio and the tree, tugging the chain tight with each circle. It was the tree my brothers and I climbed just earlier that day. Julio and I had swung from the branches and laughed until our bellies ached.

Amá grabbed Apá's shoulder. "Julio! No. Don't do this."

He pushed her away and told her to shut her mouth.

Julio's small arms were snug to his sides as the chain pulled him tighter into the bark, his face shiny with tears.

"He didn't do nothing wrong!" David's voice cracked.

"Leave him alone!" Dolores screamed. "Amá, do something!"

"Apá, please stop," Irma yelled. She held little Sammy on her hip, covering his ears to muffle the cries and screams.

"*Cállate!*" Apá yelled.

I squeezed my eyes shut, willing it all to stop, willing my father to disappear. Two little arms wrapped around my leg. I looked down to see Ruben, his sweet, innocent face pinched with fear, tears peppering his flushed cheeks. I pulled my little brother's shoulder to me to comfort him as much as I could.

Apá grabbed hold of the excess chain from one end. He gripped it tight, his forearm tense. He swung the chain at Julio, snapping it on his chest. Julio cried louder. Apá yelled hurtful and cruel words that could never be forgotten, and my siblings' piercing sobs from across the yard will forever haunt my memory. I wiped my eyes again and again, but the tears didn't stop.

"Amá, do something!" Esméralda yelled.

Our mother paced back and forth, her hands over her mouth and nose. I scanned the vast desert for help, for anything that could have saved us—nothing but quiet dirt fields and the dimming sky. No neighbors next door to hear the turmoil. No places we could run and hide. I could stand in front of Julio and take the beating myself, but I wouldn't last against my father. There was nothing I could do. Nothing.

Please, God, make it stop. Make it stop.

With Apá's next windup, Dolores grabbed his arm from behind him. He pulled out of her grasp and threw her to the ground.

"You too, Dolores?" he yelled.

He lashed the chain onto her side. She screamed, trying to crawl away.

Amá grabbed Apá's shoulders. "Julio, enough!" she yelled, her eyes wide.

He glared at her with red-rimmed eyes and threw the chain to the side, ping-ponging his gaze at the rest of his children scattered around the scene. Terrified faces reflected back at him.

Apá slowly turned and stomped to the truck parked in the drive. Climbing in, he revved the engine and gunned it. The tires tore against the dirt road, leaving a cloud of dust in its wake.

Amá and David untied Julio from the tree. For several moments he stood still, wrinkled in pain. His eyes were puffy, blood oozed from his nose, and his shirt was torn. He limped across the yard toward the house without looking at anyone.

Irma, Esméralda, and I helped Dolores up from the ground. She had cuts on her hand and arm.

The daylight faded, and the sky went dark. In the farmhouse, Amá slathered her palms with juice from an aloe vera plant and lathered it on Julio's and Dolores's wounds. Their skin would heal, but the scars would never disappear.

Julio sat with his arms wrapped around his stomach, his face defeated. There were no words for what had just happened. I was sad for all of us.

The Waddell farmhouse was quiet the rest of the evening, but my thoughts were deafening. I loved my brother. I wanted so badly to take his pain and misery away from him. I hated Apá for what he did to him, what he did to our family.

The next morning, I told Amá she had to leave Apá.

"How dare you? He's your father." Her voice was in between irritated and exhausted.

"Amá—"

"*Las cosas malas nunca mueren.*" Bad things never die. Amá often said those words when she felt lost about what to do "I can't leave him, Minu. I won't. I've made my bed, and now I must lie in it."

Amá and the nine of us kids packed up the Waddell farmhouse and drove back in Cashion the next day, the hole in my heart still there. We rode in the station wagon with the windows down, letting the warm summer air whip through our hair. No one spoke.

Julio's bruises were now a dark purple. He leaned his head against Dolores's shoulder. She stared out the window with somber eyes and a soft face. I never told her, but I admired Dolores for what she did for our brother. Through threads of bravery, she stepped up to the fear we all felt and acted like the leader we needed—a true hero.

Apá stayed away for several days. We didn't know where he went, and Amá didn't go look for him.

When he finally did come home, he seemed like an angry-eyed stranger to me—a father who didn't protect his family but brought pain and agony.

"Good news," he said that first day back. "I found a farm that needs pickin'. We start tomorrow. All of us."

10

That was when Julio began running away. Most nights, he stayed in a backyard shed in a nearby trailer park. The owners found him and loaned him a pillow and a blanket. As though he were a lost puppy, they fed him and sometimes even allowed him to sleep on their couch. Julio called these white folks his adoptive parents. He didn't want to take advantage of their generosity, so after a few days he'd come back home. And when Apá gave him another beating, he would leave again.

No one seemed to notice when he was gone. With eleven people living in a small house with only two bedrooms and one bathroom, there wasn't much space to rest your elbows, let alone sleep. Irma, Dolores, and Esméralda shared one room, while my parents, my brothers, and I crammed into the other. My parents slept on a scruffy queen-sized bed packed in the corner, the boys shared bunk beds, and I slept on a tiny cot by the door. I didn't mind it, even though it was low to the ground and had minimal cushioning. I was lucky since I didn't have to share a bed with anyone.

Despite the intense heat most of the year, we escaped the cramped house as much as we could. Since we spent so much of our childhood working the fields, our imaginations came alive on the days we were allowed to run wild and simply be kids. We made mud pies and played hide-and-seek and unnamed games that involved running around the backyard and not crying if you got hurt.

Julio once built an underground fort in the neighborhood side alley. He filled tons of buckets of water from the gardening hose and dumped them on the area, softening the dirt so he could dig. He dug and dug and dug until he formed a tunnel that opened into a six-foot-wide buried cave we called the Hideaway. We marked the entrance of the passageway with palm tree fronds to keep it hidden from adults. My younger brothers and I spruced up the Hideaway with a round wooden piece I found at the dump and topped it with full-bloomed bougainvilleas as a centerpiece.

When Julio noticed the new décor, he said, "Don't get any ideas, *cabrónes*. This place is strictly for me and *mis amigos*. And someday, I'll bring my girlfriends down here to make out."

I rolled my eyes. Yuck.

Sometimes our playtime was postponed when Amá assigned us chores. My sisters cleaned the house, little David swept the driveway, and across the yard, and Julio picked up the scattered debris from Apá's latest yard project. I usually gathered the clothes from the clothesline. I leaped up to snag the dry, stiff laundry, threw it into a basket, and brought everything into the house to fold.

I couldn't wait to grow up and never have to pick and pluck and fill another burlap sack again. Or complete another English assignment. Or do another stupid household chore. I pretended I had an aunt who lived an extravagant lifestyle in a big city, enjoying hot cinnamon tea in expensive shops and wrapped up in lavish fur coats with sparkling silver jewelry. She would come for me and we'd go to her enormous mansion with a wrap-around balcony and a chef who baked desserts every day.

"Well, darlin'," my imaginary aunt said one afternoon, sipping her cup of steaming hot tea with her pinky raised delicately in the air. "Be gone to those rubbish chores. What do you say? Shall we wander through the garden out back today? See a Broadway show tonight? The ladies at the hair salon have been absolutely raving about—"

My make-believe world was interrupted when I noticed our next-door neighbor staring at me from the fence dividing our yards. She had the reputation of being nosy, always lurking. A burning cigarette hung from her bottom lip, and her tanned, rubbery skin looked like fruit leather. She had stretched the garden hose across the yard and was dumping water onto her sorry-looking Chihuahuan sage shrub.

Trying to ignore her, I jumped into the air and ripped another shirt from the line. I tossed into the basket, straining to see her out of the corner of my eye. She was still staring. Then her hoarse voice yelled across the lawn, "You should ask your mama some questions about yourself." She took a puff of the cigarette and held it between her two fingers the way Apá did, water still falling from the hose. She cleared her throat and went on, "Ask her about who you are. Ask her who your papa *really* is. Look at yourself, *mija*. You're a white girl. *Una chica blanca*."

What was she saying? "No, I'm Mexican."

She scoffed and chuckled at the same time. Her nostrils flared as she breathed in deep. "Believe what you want, white girl. Just ask your mama. Maybe she'll tell you the truth." She sucked the cigarette, the end glowing a bright orange. "Ask her." She disappeared into her house.

That wasn't the first time someone had questioned me about my appearance. For as long as we lived in Cashion, rumors of the white girl living with a Mexican family seeped through the neighborhood. When the Sánchezes or the Alemans asked my sisters about my skin color, they said of course I was Mexican. Or when someone asked my brothers if I'd been adopted, they simply said no.

The previous month, a neighbor from a few houses over stopped by to ask Amá for a cup of milk. When the neighbor saw me running around with my brothers, I overheard her ask Amá, "Who's the little white girl?"

Amá looked at her confused and said what she always said, "That's my daughter. She gets her lighter skin from my mother's side."

At school, I had read *The Ugly Duckling*, turning the pages intensely. I related to the little duck's frustration when his feathers didn't blend in with the color of his family's. I understood his curiosity in asking questions to find out where he came from, and in the end, I felt his happiness when he discovered his family was a flock of beautiful swans— his true identity was revealed.

Like the little duck, my longing to fit in grew. I'd sit for hours thinking of all the possible answers to make sense of the ongoing puzzle. I must have been adopted. Maybe Amá wanted more kids but couldn't. Wait, no, that couldn't be. With a brood of nine children, all within a few years of one another, she didn't appear to have any trouble. Perhaps my parents adopted me from another family.

Maybe I was a rare case of an accidental baby swap at the hospital. When little Sammy was born, we stood in the hospital hallway looking through the tall window of the Neonatal Intensive Care Unit at the sea of babies, all defined by only a pink or blue blanket. Putting a baby in the wrong bed with the wrong name tag could be an easy mistake. What if the real Minu was out there in the world somewhere? And here I was, trapped in this awful life I wasn't supposed to be living.

But the chain-smoking neighbor lady brought a new thought to mind. It had been the first time someone mentioned *my father*. Was there a bigger secret behind it all? My stomach twisted into knots. Maybe she really did know something I didn't. I'd take her advice and ask my mother.

I found Amá in the living room, sewing a dress for one of my sisters. She didn't look up when I sat on the arm of the sofa. Anxious for an answer, I picked at a seam on the cushion. "Amá, the neighbor lady said I should ask you who my papa is. Why would she say something like that?" I held my breath.

Amá raised a single eyebrow and pursed her lips, not taking her eyes off the fabric and needle. She began to sew faster, her hand lashing up and down, and then let out a long sigh. "That woman is a gossip, *mija*. A sloppy, jealous, fat, old hag. *La chimosa gorda*. Don't you go believing that bullshit, you hear me?"

I looked down at my arm, a tinted pink from my brief time in the afternoon sun. It didn't match my mother's bronzed complexion. I was ashamed of my skin. "But why am I white, and you, Apá, Irma, Dolores, Esméralda, Julio . . . are all brown?"

She stopped sewing and lifted her head to meet my eyes, giving me a hard stare. "How many times do I have to tell you? You look like my mama—*tu abuela*. Now stop being so sensitive."

11

It was a breezy Friday night in early September, a little over a month since we were at the farmhouse. My parents were at a friend's house, and the boy from across the street, Pachi, came over. He and Julio had cooked up a plan of baking homemade donuts.

"Do you even have a recipe?" I asked them, putting my hands on my hips as they scavenged for the ingredients in the kitchen.

"No, we don't need one," Julio said, whipping bowls out of the cupboards and utensils out of the drawers. Just mix up flour, milk, eggs, and sugar. Lots and lots of sugar. Roll them and bake them in the oven. You'll see, Güera!"

"Sounds like the only thing you're baking up is a bad idea," I said. "Apá isn't gonna like this."

Julio measured a cup of flour. "Oh, *cállate*. Apá loves donuts. He'll be so excited to eat one, he'll forget he's mad."

"That flour is for Amá's tortillas, Julio."

He ignored me and poured the cup of flour into a glass bowl. Pachi shook some sugar and cracked two eggs into the bowl, and Julio added a bit of milk. He stirred the mixture with a wooden spoon, and once the muddled concoction turned into a gooey dough, they dropped it in small circles onto an ungreased pan and stuck it into the oven.

Thirty minutes later, when the timer went off, they opened the oven to see dry, shriveled-up dough across the pan.

"Yuck," Pachi said. "I ain't eating that."

"Needs more milk," Julio said, tossing on a mitt and taking the pan out of the oven. He threw the sorry-looking donuts into the trash can and started on the second batch. I helped this time.

Once again, Pachi sprinkled sugar and cracked two eggs into a bowl while Julio measured the flour and poured the milk. I stirred. We shaped the doughy mixture into circles, increased the oven temperature to 450 to speed up the process, and placed them in the oven.

Twenty minutes later, we opened the oven to see a burned batch of scraggly donuts.

Julio slammed the over door. "*¡Mierda!*"

"Apá's gonna be so mad," I whispered.

"Yeah, I'm outta here," Pachi said, heading toward the door. "I don't want to be here when your dad comes home."

The kitchen was a mess. Flour covered the dingy white linoleum floor, piles of sugar scattered across the counters, and the demolished batches of donuts laid at the top of the trash can.

Julio tipped the flour bag into the measuring cup to start the third batch.

I put the milk carton back in the refrigerator. "Forget the donuts, Julio. We gotta get this place cleaned up before Amá and Apá get back."

"One more batch. We need to use more flour. This time, they'll turn out." He tipped the flour bag too much, spilling it all over the counter and floor.

"No, we need to clean up!" I yelled, slamming the refrigerator closed. The handle snapped off and fell to the floor.

Julio pointed. "You broke it!"

"I didn't mean to!"

Just then, we heard the roaring engine of Apá's truck approach the driveway. Julio jumped on the counter to look out the window. "They're here!" The engine turned off.

Julio jumped down from the counter and shoved the burned donuts deep into the trash. I hurried around the kitchen, frantically putting the ingredients back into the cupboards.

The front door swung open, and Apá's heavy footsteps tromped into the house. Julio and I held our breath, standing tall and stiff. When

Apá walked into the kitchen, his eyes almost popped out of his head. Amá stood behind him, giving us a withering look.

"What the hell is going on?" Apá asked.

"We were making donuts," I said, my voice so soft I didn't think they'd heard me.

Apá saw the broken handle on the floor. "*¡Estúpidos malditos niños!*" he yelled. "Wasted food *and* you broke the fridge!"

Julio's eyes shifted as if looking for an escape. Apá pounded his fist on the counter. In the same beat, Julio darted to the front door, and I was right behind him.

"Don't you dare run away, *niños*!" Apá screamed as he ran after us.

Julio flew out the front door, ran across the yard, and into the night. I stopped and turned back.

"Julio, you son of a bitch. Get your goddamn ass back here!" Apá's scream echoed down the street.

"Keep your voice down," Amá said. "The neighbors will hear you." She followed Apá out the front door, pulling her jacket tight around her.

Apá stood in the yard, his fists clenched, staring out into the darkness. A full moon lit up the night, and dim lampposts lined the street.

"Fine. Run, boy! We don't want you, anyway. Don't you come back here, or I'll beat your ass."

Apá turned to me. "As for you, Güera, get your damned ass back in the house." He stomped toward me and smacked me on the back of my head. "Clean up the mess you made. And tell your *hermano* not to come back. We're better off without him."

At that moment, I wanted to be anywhere else but there. It would have been the perfect time for my imaginary aunt to come rescue me.

My brother would be okay, I kept telling myself. The few times he had run away before, he assured me that he always found a comfortable place to lay his head for the night. Once, he had dug a hole below the house—he called it his secret place and only went there in runaway instances like this. He kept a blanket and flashlight there and made a pillow out of the dirt.

Other nights he stayed in the neighbor's shed, and a few times, he even slept on the roof. He told me it wasn't so bad up there. It was the best seat for watching the twinkling desert stars.

Julio was gone the following two days. Apá and Amá never went to look for him.

It was late September and another hot afternoon, though it had cooled to the mid-nineties. Still, I swore we could hear our bare feet burning on the backyard dirt.

My parents had gone to town to run errands and left my four younger brothers under my supervision, once again. With me in charge for a day, it was a perfect time for the boys to act like hoodlums, and they knew it. They migrated from the house to the backyard, to the Hideaway, and one time I found them on the roof. I tried to tame them until I learned it was easier just to join the fun.

As the sun lifted in the sky, we started playing hide-and-seek.

"*Uno, dos, tres, cuatro, cinco, seis,*" Danny counted from the other side of the house.

Ruben and Sammy darted toward the front as David and I searched around the backyard for the sneakiest hiding spot.

"Minu, over here," David called. "I found one!"

I followed his voice to meet him behind the chicken shed. He stood in front of the refrigerator with the broken handle. Apá had plopped it back there after the donut catastrophe. The intense sun had already turned it a dim yellow.

"Try it," David said, opening the creaking door.

"You think I can fit?"

He cranked the door wider. I leaned my head into the darkness. The dampness trapped on the inside seeped out, hitting my face while the smell of mildew filled my nose.

"Yuck. I'm not getting in there."

Before I knew it, a hard shove pushed me into the fridge.

"No! Dave!" I yelled.

He slammed the door shut before I could put up a fight. Pitch darkness. I sat scrunched into a ball with my knees to my chin and my neck craned to the side. The surrounding walls were just a couple of inches from my face.

David laughed from the other side of the door. "Hey, guys! Come look. I pushed Minu into the fridge."

"Not funny, David. Let me out!" I roared, pushing against the door. The humidity hugged me, and I could now taste the mildew on my tongue.

Footsteps from the rest of the boys approached. Hysterical laughter came from the other side.

"Let me out!" I screamed again.

The boys continued to laugh. A droplet of salty sweat trickled down from my hairline to my ear.

I felt the refrigerator shift as the boys tugged on the door handle. They yanked the door again; the fridge nudged forward off its back two pilings. And again. The laughter stopped.

"Minu, the latch isn't opening," David said through the door. His voice sounded panicky. "Push the door from the inside."

I pressed my shoulder against the door. Then again, with every ounce of strength I could muster. It was getting harder to breathe. I opened my mouth wide and wheezed.

"Open up! I can't breathe!"

"It won't open. It's stuck. Help!" David screamed. "Danny, run and get help!"

My heart thumped wildly. Surely, it would pound through my chest and hop next to me. The tight space closed in around me. My lungs screamed for air. My head felt as light as a feather, and my body went numb as if I were paralyzed.

Life went dark.

Beeping in the distance. As I blinked, an orderly room with white walls and a small TV in the corner showing a baseball game came into view. I moved my fingers, scratching at thin sheets. My tongue swished around my mouth to feel a tube taking up space. I tried to talk but only a moan came out.

Across the room, Amá sat in the wooden chair looking out the window. She turned to me, her lips pressed in a thin line.

Just then, a doctor walked into the room. He was dressed in a white coat and had a stethoscope hanging around his neck.

"Hello, little one. How are you feeling?" He touched the top of my forehead with the back of his hand, reminding me I was indeed alive. I nodded slowly to show him I'd heard him. He took a seat at the end of the bed, crossing his legs and folding his hands in his lap.

"You're lucky to be alive, Minu," he said. "You nearly suffocated to death."

Memories flashed in my mind: the rusty fridge, the broken latch, the dark space, the urge to breathe. I strained my eyes to the corner to scan Amá's face for a reaction. Her stare was icy. Was she mad at me? Mad at my brothers?

The doctor gave me an apologetic smile. "Good thing your father was nearby. He used a crowbar to open the fridge and called an ambulance when you weren't breathing." The doctor looked at my mother and then back at me. "He saved your life."

12

*A*má and Apá never took us to a dentist. It didn't matter how serious our problems were. They couldn't afford it and figured it wasn't a matter of life and death.

Soon after Sammy turned two, he jumped off the top bunk bed and knocked out his four front teeth. My parents didn't have the money to replace them, so he had to wait until his permanent ones came in. We nicknamed him Toothless.

Just a couple of months later, an abscess grew on the gum of my upper back tooth. I begged Amá and Apá to take me to a dentist, but they told me I had to deal with the pain. It was unbearable. The herbal concoction Amá gave me didn't help. The left side of my cheek swelled up so big it looked as if I had a large marble on the side of my mouth.

That week at school, during Mrs. Cable's science lesson, she stopped mid-sentence and glared at me from across the room. "Miss Becerra, spit out your gum."

I swallowed the excess saliva lingering in my mouth, and spoke slow, making sure to pronounce each syllable clearly. "I'm not chewing gum, Mrs. Cable."

Her eyes narrowed and she cocked her head as if ready to pounce. "I won't ask you again. Spit the gum out."

"I don't have gum. It's my toof," I said.

Some students giggled at my pronunciation. Mrs. Cable pressed her lips so tight they turned pale.

"Miss Becerra, out in the hall. Now!"

The class stayed quiet as I trudged out the door. Mrs. Cable slammed the classroom door behind us. This cantankerous, bitter woman was a bigger pain than the abscess itself. Earlier that school year, she had forced me to eat the soggy spinach that was plopped on my lunch plate. She told me that since I was on the free lunch program, I had to eat every piece of food they gave me.

"But I don't like spinach," I told her, wrinkling my nose at the look, the smell, and the thought of those disgusting leaves trickling down my throat into my belly.

I had tried spinach the last time it was served at lunch. I realized quickly it tasted like nothing but a hunk of grass. If I wanted to eat grass, I'd go to the rich houses on the other side of town and cut a wedge from their lawn.

"But it's good for you, Minu," Mrs. Cable said. "And we have strong, healthy students here at Littleton Elementary. Don't you want to be one of them?"

I stared at her. Did she *really* want me to answer that?

"I don't want to have to tell your parents that you're wasting food, Minu."

My parents won't mind, I thought. I stared at the spinach. The spinach stared back. She slammed her hand on the table, and I jumped out of my seat. "Eat it, Minu. Eat it!" she yelled. I swear steam blew out her ears.

I was cornered, and there was nothing else I could do, so I pinched the mushy green leaves from the plate, dropped them into my mouth, and chewed fast, hoping the faster I chewed, the faster I could swallow and get the nasty vegetable off my tongue. I shuddered. The taste was even worse than I remembered. The texture made me dry heave, but I choked down every leaf that day.

Now here we were again, squaring off in the hallway. She flashed that wicked smile I'd seen many times before and, with no words, slapped the left side of my face. The abscess burst open, and blood splattered from my mouth onto the floor. Her small beady eyes grew wide and her mouth opened to inhale as much air as she could gasp. Just as shocked as Mrs. Cable, I patted the side of my cheek, and the lump was gone. She looked at the droplets of blood on the floor and back to me.

"I thought—oh, my goodness, Minu, I thought you were chewing—"

Before she could finish her sentence, I was sprinting down the school hallway for the front doors. "Minu! Come back here!" she yelled after me.

I bolted out of the building, my heart pounding against my chest. I stopped and rested my hands on my knees to catch my breath. My cheek throbbed, and the coppery taste of blood filled my mouth. Tears fell to the ground mixed with splotches of red.

I sprinted home, the entire mile, not stopping until I stumbled through the front door. I stretched my head over the kitchen sink, wiping the blood with a towel and groaning in pain.

"What happened to you?" Dolores asked from the dining room table. She was home from school for lunch and munching on a leftover chorizo burrito. I told her through the soaked towel pasted to my mouth about Mrs. Cable's accusation and her slap. Dolores' eyebrows raised to the middle of her forehead.

"*¡Pinche cabróna!* I'll take care of this," was all she said before storming out the front door. She had dealt with Mrs. Cable when she was in her class and had despised every minute.

The next morning, Mrs. Cable walked into the classroom with a black-and-blue half-moon bruise just under her left eye. Whispers and giggles trickled around the room.

"All righty then," she said, picking up her math book. "Shall we get started?"

Not once did she look at me. Dolores showed her what happened when someone overstepped a boundary in the Becerra family. I didn't have to worry about Mrs. Cable again.

13

When spring rolled around, it meant that yellow onions were ripe and ready for picking. After the usual three-in-the-morning wake-up and the long drive to the onion farm, Esméralda, Julio, David, and I scattered across the field, each with a pair of clippers, torn gloves, and a dirty bucket.

The onions ripe for plucking had luscious green leaves that sprouted from the top of their heads. We'd pluck a bulb, hold it up to the morning light to make sure there were no signs of insects or rottenness, and then snip the excess leaves and roots before plopping it into the bucket. Sometimes we stumbled across a rotten onion that reeked of decay and mold. Flies buzzed over the stacks of the old, wet vegetables, and we scurried around them holding our shirts over our noses to keep from heaving.

The late May desert temperatures reached up to the nineties and often triple digits. Beads of sweat made clean streams on our dusty skin as they dropped from our hairlines to our chins. To keep my mind off the desert sun frying my face and limbs, I fantasized about spending the day at the local community pool. I pictured myself wearing a bright pink swimsuit with a flowery cap wrapped around my head, leaping off the diving board and splashing into a pool of ice-cold water. I floated to the top, my nose leading, as composed as those fancy ladies I saw on the television.

After a nice cold swim, I'd work up an appetite. I thought about my favorite snack: a pickle (most kids were into sweet stuff, but I wasn't a candy girl). It wasn't just any pickle. I loved the five-cent pickles from the Asian grocery market down the road or, as we called it, the Chinito Store. We didn't get allowances, so I'd pocket the loose change I found in Apá's truck or while cleaning the living room sofa cushions and store it in a jar under my cot. Whenever I saved up five pennies, I'd walk to the Chinito Store.

One especially exhausting afternoon in the field, I couldn't stop thinking about those pickles. I pictured myself running through the aisles of the rows of canned foods and past the produce to the meat section, where a large jar of pickles sat on the counter. I'd ask the man behind the counter for "one pickle, please." He'd untwist the jar and pull out the plumpest, juiciest green pickle. My mouth would salivate and I'd reach for—

Just then, something smacked the back of my head, interrupting the happy scene. I looked at the ground to see an onion rolling to a stop.

"Quit daydreaming out there, Güera. Back to work!" Apá yelled from across the field, shielding the sun from his eyes with his hand.

He sometimes picked with us, but most days he stood at the end of the field observing. His hands behind his back and eyes narrowed, he ordered his workforce like any good army drill sergeant. Rubbing my head, I did as he said and kept picking.

When we kids weren't lost in our imaginations, sometimes we had competitions. We'd race to see how many onions we could clip in ten minutes. David, a sly son of a gun, wouldn't clip the top stem, filling his bucket up quicker than the rest of us.

"I'm the champion onion picker," he would shout, flaunting his full bucket.

Sometimes, wars broke out.

"Onion war!" Julio would shout as he chucked an onion across the field like a grenade, often aiming at David. Then David would side-arm one back at Julio, who always managed to duck below the row of onion stalks, whooshing a dust swirl into the air. I'd hurl one at Esméralda, hitting her arm, and she would laugh and pitch one back.

"¡Ándale, cabrónes!" Apá would yell. "Knock it off and get back to work!"

We never say a word. Just went back to picking.

"He never lets us play," I'd mumble, wiping my forehead with my forearm. "It's no fun picking every day. He can be so mean."

One day, David said, "He ain't right in the head, Minu. Don't you know that by now?"

I nodded, but I didn't want it to be true.

On our way home, Apá often stopped at the local Circle K gas station a few blocks from school to fill up the truck and buy a pack of Marlboro Reds. I crouched down in the truck's bed to avoid anyone seeing me. The last thing I needed was any of my classmates catching sight of my dirt-caked fingernails and raggedy clothes or, worse, smelling me.

David didn't care. He leapt over the side of the truck. "I'm gonna see if Apá will buy me a candy bar."

"Not a chance," Julio said. His lips were chapped from too much sun, and dust coated his face, shirt, and arms.

As Apá climbed back into the truck with his pack of cigarettes and revved the engine, David hopped into the bed. He flaunted an Almond Joy bar with a smirk.

"Apá bought you one?" Julio cried.

"Nah, took it for free."

"What! I'm telling," I blurted out. "You'll go to hell for that kind of thing, David!"

I yelled to Apá through the back window, telling him what David had stolen from the store.

"So what?" Apá yelled back. "They charge too much. They deserve to lose it."

David snickered, ripped open the candy bar, and took a big bite.

14

*M*y brothers were like the pack of coyotes we sometimes spotted in the desert—wild, testy, and rough. Julio and David—the alphas—challenged each other relentlessly and ordered the younger brothers around. Danny, Ruben, and Sammy—the pups of the pack—followed the leaders and tried their darndest to keep up.

The five of them wrestled and roughhoused constantly, most fights ending with one of them smacking their head into a wall and someone crying. Amá told them to deal with it themselves, while Apá smiled and said pain was good for youngsters. At other times, Apá's fuse was way too short.

Since Julio received the brunt of our father's anger, he was an expert at reading him. "If you look into his eyes," Julio whispered to me one night, "and they're beady and droopy, he'll explode like a pinata if you tick him off. That's when he's Crazy Eyes, not Apá."

I knew exactly what he meant. Just the week before, while I was washing the dinner dishes, it got dark in the kitchen, so I turned on the light. Within minutes, I felt a hard smack to the back of my head, and I nearly dropped the plate I was rinsing. I turned around to see Apá. His dark eyes were smoldering. Crazy Eyes.

"Wha—what'd you do that for?" I asked him.

"Do you pay the electric bill?"

I wanted to tell him that, yes, I *did* pay for the bill because if it weren't for us plucking and picking in those fields day after day, we wouldn't have money to have lights on in the house. But I knew better than to cross him. I shook my head.

"Then keep the damn light off," he said with steel in his voice.

A couple of months later, after a long day of working the fields, David accidentally dropped a glass of milk in the kitchen. Apá took his belt off and lashed him with it. David tried to stand up to our father, to fight back, but Apá hit him harder. Then Apá handed the belt to Amá, and she snapped the belt on his behind several times. When Apá felt he'd gotten his point across, he stormed out of the house and headed to his truck, slamming the door and revving the engine before disappearing to who knew where.

Another evening, I lay on my cot doing homework when all five of my brothers ran into the bedroom in sheer panic. I sprang up. "What'd you do?" The house shook when the back door slammed open.

"Danny did it," David whispered.

"I didn't mean to," Danny said.

"Where are you, *cabrónes*?" Apá yelled, his voice shaking the walls.

"He's got them crazy eyes, Minu," Julio said, his face frantic.

Leaping across the room, I grabbed yesterday's shirt from the floor and shoved it down the back of my pants—an attempt to shield myself from the incoming attack. "Quick, stuff your pants!" I said.

My brothers flew around the room, stuffing their pants with any shirt or sock they could find.

Apá's barged into the room, his pupils ignited, and his neck veins bulging so thick I thought they would tear open his skin. He stomped across the room and seized Julio by the shoulder. Apá slid his belt from his pants, twirled it in the air like a lasso, and slashed it to Julio's backside, the belt buckle jingling with each thrash. Julio held his hands over his face and a shrill cry escaped his lips.

David was next for the beating. He flinched with each snap of the belt. The rest of the boys took their turns, bearing the whips, the clothing beneath their pants buffering each beat. I stayed on my cot still as a statue, knowing if I left the room or made a movement, I'd be next.

When Apá finished whipping each son, he said through clenched teeth, "*Niños, estupidos.*"

On his way out of the bedroom, Apá grabbed my arm and threw me to the floor.

"What, Apá! What'd I do? I was just sitting on my bed." My cheek pressed into the wooden board.

"For being here, that's why!" The belt lashed into the air and down onto my rear with a crack.

Apá kept violence front and center in my brothers' lives.

One afternoon, he used a stick to draw a wide circle in the backyard dirt to make a boxing ring. "Let's see who the toughest Becerra boy is. You must all learn how to be strong Mexican men. David. Julio. You two are up first. Danny, Ruben, you're next. And little Sammy will take on the winner."

Apá sat in a lawn chair poker-faced, a burning cigarette dangling from his lower lip.

The boys hated it when he did this to them, but they knew better than to banter or they'd be fighting him instead. Julio and David stepped into the dirt ring, circling one another with their scrawny hands balled into fists and swaying in front of their faces. I watched through the back screen door, positioning myself strategically away from the scene.

"C'mon, Julio," Apá said. "Uppercut. Knock him on his chin. David, you gotta go for his head. Knock some sense into his puny brain."

David threw the first jab. Julio ducked out of the way and punched the side of David's face. Danny, Ruben, and Sammy stood to the side, flinching with each move.

"¡Andele!" Apá yelled, taking a puff of his cigarette.

As I peeked out the window, Amá stood next to me, drying her hands on a towel and mumbling under her breath. Together, we watched Julio take a hit to the nose.

Amá opened the door and stood with her hands on her hips. "Julio, enough of this."

Apá shot her a stifled look. "Put a sock in it, *cabróna*! Let the boys show me who the men are."

David pummeled Julio to the ground. A cloud of dust sailed into the air as they rolled across the dirt, throwing punches into one another's stomachs.

Apá leaned closer, his arms on his knees, cracking his knuckles. "*Si hermanos*, make the other tap out. Who's the strongest Becerra son? I don't raise no *cobardes!*" he yelled

David positioned Julio into a choke hold and tightened his arms with a grunt. Julio scrunched his face tight and gasped for air. He finally let out a muffled yell and tapped David's forearm to forfeit.

"David, *el ganador*, the winner!" Apá clapped with a belly laugh.

Julio rested on his knees, trying to catch his breath. He let out a wheezing cough. David closed his eyes, looking relieved the fight was over.

"Danny. Ruben. You're next," Apá said. He tightened his mouth around another cigarette and lit the end. Danny and Ruben looked at each other with fearful eyes, knowing they didn't have a choice.

Apá's constant push for fighting spilled over into our daily lives. Julio and David shared the bottom bunk, and sometimes in the middle of the night, I'd wake up to hear trash-talking whispers from across the dark room.

"I'll beat you next time. You'll see," Julio would hiss at David. "I'll show Apá who's the toughest son."

"Yeah, kick me again and see what happens."

"Psst," I whispered from across the room. "You guys better knock it off. You know what will happen if you wake Apá."

Nothing I said would stop them.

15

*B*ut then Apá would surprise us. We all stood stunned the day he unloaded a blue Stingray bicycle from his truck. He had bought it at a thrift store for a few bucks and gave it to David . It had rust spots peppered on the handlebars and a white banana seat. The rest of us siblings watched with envy as David rode the bike around the neighborhood—we didn't get gifts from Apá.

One morning a few months before I turned ten, I asked David if I could take the younger boys to daycare on his bike. Spring brought the best time of the year for seasonal vegetable picking, so Apá spent his days working the fields while we were at school, and Amá worked long hours at the laundromat and tortilla factory. Since my parents were both gone to work before dawn, and my sisters left for school just after them, I was responsible for Ruben and Sammy. I didn't mind—the daycare was on the way to Littleton Elementary.

Four-year-old Ruben crammed on the back pegs while three-year-old Sammy balanced on the long handlebars, and I steered from the banana seat. The slope from the driveway gave the bike momentum, and once we made it to the street, I pedaled. The bike was severely off balance and pulled us to the right, so I pedaled my skinny legs faster to center the bike and soon we were soaring. As we turned the corner, I stretched my neck to see over Sammy's head. Ruben squirmed behind me, making the bike teeter back and forth.

"Stop moving!" I yelled.

I locked my arms on the handlebars, but the bike jerked fast and tumbled over. Ruben and little Sammy skidded across the road. Pebbles and stones stabbed into my knee and palms as I came crashing down.

The neighbor, Mrs. Sánchez, had been watering her flowers when she saw the tumble. "Oh no, *niños*. Don't move," she yelled from across the yard. She threw the watering hose into the bushes and ran into the house. Sammy cried as loud as his little lungs allowed while drops of blood covered his knees.

Ruben sat up from the pavement. "I'm telling on you!" he yelled, holding his hand over his scraped arm. "You're going to get in so much trouble." His voice was somewhere between crying and angry. "I'm telling Apá."

"It was an accident!" I yelled back. Brushing off my hands, I picked up Sammy and hushed him. His screams made it hard to think, but one clear thought came through: Ruben was right. I'd get in big trouble for this one—big, big trouble.

Soon Mrs. Sánchez came barreling out of her house. Her fluffy hair spilled out of her white visor and bounced on her head as she ran to us. She held a box of Band-Aids, a bottle of peroxide, and a handful of cotton balls.

"You *niños*, okay? Let me clean you up."

She tended to Sammy first, carefully dabbing the cotton ball on the wound on his knee. Sammy cringed and then cried louder. Mrs. Sánchez hushed him and wrapped him in her arms.

"There. There, *mijo*," she said calmly. Sammy's wails quieted down. He wasn't used to hugs.

"I didn't mean for this to happen," I said to Mrs. Sánchez, hoping she wouldn't tell my parents.

"Yes, she did. It's all her fault," Ruben said. "She almost cracked my head open."

"You kids shouldn't ride all crammed on a bike like that," Mrs. Sánchez said. "Do your parents know what you're doing?" She wet a cotton ball with peroxide and rubbed it on Ruben's wound. He clenched his teeth and inhaled.

"They don't care," Ruben said.

Again, he was right. Our parents didn't care how we got to school. I was convinced they didn't care if we even *went* to school.

"Well," Mrs. Sánchez said, scooting over to Ruben to bandage his arm. "I wouldn't be letting my little ones ride to school that way."

She had ten kids of her own who all went to the private Catholic school in town. Apparently, they received a discount for having so many kids attend the school: pay for three kids and get one free or something like that. I'd watch every morning as her husband in his fancy suit led the kids to the station wagon to drop them off at school.

Mrs. Sánchez sighed. "Just be careful. I worry about you Becerras." She stuck a bright green Band-Aid on Sammy's knee and patted him on the top of his head. "There. All fixed. Good news: he'll live."

Sure, Sammy would be fine. I'd be the one dying tonight.

The three of us hopped on the bike once again, assuming our positions, and we were off, wobbling to their daycare.

The rest of the day at school, I thought about the beating I had coming. My brothers would surely tell Apá about the bike crash and Sammy's injured knee. Thrash! Snap! Slash! I winced thinking of the belt whisking into the air and lashing down on my behind. I'd stuff my pants, so it wouldn't hurt as much. Or maybe I'd lie low in the Hideaway for the night. Or I'd walk and walk and walk until my legs cramped up and I had blisters all over my feet. I bet I could make it to California.

I should never have piled my brothers onto the bike. But it was the easiest way to get them to school, and it was my responsibility. If my parents didn't like it, they shouldn't let me supervise them. I'd tell Apá it was an accident because it was. I didn't mean to hurt my little brothers.

After school, I walked home, bracing myself. From a distance, I could see my brothers wrestling in the front yard. Amá hung clothes on the line, and there, trenching a patch of the dirt yard with a hoe, was Apá. As if the situation couldn't get any worse, he was equipped with a weapon.

I might as well get it over with.

"There she is!" Ruben yelled, pointing to me as I walked up the drive. "She almost killed us this morning when she crashed the bike!"

He held up his scraped arm in my direction. "Remember this? 'Bout to get in *big* trouble."

I moped up the driveway. "It was an accident! I didn't mean to." My body was clammy and salty from working myself up all day.

Apá looked up from his hoeing with a sweaty face. I stiffened, waiting for his next move—like anticipating a loose cannon to launch into action. Yet instead, he laughed so hard, he bent over and held his stomach.

My brothers watched him, their mouths open.

"You're not in trouble, Guëra," Apá said, leaning against the hoe's tall handle. "You fell off a bike. It happens. I have bigger things to worry about."

I went to sleep that night, thankful Apá hadn't lost control. I wasn't hurt, and I didn't die.

16

*I*n the sizzling months of June and July, when the vegetable picking was slow around the Southwest, we drove down to Consuelo, Mexico, to stay with Amá's parents. My family would pile into the truck, some of us squeezing into the uncovered bed. We bought one large suitcase full of everyone's clothes to wear over the next several weeks. Sitting on lumpy pillows and quilts Amá had made, we watched six hundred miles of desert full of saguaro cacti and wooden telephone poles snap past.

There was always something special about heading down to Mexico, but the summer I turned twelve, I was the first one in the truck, chomping at the bit to leave. I couldn't face another day in the fields, and our trip was the closest thing to a vacation we knew. We'd see aunts, uncles, and cousins and find any reason to get together and fiesta. The grownups celebrated with *copas* of tequila, loud music, and dancing while we kids ate enormous piles of homemade beans, *carne asada* tacos, and homemade corn tortillas. Better yet, we loved seeing Abuelito Rosalio and Abuelita Ángela—well, maybe just Abuelito Rosalio.

I could always tell when we were getting closer to my grandparents' house. The sun slept, the truck bounced over the potholes, and the silhouettes of the towering surrounding mountains made us feel like we were a speck in a bowl. We'd arrive at my grandparents' small tan adobe house just before midnight, sleeping the rest of the night in the truck under the clear Mexican sky. The only sound was the crickets singing their lonely songs.

As the red sun rose over the foothills in the morning, Abuelito Rosalio tapped his fingers on the truck. "Wake up, Minukies," he whispered to me. And then he said louder, "Wake up, *chiquitos. Tunas* for breakfast."

Tunas were fruit from the prickly pear cactus. He always picked a bunch from the cacti growing in his yard when he knew we'd be in town. Once he removed the needles, he would carve up the paddles, soak them in water, and top them off with tomato, chile, and onion seasoning, creating my favorite treat: *nopalitos.*

"Abuelito!" we yelled, perking up with big, wide smiles. Abuelito Rosalio laughed his contagious, hearty laugh. He was a lean, robust man who wore his usual attire: a stiff white cowboy hat, a perfectly ironed button-up shirt, faded jeans with a shiny silver belt, and the warmest smile.

He held out a bowl filled to the brim with fresh fruit. We'd bite into the delicious prickly pear, the guts of the fruit breaking free and juice dripping from our chins and down our arms, leaving our fingers sticky. *Nopalitos* left its print on us, staining our teeth and lips bright red—it was the taste of summer in Mexico.

Apá opened the door, awakening from his slumber in the front seat of the truck. He still had sleepy eyes.

"*Bueno días*, Julio," Abuelito said.

"Same to you, Rosalio."

Abuelito shook Apá's hand in what looked like a forced greeting. It was obvious he still disapproved of Amá's choice for a husband. Despite the tension between the two men, they always did their best to stay cordial during our time together. Abuelito didn't cross Apá, and Apá didn't cross Abuelito.

Amá stepped out of the truck and hugged her father. "*Hola*, Apá."

"*Ah. Mi hija hermosa.*" He gave Amá a warm hug.

Since Amá was the only daughter Abuelito raised, she told us she grew up *la niña de papa*, daddy's girl. I pictured her as a little girl, spending her days alongside Abuelito Rosalio, feeding the farm animals, milking the cows, and picking the fresh guavas from the garden. She would have been the luckiest daughter in the world to spend her childhood days with a patient, gentle, and happy father like Abuelito Rosalio. A contrast to my own father. It made my heart ache.

Abuelita walked out of the house, drying her hands on her apron. Her thin hair was wrapped in curlers, and she wore her usual frown on her squinty face, hiding her crooked set of teeth. As Amá always said, she had lighter skin, but I was reminded again when I saw her, that it wasn't as light as mine. Even so, that's where my similarity with her ended.

Unlike Abuelito, Abuelita was a person of few words and kept her distance from her grandkids, finding things to do around the house to avoid contact with us, like cutting up and canning vegetables and making Mexican cookies that tasted like Styrofoam. The cruelest thing you could do to a Mexican lady was to refuse her food, so I always choked it down.

A part of me understood Abuelita's coldness. Amá told us that at only thirteen years old, Abuelita had lost her mother. On top of that, Abuelita and Abuelito had lost two children: a two-year-old daughter to an illness and an eleven-year-old son who was struck by lightning. Other stories floated around the tight-knit community about Abuelito's wandering eye and how he had two other children from two separate affairs he had pursued a few years earlier. Maybe Abuelita had reasons to be irritable all the time.

Scrawny chickens, dirty pigs, bloomed fig trees, and bougainvilleas with thick red flowers filled every inch of my grandparents' yard. Their house smelled of lamp oil mixed with the fresh rainstorm water Abuelita sprinkled on the dirt floors to keep the dust at bay.

Along with no electricity, the farm didn't have running water for cooking or baths. We fetched water from the nearby riverbank with a carrying pole resting on our shoulders and buckets swinging on each side. When I scooped the water from the river, I could fill the buckets only halfway before they'd get too heavy, and I'd lose my balance and tumble. Abuelito Rosalio would help me carry the water back to their bright blue kitchen, where we'd pour the water into a big red clay pot—our drinking water always had a hint of clay to the taste. For baths, we'd fill up an old horse tub and wash off in there.

The neighbor's house down the street served as the local grocery store. We'd go there almost every day to buy the ingredients needed for the day's meals, like freshly butchered meats and canned beans. When Apá was in a good mood, he'd give us a dollar to buy chile suckers. It was tough to figure out where all eleven of us would sleep in such a small space. My parents had it easy and slept in the second bed in the same room as my grandparents, which was fine by me since Abuelito's appendix sat in a glass jar on a shelf, freaking me out. Most of my brothers slept in the truck bed, and my sisters and I slept in the house on the dirt floor with one of the lumpy pillows we brought from home. Most nights, the sweltering summer air made it impossible to sleep.

As for the toilet, there was an old wooden outhouse Abuelito had built out back hidden behind the fig trees. And next to the outhouse, far enough away to avoid any vile smells, was a small shed where Abuelito created his magic.

He was a handy craftsman and a reputable blacksmith in the town of Consuelo. When the rustling of tools and the clanking of steel came from Abuelito's shed, I ran out to join him. The stench of coal hung thick, and smoke bellowed from a flue that opened through the ceiling. Tools of all kinds dangled from tarnished nails and covered the thin boarded walls. In the corner were rusted old remnants and trinkets of a different time: horse saddles, a metal saw, and wrapped-up wire and ropes. And there, swinging his hammer with brute force, was Abuelito.

I watched him for hours as he heated pieces of iron over the forge. Little by little, he'd share tidbits about the craft, his tools, and how important it was to stay calm and steady. When the metal became soft enough, he'd shape it with a chisel or hammer that sent sparks flying through the air like a shooting star. And once the shaping was complete, he let me blow on the metal to cool it down.

He held up a sturdy metal horseshoe. "Look at this piece of art, Minukies." A day's worth of dirt lined his fingernails, his hands rough and leathery. I imagined he once ran as wild as the untamed desert horses.

"A masterpiece," I whispered, grazing the warm horseshoe with my hand, its matte black finish as dark as night.

"Horseshoes symbolize *suerte*. Luck." Abuelito smiled. A map of wrinkles formed around his coffee-brown eyes. "We could all use a little extra luck in this life. Don't you think, Minukies?"

I nodded. Every precious minute I spent with Abuelito was a sliver of luck.

"I'd like to be just like you, Abuelo."

"Ahh, with a heart like yours, you'll do great things in this life, Minukies." He winked. "You have the strong Escobedo blood in you. *Chica fuerte*."

As the sun set low in the west, my brothers, sisters, and I gathered around Abuelito and a burning campfire to hear of his wild Mexican Revolution days. We must have listened to his legendary stories a dozen times, but they never grew old.

"Tell us about Pancho Villa again, Abuelo," Julio said.

"No, no, you've heard that one so many times," Abuelito Rosalio said. The fire crackled, lighting up Abuelito's face.

Julio laughed. "One more time!"

"*Sí. Por favor*, Abuelo," Ruben chimed in.

"Did you kill people, Abuelo?" David asked with wide eyes.

Abuelito nodded. "But only the bad guys."

"The bullet one! Tell that story." Julio clapped.

Chuckling, Abuelito held up his hands. "Okay, okay." Once again, he told the legendary tale. I'd heard it so many times I could recite it myself.

During one of the Mexican battles, Abuelito had been shot three times. One bullet just missed his head, and the other two hit him on his left side. The two pieces of lead had lodged themselves in between his ribs, and since Abuelito had received no medical attention, the bullets remained in his side.

"Can we feel them again, Abuelo?" Julio and David both asked.

Abuelito lifted the left side of his pressed shirt to show us the two small splotchy scars on his tan skin. I carefully grazed my fingertips over them, as I had done many times before.

"It's a reminder of the fight I have for this country," Abuelito said, his strong jaw tightened. "I thought I was a goner after getting shot, but with your grandmother's care, I lived to tell the tale."

Abuelita was listening through the kitchen window. She rolled her eyes.

When Abuelito told his stories, I studied him under the twinkling silver stars. I couldn't fathom the unspeakable, terrifying things his eyes had seen. The war years, the bullets, and the struggle to survive had created the wisest, bravest, and kindest person I had ever known. He was like a jacaranda tree we occasionally passed on the drive through Mexico—sturdy, rugged, and blossomed with life. I desperately wanted to take him back to Cashion to live with us.

"Abuelo, why don't you live in our country?" I asked.

Abuelito laughed that hearty laugh and patted the tangled hair on the top of my head, just like he always did.

"I wouldn't be caught dead on the other side, *el otro lado*, Minukies. I disagree with how those foul Americans live."

Abuelito lived his entire life without stepping foot in the States. And he never learned English. He stood firm in his Mexican culture, determined to make a positive difference in the unstable economy. Along the way, he became an advocate for the small town of Consuelo, working to build a sense of order by hosting town halls to hear out the complaints and hardships of the residents. He replenished the town with resources for residents, religiously carrying buckets of water from the riverbank. He even engineered community showers.

Everyone in the town loved him. He was their leader, their hope. Mine too.

Among all the other things, he was also the mail carrier. Once a week, at four in the morning, he met the train to pick up mail and supplies for the residents of the community. I joined him on the early-morning two-mile trek, walking along the creek that poured water like a Spanish lullaby, soft and peaceful. We held dim lanterns in front of us that swayed from side to side, lighting the path we followed. Once we arrived at the train tracks, we'd wait, whispering to one another, careful not to wake the night. Soon enough, a bright round light appeared in the distance, and the whistle of the train announced its arrival.

As the train screeched to a slow stop, the conductor tipped his hat at us, and Abuelito grabbed the mailbags hanging from the train. On the walk back, vibrant yellow and orange streaks smeared across the sky as the sun rose above the velvety mountains. Our hands were full, and the lanterns dangled in the grasp of a single finger. We walked to town, passing adobe houses painted vivid colors of blue, pink, and red, and delivered the mail to one of the residents' homes that operated as a post office.

"I feel like we're noble people, Abuelo," I said once the last envelope was dropped off. "Those envelopes and packages hold important information, and it's up to us to get it to the right person."

His pearly white grin showed under his thick mustache. He patted me on my head. "We're very noble people, Minukies. Never forget that."

Mexico was my safe place, and Abuelito Rosalio was the gentle warrior I needed.

17

It was the night before our drive back to Arizona. Along with being the bandit-hero of the area, Abuelito coordinated dances at the local hall in downtown Consuelo. The events usually evolved into a night filled with loud Mexican music while the crowd tossed back bottles and bottles of tequila and danced until the sun rose.

Amá pinned her hair up on one side, studying herself in Abuelita's silver framed mirror, humming a song in her tender voice. She glided the lipstick across her parted lips and rubbed her lips together to spread the bright red color. Her peach dress exposed her soft, sun-kissed shoulders—her dark skin always popped next to shades of orange. Dark curls bounced around her face, a dainty amount of mascara complimented her eyes, and her perfume matched her romantic mood.

I stared with disgust at my reflection. "I look ugly when I stand next to you."

Amá gave me a quick smile, only half listening. Leaning closer to the mirror, she inserted big silver hoop earrings into each ear. Her humming continued.

I unscrewed the top of her face powder, dabbed the sponge into the powder, and tapped it onto my face, as I saw Amá do. Powder particles lingered in the air as I studied the result in the mirror. The color of the powder made me look dirty, as though someone had smeared mud on my forehead, chin, and cheeks. Like a reflex, I quickly rubbed the back of my hand across my face to wipe it off.

"It looks better on you," I said.

She slipped on her heels. "Come on, *mija*. We're going to be late."

Apá didn't come with us to the dance hall. He said he wasn't in the mood. Although he had been relaxed and calm since we arrived, that day he kept to himself, not saying much. Irma, Dolores, and my three youngest brothers stayed home with Abuelita, while Esméralda headed out to a house party with some of our cousins, most likely to find boys.

The dance hall had plain white walls with sticky marble floors and smelled of overpowering cologne mixed with sweat. Julio, David, and I sat at a table slurping red punch. On the stage, the bushy-mustached mariachi band balanced sombreros on their heads as they shook maracas and strummed the vihuela. I always hated those Mexican songs the drunks liked to dance to—making sad tunes sound happy.

Amá had made her way out to the dance floor a few songs before. She swayed her shoulders and hips elegantly back and forth, her dress moving with each poised stride. A tall man with chest hair bulging over the collar of his low-cut shirt weaved his way to Amá and placed his hands on her hips. She leaned her head back with a loud laugh and put her arms around the man's neck. They danced in rhythm, looking natural and fluent, like two trees swaying in a subtle breeze.

"Should she be dancing with him like that?" I asked my brothers. They both shrugged.

For the next song, the maracas and vihuela slowed down and the tempo turned seductive. Amá and the hairy-chested man matched the mood, pressing their bodies against each other. I looked at Julio and David sipping their punch, not at all fazed that our mama was out on the dance floor practically cuddled up with another man.

I thought about Apá back at the house, not knowing his wife was flirting on the dance floor. Regardless of how angry I got at him, that very moment, I was disappointed in Amá.

I stood up from the table, walked toward the dance floor, and carefully weaseled my way in between my mother and the man, wrapping my arms around her waist and snubbing her dance partner.

Amá looked down at me. "What are you doing, *mija*?" Her smile was remorseful, but her eyebrows told me she was perturbed.

"I want to dance too."

The hairy-chested man chuckled. "This your daughter?"

Suddenly, Abuelito came into sight with his arms stretched out. "Come on, Minukies." He twirled me around. "Let's you and me dance."

The next morning turned blue and hot fast. My parents, siblings, and I packed up our single suitcase and plopped it into the truck. As we said goodbye to Abuelito and Abuelita, I noticed we were missing one Becerra daughter—Esméralda.

It didn't take Apá long to notice either. "Where's your sister?" he asked Irma, Dolores, and me. We all shrugged.

He marched to the end of the dirt driveway and looked up and down the road. Swearing, he shook his head and marched back to the house. "¡Vamos!" he clapped at us. "Get in. We have a ten-hour drive home. If Esméralda doesn't make it in the next couple of minutes, we're leaving without her. ¡Hija estupida!"

Just as the last of us squeezed into the back of the truck, a rusted brown car with an ear-piercing motor pulled up. In the driver's seat was a boy with greased-back hair, and in the passenger seat was Esméralda.

The two of them leaned toward each other for a kiss, and then my sister stepped out of the car wearing yesterday's shirt and skirt, leftover makeup smeared under her eyes. Her long dark hair was unbrushed and matted, and she held her red stilettos in one hand.

Apá stormed toward her.

"What, Apá?" Esméralda threw her forearm into the air as if it were a shield. I'm here. I'm here."

"You stayed out all night with this cabrón?" Apá shouted, yanking her back up the driveway.

Esméralda hurried to keep up with him.

"Get your ass in the truck," he said, pushing her. Then he turned back to the boy sitting in his car. "And you," Apá said through clenched teeth, "you aren't leaving so fast." He fumed to the driver's side of the car, opened the door, and heaved him out.

The boy raised his hands above his head. "Amigo, amigo," he said, his eyes wide in horror.

"Julio, leave the poor kid alone," Abuelito yelled from the house.

Apá grasped the front of the boy's white T-shirt and pulled him an inch away from his enraged face. "If you're going to be with my daughter all night—and do God knows what—you're coming back with us. You're going to marry her!" Apá let go of his grip and shoved the boy.

"Apá, *¡basta!*" Esméralda yelled from the truck bed. "No. Don't make him!"

"Go on," Apá told the boy. "Go tell your folks you're coming with us."

The boy nodded his head frantically and sped off. His tires crunched on the dirt road, startling the bony chickens in the yards.

Apá breathed heavily as he watched the car disappear into the distance and then mumbled, "A disgrace to the family."

Esméralda cupped her hands over her eyes as if to hide the tears that might fall. The rest of us sat slouched in the truck bed, surrounded by the lumpy pillows and scratchy blankets.

"You really think he'll come back?" I whispered to Irma.

"He better not come back," Esméralda said. "I'm not marrying him."

"Should have thought about that before you stayed with him last night, *tonta*," Dolores piped up. Esméralda kicked her.

"He'll be back," Irma said. "It's a free ride into the United States. His family would be happy to have a son there. He'd be stupid not to come."

"But won't his family miss him?" I asked.

"He'll send money to them with whatever job he finds."

Abuelito leaned over the truck bed with a bowl of fresh *nopalitos*. "Here's a snack while we wait. Save some for the road," he said with a wink.

Twenty minutes later, the loud car engine puttered to a stop in front of the house, this time with the boy and what must have been his mother. After a brief goodbye to the woman, the boy stepped out of the car carrying nothing but a small duffel bag. Without a word, he hopped into the back of the truck with the rest of us, taking a seat next to Esméralda, who barely made room for him.

Apá started the truck and skirted down the driveway. Abuelito and Abuelita waved from the house, their faces filled with concern.

"*Hola. Me llamo* Agapito," the boy said timidly.

He had smooth skin with no facial hair. We all took turns introducing ourselves. Esméralda stayed quiet, her cheek resting on her bundled fist.

"How old are you?" David asked.

"*Diecisiete,*" Agapito answered. Seventeen.

"Welcome, *amigo,*" Julio said, shaking Agapito's hand.

"Are you our new brother?" Danny asked.

I was glad he asked since I was thinking the same thing.

"No!" Esméralda cried out. "He's not your brother." She put her face in her hands.

Before we passed through the border check from Mexico to Arizona, Apá pulled over and coached Agapito on the protocol. Apá told him if the patrol agent asked where he was from, he was to answer simply, "Phoenix." Apá made him practice his pronunciation a few times. Agapito's English was choppy, but it would do.

When we passed through the checkpoint, the agents gave us a few waves and nods.

Later that evening, when we arrived back in Cashion, Apá began building a single room for Agapito and Esméralda. The impulsive construction of slapping an extra room onto a house was something Apá had learned from his father. For the next week, he tore down a living room wall and then added plywood, a roof, and a door. It wasn't too sturdy, but it did the job.

After a few months of living together and sharing a bedroom, Agapito and Esméralda realized they weren't cut out for dating, let alone marriage. With the money Agapito had earned working at the local train station, he moved out and rented a room in one of the nearby towns.

But it wasn't the last we'd hear of him.

18

*D*olores got pregnant just shy of turning nineteen. I thought she had just gained a bunch of weight, but it turned out that her new boyfriend had knocked her up. When the Baptist Church found out, it raised a big hoopla in the congregation. Pastor Gonzalez took Apá aside one morning after the Sunday service and told him our family was no longer welcome because of her immoral sin.

Apá's eyes grew wide, and a vein stuck out of his forehead. Church was the one thing in his life that brought him a smidgen of joy. He puffed out his chest and poked Pastor Gonzalez's shoulder as he mumbled ungodly words. Before anything bad happened, Amá grabbed Apá's shirt and dragged him outside.

"*¡Carbróna estúpida!*" Apá yelled in the car. "Who does Gonzalez think he is? He can't banish us from the congregation!

After that, Apá stopped praying and reading the Bible, and as a family, we stopped going to church. Bitterness and violence so often found their way into our house, and that hour or two on Sunday was one of the few times we had some peace. I was just as upset as Apá. With a snap of a finger, my comfort, my church, a community I had been excited to be a part of, vanished.

A few weeks later, Dina, a classmate of mine who lived in the house on the corner, asked me if I'd like to join her and her family at their church. She had heard about our family's recent expulsion. At that point, I was desperate to fill my Sundays with God again, so I quickly said yes.

"It's the Pentecostal Church in Phoenix. We'll pick you up at eight sharp," she said. "Oh, and wear something nice!"

The following Sunday, I found Irma's long black prairie skirt buried in the closet, and Amá offered a white button-up blouse she had bought at the thrift store ages ago. I tried it on, and it fell to my knees, so Amá knotted the back of the shirt, tightening the slack.

"Well, this will have to do," she said, studying the frumpy outfit in the mirror.

The Millers picked me up in their polished charcoal gray car at five to eight. Both nervous and excited, I slid into the back seat next to Dina.

"Well, don't you look nice this morning, Miss Minu," Dina's mother said from the passenger seat. I smiled, letting out a breath of relief at her approval of my outfit, even if it was four sizes too big.

The Pentecostal Church had colorful stained-glass windows, and the music was louder and more old-fashioned than the Spanish hymns I was used to. The preacher was different too. He yelled heartily and passionately during his sermon. At times, it sounded like gibberish, but Dina whispered to me that he was speaking in tongues. Why would people sit through a church service they couldn't understand?

After the sermon, some of the congregation formed a line in front of the pastor who stood at the altar. The pastor laid his hands over each person's forehead, and spoke in tongues again. I sat at the edge of my seat and craned my neck to get a better view.

Dina must have noticed my curiosity. She leaned toward me, her words soft and serious, "They're receiving the Holy Spirit."

"I'd like to receive it too," I whispered, not taking my eyes off the pastor. "Maybe I could get baptized here."

"It takes time to receive the Holy Spirit," Dina whispered back, patting my knee.

After church, I went back to their house. It was neat and organized and decorated in shades of blue with enormous plants in every corner. Soft classic piano music played from the record player in the living room, and on the wall was a collage of Dina's school portraits.

My mouth dropped when I saw their bookcase. I'd never seen so many books in one place. I stared, mesmerized.

"Minu, do you like to read?" Mrs. Miller asked.

I nodded vigorously.

"Here, take these home." She handed me a stack of Harlequin Romance novels. "You can keep them."

I'd never read a novel before, let alone owned one. My heart almost burst at her kindness.

Dina and I sat across from her parents at a fancy dining room table. Before us was a feast of oven-roasted chicken, buttery green beans, and sweet potatoes topped with brown sugar. We passed the dishes around clockwise, and her parents asked us what was on our schedule for the week ahead. Dina answered with her after-school plans: tutoring after school and band practice Tuesday and Thursday. Her parents even asked what we were learning about in school.

How I wished my parents would ask me about my day, if it was good or bad, or if something exciting happened.

What I admired most about Mr. and Mrs. Miller was their formal yet warm manner. If Dina made mistakes or spilled her water on the dinner table, her parents didn't yell or swear or lose their temper or beat her with a belt. All they did was flash a look of disappointment.

After we finished eating, Dina's father prepared his briefcase for work the next day, shuffling papers into neat piles and sorting through manila folders with words like "Proposals" written in black marker. Dina's mother made a turkey club sandwich and packed it in a brown paper bag for his lunch the next day. It baffled me that the Millers didn't have to turn the lights and swamp cooler off to save money.

Families like the Millers were the reason I rarely invited the neighbor kids or any friends over to my house. I was too embarrassed and ashamed of the chaos and havoc in our home. I felt tense and anxious all the time, and I hated it.

When I told Amá about the pastor speaking in tongues at the Pentecostal Church, she forbade me to return. "Speaking in tongues is the Devil's work," she said.

I never went back.

But Dina kept feeding me her mom's Harlequin Romances. Along the way, I learned about falling in love and French kissing.

Rachel, another classmate, went to the Jehovah's Witness Church, and I asked her if I could try it. Inside the building was a large room filled with folding chairs lined up in tight rows. Every service included something about going to hell. That scared me, but I told myself to give it a chance.

A few times after school, I tagged along with Rachel and a few other Jehovah's Witnesses as they went door to door passing out pamphlets and preaching the word of God. They did all the talking since they were the experts.

"Thank you for sharing," some strangers said. Others slammed their door in our faces or peeked through the blinds and pretended they weren't home. After a few weeks of attending Rachel's church, I knew it wasn't for me.

When my parents decided to return to the Catholic Church, I joined them. I was trying out religions like new pairs of shoes. The brick building had long stained-glass windows decorated with people dressed in what looked like tablecloths. As we opened the door, the smell of incense and flowers filled my nostrils. I plugged my nose and breathed out my mouth. A roaring bell rang from the steeple, shaking the church so hard I thought the windows would shatter.

Facing the front, my mother knelt quickly on one knee, and I mimicked her. Then the three of us slid into one of the back pews. The choir's voices filled the air.

My understanding of Catholics growing up was that they drank, smoked, and confessed their sins to a priest, who wiped their sins clean. I thought you confessed your sins only to God himself, but I didn't say anything. I was seeing a glimpse of the Sunday normalcy I longed for.

Throughout the mass, we knelt, stood, and sat a lot. The constant moving kept me alert. The priest stood at the podium and read a story from the Bible, a parable of an injured traveler who had been beaten, stripped of his clothing, and left alongside the road. Two men passed by the wounded traveler, not stopping to see if he needed help. The traveler would certainly die if no one helped him. It wasn't until a man the Bible called the Good Samaritan stopped his donkey to check on the traveler. The Good Samaritan cleaned the man's wounds, put him on his donkey, and took him to an inn for the night.

I peeked over at Apá. He sat tall and stiff, his eyebrows crinkled. I sure hoped he was listening.

Afterward, one by one, my family and I went to confession. When it was my turn, I sat in the creaky wooden chair and faced a thick red curtain.

"And what brings you here today, young lady?" a deep voice asked through the curtain.

"Bless me, Father, for I have sinned." Irma had prepped me on what to say. "I yelled at my brother Danny last week. He was teasing me, and I couldn't take it anymore, Father. I screamed at him and called him names." I glanced down at my hands folded tightly in my lap. My white knuckles looked as if they would pop through my skin.

"Your sins are forgiven, my dear," the voice responded. "Please say three 'Our Father' prayers to be reconciled with God and the church."

Well, that was easy.

I said my prayers later that evening, reading off the card the priest had given me. A few weeks later, we stopped going to church altogether.

19

By that time, Julio was struggling badly in school. His teachers said he was behind in everything, so at the start of the new school year, they held him back, placing him in my eighth-grade class. He shrugged it off. Education wasn't important to him.

But he excelled with girls. He had become quite the ladies' man, always surrounded by adoring fans. Whenever we returned from the fields, he'd scrunch down in the truck so none of them could see him.

In the spring, Dolores had a baby girl, and Apá built an additional bedroom onto the house for them. I moved into the room that was once occupied by Esméralda and Agapito, leaving the boys with my parents. But I quickly found out I didn't like being alone and slept in Esméralda's room. Sharing a room with her was like taking a home economics class but in the subjects of boys, alcohol, and what it was like to be a señorita.

"Have you gotten your period yet?" she asked me one night as she climbed into bed.

"Not yet," I said.

"You'll start soon enough. Give it a year."

"I'm in no rush." But I was in a hurry, secretly waiting for the day I'd become a woman.

Three years before, at the beginning of fifth grade, my teacher showed the class a movie about puberty. The boys and girls kept giggling the whole time. I laughed a little but tried to focus on what it was saying so I would be ready.

All my sisters went through puberty in sixth or seventh grade, and here I was in the eighth grade still looking like a little girl. When they suffered from cramps, Amá boiled water and added mint and sugar for them to drink. It was her magic potion to clear the stomach aches and pains. Amá also kept a box of Kotex in the bathroom cupboard for them.

"Use a Kotex pad when you bleed. Only whores use tampons," she would say.

As the last Becerra daughter to go through puberty, I was able to learn from my sisters' bodily changes. For one, their breasts grew to the size of mangos. Amá bought them bras at the thrift store and sewed the loose elastic straps tighter for support.

One morning, I saw Esméralda shaving her legs over the bath, and thought I'd try it. I lathered my legs with the bar of soap and glided Apá's Gillette razor from my ankles up to my knee. On one of the upward strides, just as the razor glided over my knee, I pressed too hard and cut myself. A trail of blood streamed down my leg. I jumped out of the bath and dabbed toilet paper on the cut, practically using an entire roll before wrapping it with an old rag. If I told Amá I shaved my legs, she'd be angry, so I threw the bloody rag into the garbage and didn't wear shorts or dresses for days to cover the gash.

Amá deflected awkward maturity questions, providing no guidance to her daughters. "Just don't do it," was all she told us when we asked about alcohol, drugs, or smoking pot. She danced around the topic of where babies came from and preached that birth control was bad and wouldn't be discussed in her household.

When I used deodorant for the first time, borrowing it from Esméralda, a red rash formed in my armpits. I showed Amá and asked her how to get rid of it.

"Don't use that crap! It makes you smell even worse."

Kids at school would have killed to have parents like mine who didn't breathe down their necks, but as an almost-fourteen-year-old on the verge of womanhood, I longed for advice.

One day after school, I was devouring another romantic novel when Esméralda asked me if I wanted to go shopping with her at Uto-teM, the convenience store. Thrilled to be included, I threw my book aside, dressed in a clean tank top and jean shorts, and was ready in five minutes.

Esméralda's friend, Cristina, who lived a few blocks away, came with us. She had green eyes with golden brown skin, and her large breasts filled her white T-shirt with confidence. Esméralda told me stories about her—she smoked a ton of pot and canoodled with boys in alleys after school.

On the walk to the store, Esméralda went on about the bottle of liquor they would drink that weekend while Cristina gabbed about how far she let her boyfriend go with her. I listened intently but stayed quiet.

The UtoteM sign flashed in red and green, and the words "Groceries, Milk, Beer, Ice" lit up the awning. As we walked in, a woman behind the register gestured a quick wave and the three of us wandered through the aisles of candy bars, bags of chips, and liters of sodas.

As we passed the magazine aisle, I spotted Mrs. Sánchez's husband with his face rammed into a magazine. On the cover was a naked blond woman kneeling on a beach with her large breasts exposed. I gasped in disgust. What a sicko! Surely Mrs. Sánchez had no clue her husband flipped through nude magazines. I bet he didn't even buy them, just snuck a peak after work and then he went home to his ten kids and Catholic wife and worked in his garage, like I saw him do in the evenings. Grossed out, I scurried up to the girls who were browsing the small shoe rack.

"Oh, I love these," Esméralda said, picking out a pair of flat brown sandals with braided straps. She slipped them on her feet and took a test trot down the aisle.

Cristina dug through the inventory for her size. She stepped into the sandals, rocking back and forth and wiggling her toes. I stood with my hands in my pockets, watching them. I didn't have any money on me, and if I did, I wouldn't be wasting it on a pair of shoes. I'd browse the pickle section for a snack.

I flinched when Esméralda and Cristina ripped the price tags off the sandals.

"What're you doing?" I asked in a loud whisper.

Esméralda nudged me as if to follow along, and Cristina shot me a keep-your-mouth-shut glare.

"¡La alarma! The alarm will go off," I said, my voice turning into a high-pitched squeal.

"Dammit, Güera. Keep your voice down," Esméralda spat.

"Don't you remember what the Bible says? Thou shall not steal!" I whispered.

"Get away from us, Güera," Esméralda whispered back.

They both walked toward the store's entrance. My stomach churned. They were going to get caught!

As Cristina stepped through the door, I held my breath. Esméralda followed. Nothing. No alarm. I looked at the woman behind the register flipping through a magazine. She had no idea unpaid merchandise was walking out the store.

Esméralda and Cristina continued through the parking lot. I ran to catch up. "I can't believe you got away with it," I said, my voice wobbly.

"Believe it," Esméralda said. "And just so you know, this'll be your last shopping trip with us—ever. You almost blew our cover."

"*Piérdase*. Get lost, Güera," Cristina blurted out.

That was Esméralda's way of punishing me, but I didn't care. I wanted no part of their crime.

When we made it home, Amá was there. My nostrils burned from the pungent scent of roasting spicy chilaquiles drifting from the kitchen. This was good. Amá would lecture Esméralda on her stealing and how wrong it was—a lesson she would never forget. Like clockwork, Amá immediately commented on her new sandals.

"You like?" Esméralda asked. "From UtoteM."

"Yeah, tell Amá how you got them," I said.

"*Callarse la boca*," Esméralda said. "Shut up."

I did the exact opposite. "She stole them. She stole the shoes."

"*Para que te apuras*," Amá said. "Why do you worry?" One of her favorite phrases. "That store makes plenty of money. Why didn't you grab a pair too, *pendeja*?"

❖

Early one Sunday morning, I woke up to Esméralda stumbling into her bed. It was just before dawn, and the desert sparrows were beginning to chirp outside the window. I glanced at the clock across the room—a quarter to six—and fell back to sleep.

A while later, Amá stormed into the room, banging the door against the wall. I shot up from my bed in a panic.

"*¡Un montón de putas!* A bunch of whores!" she yelled. "Both of you! You've been out all-night screwing around." Her hands were balled into fists.

Esméralda pulled the blanket over her head and turned to face the wall. I sat up in bed, confused—what had I done? Then out of nowhere, Amá threw a can of Raid at Esméralda's bed.

"Here. Spray your *coños* with this. You better hope Apá doesn't find out. He'll give you the whipping you both deserve." She looked at me with a piercing stare, her face flushed with rage, and then stomped out of the room, slamming the door behind her.

"Es, *¿qué demonios?*" I whispered. "What did you do last night?"

Esméralda sat up with snarled hair and bags under her eyes the size of orange slices. "Something I guess Raid is going to fix." She scoffed and threw the can on the floor.

"What does Amá mean? Spray our *coños*?"

Esméralda lifted herself onto an elbow and rubbed her eye with a knuckle. "She means sex."

"Have you had it?" I asked.

She nodded casually, almost like she was proud.

I hesitated to ask a question that had been on my mind since I first heard the word from the kids at school. Finally, I asked it, whispering so softly I wasn't sure she even heard me. "What does it feel like?"

"It sucks the first time. It feels like a knife being shoved into you."

I gulped. "That sounds awful. I'll go my whole life without it."

"Yeah, here's your 'birds and the bees' lesson, Minu. Sister to sister. Don't do it."

She pulled the covers back over her head.

20

I hadn't seen Julio for a long time. Soon after starting ninth grade, I spotted him at the park on my way home from school and ran over to him.

"Minu!" He hugged me, smiling.

"Where have you been?" I punched him playfully in the arm. "I've missed you."

He looked away and then back at me, his eyes filled with sadness. "I dropped out. School is too hard for me." He told me he had officially moved in with his adoptive parents. "Apá is always hitting me. I can't take it anymore. I'm not coming back."

"Oh, Julio . . ."

We hugged again and I left for home, angry at him for leaving. For not taking me with him. He was my protection and pillar in the violence and chaos. He was my best friend.

It was all my parents' fault. They simply didn't care. They were the ones who made our lives hell on earth. Julio had no choice but to go. It was as though they accepted that they had lost one of their sons.

Tears spilled down my face.

A part of me broke that day. But I also became more determined than ever to move away from my parents, to leave Cashion. The first step was to graduate from high school. Education would be my golden ticket out of that dead-end town.

Irma had moved out after graduation and into an apartment, but I wanted to get farther away. I'd be a stewardess and let the planes carry me across the globe—Europe, Australia, Thailand, Brazil. I wanted to explore the cultures I read about in books and learned about in history class, to taste the food, meet the people, and hear the hustle and bustle of a different place. All I had to do was survive Cashion for four more years.

By 1972, most of the gringos had left for the big cities, and Mexican families had taken their place. Some houses were filled with a couple of dozen people, and the orderly lawns that once lined the neighborhood roads were now littered with broken beer bottles and plastic toys bleached by the Arizona sun. Spanish music blared in every direction throughout the streets, and unfed dogs roamed loose, growling and jumping at cars as they passed by.

Like the Cashion neighborhood, our household income tanked. Or maybe it was the growing children my parents had to feed. David, Danny, Ruben, Sammy, and I worked most days after school, plucking vegetables and filling burlap sacks, but we still couldn't keep up with expenses.

A few times, we relied on government and welfare agencies for food. We'd wait hours in a large room crowded with families, hard chairs, and agency literature as we listened for the number to be called. We would receive our box filled with powdered milk, stale cheese, canned soup, eggs, and days-old bread. The food only lasted a few days, but anything helped.

To help pay for school lunches, I worked during the lunch hour, emptying dirty trays, washing the cafeteria tables, and taking out the heavy trash bags. At first it was embarrassing, but Amá told me the few bucks off my lunch tab would help the family, so I stuck it out.

During those days, David and I grew closer. He had gone from the rowdy trouble-making little brother to a fiercely loyal and responsible ten-year-old, a transformation that happened overnight. We bonded over the schoolteachers we despised, songs we liked on the radio, and our desire to leave this no-good town.

"Time stands still here, Minu. I can't wait to leave," he told me one afternoon while we picked onions. I always found comfort in David's desire to leave—that I wasn't the only one who dreamed of running away. He snipped the top of an onion head, dropped it into the bucket. "I would love to buy a motorcycle and travel the world. Nothin' but the open road ahead."

I studied my brother a few rows away. His faded torn jeans hung loose around his waist, and his big brown eyes squinted under his thick eyebrows.

In a way, David filled the void of Julio. I ached when I thought about my older brother and what he might have been doing at that moment. A few weeks prior, he had stopped over at the house to see us, coming by when my parents weren't home. It horrified me when I saw the paint lining his nose. Sniffing spray paint had been a recent trend in the neighborhood. That day, I begged Julio to stay, telling him I would protect him from Apá, that I'd give him my plate at dinner and help him in school.

But he shook his head. "I can't come back. Any place is better than here."

Every night before I went to sleep, I bowed my head and prayed for Julio. I asked God to help him find the happiness he so very much deserved.

The park toward the south end of Cashion had a wooden sign etched "CPL." David and I never knew what that stood for, so we called it the "Cashion Park Locos." It seemed fitting since the drug-dealing teenagers camped out there at night, smoking marijuana and guzzling bottles of liquor in brown paper bags. Graffiti decorated the ramada where many of them gathered.

Off to the side, there was a baseball field where David would play games. It had grungy old bases, and the fences were corroded with wire sticking out like miniature knives, but to the boys on that field, they were playing for the Dodgers in the World Series. Sometimes I tagged along to watch.

One Saturday afternoon, I sat along the first baseline on the wooden bleachers. David stood in left field, his glove resting on his thigh. At the makeshift home plate, the batter swung, hitting a ground ball. The third baseman backhanded it and zipped it across the field, hitting the first baseman's glove with a loud smack!

"Out!" the first baseman shouted.

Behind the players, a group of six people walked along the field. I recognized the tawny skin and combat boots—the Gomez siblings.

One of the sisters, Pati, was the sort of high schooler who even scared the adults. She talked back to teachers when they called her out for being late to class, and just last week, she shoved a girl into the hallway lockers for looking at her wrong. The Gomez parents lived one street over and were alcoholics who drank themselves to sleep while Pati and her siblings spent most days on the streets up to no good.

The gang looped around the home plate backdrop and walked toward the bleachers where I sat. I kept my attention on the game, avoiding eye contact. The next batter approached the plate, and the pitcher launched the ball. A swing from the batter, but the ball ricocheted off the fence and died a spinning death.

I heard Pati's husky voice, "Look at her. Sitting over there. Thinking she's better than us. Who does this *pinche gringa* think she is?"

I winced at her harsh tone and gnawed at my bottom lip, keeping my focus on the baseball game. Cluck! A hit fly ball whizzed out to centerfield. The fielder leaped into the air to make the catch.

"All year I've been wanting to beat her ass," Pati said. The rest of the Gomez siblings laughed.

My heart began to pound in my head. Fear and rage took their turn bubbling in my stomach. My mouth trembled as unplanned words came falling out, "What's your problem, Pati?"

"You're my problem, *perra blanca*," she hissed.

The next thing I knew, she was trying to rip my hair right out of my scalp. The grip pulled me off the bleachers, and my head hit the dirt. A flurry of punches to my face and kicks to my ribcage made me nearly pass out. A blow crunched my jaw. Pain blasted through my skull.

In the distance, I heard David's shouts ringing through the park.

He sprinted to the ambush, swinging left and right with a bat. The rest of the baseball team followed his lead until the Gomez crew retreated.

On the walk home from the CPL, I dabbed David's shirt on my cheekbones and lips to soak up the blood that oozed through the gashes. Every touch brought fresh pain.

David put a hand on my shoulder. "You, okay?"

"I'll be fine." I was almost too weak to speak. "I fucking hate this place."

David sighed. "Me too, sis. It's not fair."

I took a shuddery breath, willing the pain to go away—maybe my imaginary aunt would finally come to the rescue and take me anywhere but here.

21

*C*ashion grew worse by the day. Teens passed drugs around like candy, and brawls broke out all the time at the park. The dogs snarled at me on my way to school, sometimes gripping my butt and tearing my pants. And at the house across the street, a sloppy man with slimy gray hair sat on his weathered porch sipping tequila out of the bottle while touching himself. Our neighborhood had become the rough part of town.

Despite all of it, families continued to move in. That fall, the Espinosas bought the brown house down the street—the one with a crooked white porch. According to neighborhood gossip, they had come from California. The recently divorced mother had received full custody of her three sons and three daughters.

One day, on my way home from school, I saw the Espinosas grabbing grocery bags from their car parked in the driveway. They were a stunning family, all tall with coal-jet black hair and russet skin. I must have been staring longer than I realized because one of the daughters called out to me with a wave, "Hey there." She had a slender face with a ski slope nose, and her thick lips framed a pearly white smile. "We're new here," she said. "My name's Lolita, but everyone calls me Lola."

"I'm Minu," I said with a short wave.

"M-ennn-uu?" she repeated, cocking her head to one side. "How do you spell that?"

After I told her, she laughed. "Sounds like you're saying 'am I in you'. Anyway, want to hang out?"

Lola cussed like a sailor, smoked pot like a chimney every day, and gripped her Budweiser bottle by the neck. Although I knew she was trouble, I so wanted desperately to be her friend. We became attached at the hip, a dynamic duo, roaming the halls of Tolleson High School.

We yakked about the obscenest things, but often the conversation would meander to genuine issues about life, love, and growing pains. I liked her bad-to-the-bone attitude, and in turn, she thought my goal to be a stewardess was cool. Her mother worked as a hotel maid, so Lola and her siblings had a lot of unsupervised time on their hands. Most days after school, I went to her house, where she, her siblings, and other neighbors passed around a joint. That's when I first laid eyes on Lola's older brother.

Alberto was just as fascinating as his younger sister. He was nineteen years old—five years older than us and handsome enough to put instant butterflies in my stomach. His skin was perfectly kissed by the desert sun, and he spoke calmly and composed as if all the time in the world revolved around him. With his devilish grin, ducktail dark hair, and long sideburns, he resembled a Mexican Elvis Presley—he even had that sexy lip curl. Girls would stop in their tracks and gawk with heart eyes when he pulled up in his '68 Pontiac GTO. I did too.

"Don't even think about it," Lola whispered to me when she saw me swooning over Alberto after school.

"I would never." I laughed.

"Slippin' into Darkness" played on the car radio. A warm spring wind blew through the windows of the red Impala, snapping my hair back and forth. It was our school lunch break, and I had skipped out on emptying lunch trays to cruise around with Lola and Carlos, a sixteen-year-old dropout.

Carlos handed me a joint. "Here, your turn for a hit, *bonita*." He winked at me and smiled, revealing yellow-stained buck teeth.

I carefully grabbed the burning rolled paper, letting it rest between my pointer and middle finger, the way Apá held his cigarettes.

"Least you can do is hold it right," Lola said from the back seat.

"Give me a break. It's my first time." I switched my grip to hold the joint with my index finger and thumb. Gray smoke curled into the air from the end like a dancing snake. I stuck it between my lips and inhaled, the warm smoke filling my mouth. Before I could blow it out, an itch crept up my throat that turned into a chain of dry coughs.

Lola laughed. "Amateur."

"Am I supposed to feel high? I don't feel any different," I said through my coughing attack.

Carlos gave me a smile. "Not everyone gets high their first time." He was getting a kick out of this.

"Good. I don't want to get high anyway." I handed the joint to Lola. "I have a chemistry test this afternoon."

She inhaled the tip, and the ash ignited to a bright orange. "You're such a nerd." She blew out the smoke, some escaping through her nose, and passed it back to Carlos.

"So, Minu, what age were you adopted?" Carlos asked, genuinely curious. He took a puff and blew it into the wind outside.

"What? I'm not adopted. Who said that?"

"Oh. Well, why are you a white girl living with a Mexican family?" He kept his gaze on the road through the cracked windshield.

"I *am* Mexican."

Carlos scoffed. "The fuck you are."

"Fine, don't believe me." I took the joint from his grip and inhaled.

"She's Mexican, *estúpido*," Lola said. "Her parents are literally from Mexico."

Carlos snickered. He shot me a flirtatious glare out the corner of his eye, complimented by a coy smirk. "Man, I like you, Minu. What'd you say you and I go out?"

I glanced over at Lola.

She shrugged.

"Sure." I took another inhale from the warm rolled-up paper. The coughing wasn't as bad this time.

"Cool," Carlos said.

Someone wanting to date me? Someone thinking of me romantically? All the Harlequin Romantic novels I read flooded to the forefront of my mind. The characters, the enticing man, the horny woman, the connection, the kiss, the intimacy—the sex?

Carlos turned his car into the school lot, parking far away from the school doors. Lola took one deeper inhale of the now short brown rolled paper and we stepped out. Carlos leaned his head out the window. "Come here and give me a kiss, *bonita*,"

I looked back at my first-ever boyfriend and shook my head. This wasn't me. I didn't even really like him. "Hmm. Yeah, I'm good. And actually, Carlos, I don't think this whole boyfriend-girlfriend thing is going to work out." Plus, I didn't find his mouthful of yellow teeth and shaggy hair attractive, but I didn't tell him that.

"What the fu—? It's been like five minutes." He threw his hands in the air.

"Sorry."

"Fine. Get your pot somewhere else, Lola," he shouted, skirting the car out of the parking spot. Exhaust smoke trailed behind him.

"What the hell was that?" Lola smacked me on the back. "Now I have to find a new dealer."

"Pothead isn't my type."

She cackled her loud, obnoxious laugh. "That might have been the shortest relationship in history."

"Like five minutes."

"Yeah, exactly. Five minutes."

After that, Lola and I gave Carlos the nickname Five Minutes. He must not have been too upset about the breakup because he started dating the snotty thirteen-year-old Mary Anice the very next day.

At lunch later that week, I emptied another dirty tray with bread crust and half-eaten soggy spaghetti into the trash. As I tied another garbage bag, I heard someone say, "That job fits you well, white trash."

I looked up to see Mary Anice holding a lunch tray, her eyes cold and hard, her nostrils flared.

I groaned inside. "What do you want, Mary?"

"This, you stupid bitch." She dumped her food on my head.

Spaghetti noodles and red meat sauce dripped down my face and onto my shirt. Cackles from the students echoed through the cafeteria.

"What'd you do that for!" I yelled.

"For wanting my boyfriend!"

"Five Minutes? Carlos? I don't want him!"

"Next time, think again before you get in his car, *cabróna*," she said through gritted teeth.

I brushed the spaghetti noodles and meat sauce from my hair and wiped the food from my shirt, but it was already staining.

Mary wasn't finished. That afternoon, as I walked home from school, she and her girl gang jumped me at the CPL. I made it just past the baseball bleachers when they came out of nowhere, pulled me to the ground, and started yanking my hair and scratching my face with their long nails.

"I don't want your stupid boyfriend!" I screamed over and over and over.

I didn't go to school the next day. Instead, I sulked around with aloe vera juice smeared across the marks.

"Why does this happen to me?" I asked Amá as she put laundry into the dresser drawers. She didn't move her eyes from the stacks of clothes.

"It's just this town," she mumbled.

"Then why do we live here?"

"It's the way it is, *mija*. You'd get this anywhere. Remember that."

Later that day, after school was out, Lola stopped over to tell me I didn't need to worry about Mary Anice and her tagalongs again.

"Why? What'd you do?"

"Took care of them myself," she said with a wink. "This town is madness. We're in this together."

22

*M*y mother and father left Mexico back in 1948 with high expectations of their new life in the States. Once Apá saw all the opportunities for himself, he was determined to bring other Mexicans too. Over the years, he smuggled in dozens of people, driving most of them across the border as we had done with Agapito. A risky business.

"American!" Apá would yell out the truck window with a wave to the border patrol agents. The agents would nod and tip their hats.

As I got older, Apá brought me along on most of his smuggling expeditions. He would have me sit next to the undocumented traveler in the truck's bed or in the front seat next to him.

"Smile and wave, Güera," he'd say. "Patrol agents don't question a white girl."

Soon after school let out for the summer, Apá told me he had been asked to cross six Mexicans. "It's too dangerous to drive them through the border patrol. We'll take the Rio Grande route this time. Big money for this, Güera. I need your help."

I nodded, knowing I didn't have a choice. Besides, it would be better than picking onions. I asked Lola to come with us. She and I piled into the truck, along with Amá, David, Danny, Ruben, and Sammy, and took off for Mexico.

We passed through towns lined with debris and garbage, collapsing shacks, and skinny kids with spaghetti legs running around in dirty clothes. Mangy feral dogs with open scabs roamed the streets. Soon the familiar flagstone church came into view, with jacaranda trees covered in purple flowers. In the distance, mountains shaped like fuzzy inverted pyramids filled the sky.

Once the truck began to teeter back and forth over the bumpy dirt road, I looked over the side to see the half-built crumbling adobe fence some Mexican farmer had started but never finished. Had he run out of money? Or gotten bored? Maybe he had died. Whatever the reason, the fence meant we were close.

Tumbleweeds bounced across the cracked dirt and the sun beat down to the ground. It was so hot the baked crows didn't want to fly. Instead, they called out in their screeching voices, speaking the language of the desert.

Five years before, Apá and Amá had bought a cheap plot of land in Juárez, Mexico, on the border of El Paso. Together they built an adobe shack, a small, unkempt space with a packed-earth floor and a single window that held a line of dead flies at the base. We'd been there only a few times as a family.

Amá kept a portable two-burner propane stove in the corner to make beans, rice, and tortillas for dinner. Next to the stove stood a tall clay jar for warm clay-tasting water we'd ladle out to quench our thirst. Along the wall was a single twin bed where my parents slept— the rest of us slept on the floor. And out back was a crooked wooden outhouse that flies buzzed around for their next meal. Just a mile up the road was the Rio Grande.

It was too risky to include my younger brothers in the smuggling scheme, so Apá relied solely on Lola and me. He would hide the six Mexicans in bushes south of the river while we acted as decoys up the riverbank so Apá could hustle them into El Paso. Lola and I both nodded in agreement.

The next day was the same—hot and dry—and the Mexico sky looked like azure glass. The river flowed like hot chocolate but smelled like dead fish. Scraggly creosote bushes with tiny yellow flowers and thin mesquite trees with dangling dead leaves hunched over the bank. The stream barreled over polished rocks and mossy logs.

Lola slipped off her sandals and dipped her feet into the river. "Don't you feel like some sort of rebel being a part of something like this?"

I peeled off my own sandals too, set them on a rock, and stepped into the warm stream, mud squishing between my bare toes. "Maybe," I said quietly. I took a sweeping glance around the eerie riverbank. Something felt off.

"I like it." She skimmed her fingertips across the top of the water.

Just then, a twig snapped. Leaves crackled. We turned to the north side of the bank to see two American border patrol agents with campaign hats and shiny belts. One had a clean-cut face, the other a bushy mustache that spread down to the corners of his mouth. They both stood with their hands on their belts.

"Hello, ladies. Can we help you two?" the clean-cut agent asked, taking a stride forward.

I held my breath, and my heart pounded in my temples. I couldn't speak through the lump in my throat. Instead, I waved innocently, although there was nothing innocent about two Mexican girls standing in the Rio Grande.

"No help needed here, sirs," Lola said cheerfully. "We're just cooling off from the heat."

"Y'all out here by yourselves?" asked the older agent with the bushy mustache. They kept their eyes on us like starving hawks.

I pointed toward the shore touching Mexico. "My father is back at our shack just a short walk that way." I hoped they couldn't hear the fear in my voice.

"Y'all comin' from the Mexico side?" the younger agent asked.

"Yes, but we're both American," Lola said.

The agents glanced at each other and chuckled. "Both American citizens, huh?"

Before Lola and I could say another word or put our shoes back on, we were headed to the El Paso Juvenile Hall.

To our surprise, we lived like queens. We were the only ones there, so Lola and I took advantage of what felt like a vacation at a five-star hotel. We put puzzles together and played Go Fish and board games. We even had our own cells with ice-cold air conditioning and a bed comfier than mine back home. And we had plenty of food. We left each dinner fuller than we ever dreamed. Beans, mashed potatoes, and beef with gravy was the typical meal, and to top it off, we chugged two cartons of chocolate milk.

"The clothes are comfy too," I told Lola from across the cafeteria table as she slurped her milk. We both wore beige shorts, a white T-shirt, and black closed-toe slippers.

"I could live here forever," she said, tilting the carton to get the last swig of milk. She held it in the air. "Cheers to certified juvie delinquency."

"Cheers." I tapped my carton to hers.

Though we were living happily in jail, I wondered if my parents were looking for me. Did they even notice I was gone? Or were they happy they had one less mouth to feed? They must be searching for me, I told myself.

After a week of multiple completed puzzles, delectable meals, and cool sleep-filled nights, a security officer called Lola and me into a small room. The officer told us that since we didn't have a pending court case, the hall couldn't keep us any longer. He called Lola's mother on her home phone, and she answered immediately. It turned out that for the past week, she had been searching frantically for her daughter.

"I haven't been able to get ahold of the Becerras," I could hear her high-pitched voice over the phone. She promised she'd send a ticket for Lola to hop on the next Greyhound bus back to Arizona. When it arrived, Lola left the next day.

When the officer called the landline at my house, there was no answer.

"No one's going to answer," I told him. "They're in Mexico. There's no way to reach them."

He called again later that evening and the next day three more times. I gnawed at my lower lip with each call. Did my parents call someone to let them know about my disappearance? Did Lola's mom reach them, and they were on their way to get me right now?

"What about grandparents, aunts, uncles?" the officer asked.

I shook my head. No one had a telephone, and I didn't know Abuelito Rosalio's address to send a letter.

"I'll try one more time," the officer said on the third day of no answer.

I sat across from him at the table and watched him punch the numbers on the phone. I gnawed at my cracked lip again, this time so hard a faint taste of salty blood lingered through my mouth.

Please, God. Please. Please have Amá answer. Please make her be there. Let her answer the phone.

The security officer took the phone from his ear and placed it back on the cradle with somber eyes. "There isn't much else we can do."

Later that day, I dressed in my original clothes but kept the cheap slippers since I had forgotten my sandals at the river. A secretary from juvenile hall drove me across the border to Ciudad Juárez. The streets echoed with blaring horns and people shouting from their meat, fruit, and jewelry tables. The secretary weaved the bumper-to-bumper traffic and pulled in front of a line of colorful buildings with red terra-cotta roofs and parked. Rummaging in her purse, she pulled out a five-dollar bill and handed it to me. "This should get you where you need to go."

I rubbed the bill between my thumb and finger, realizing this was where my journey with her ended. "But I don't know how to get home," I said, barely above a whisper.

"You'll figure it out, darlin'. Now, out you go."

I stepped onto the sidewalk, the rancid smell of exhaust from the cars, trucks, and taxis soaking into my skin and hair. The secretary drove off, disappearing into the hazy cloud of traffic.

On the corner of a nearby intersection was a burrito stand. My stomach roared with hunger. I hadn't eaten since dinner the night before, and it had been just before noon when the secretary dropped me off. I ran to the stand and ordered a burrito.

"*Sies pesos,*" the man said. Sweat beaded across his forehead.

"And for American money?"

The man cocked his head and smirked, practically licking his lips. Grandpa Rosalio had warned me the dollar bill was sought after in Mexico.

"*Un dólar,*" he said.

I handed over my five-dollar bill. He reached into his wallet and pulled out four dollars, and then handed over a burrito wrapped tightly in aluminum foil. My mouth salivated at the smell of the greasy meat mixed with spicy peppers.

"*Comer lento*, eat slow, *mija*," he said. "You're going to make yourself sick."

"*Para que te apuras*," I said, just like Amá always had.

A taxi was parked across the street. The driver, *el chofer*, must have sensed my situation and pulled up next to me, cracking down his window.

"*Paseo?*" *el chofer* asked. He had eyebrows thicker than the cotton bushes in July.

"*Si, por favor.*" I opened the car door and slid into the back seat.

"Where to?" he asked in Spanish.

I didn't know the way. I barely knew where I was. The only thing I did know was that Apá's shack was near the river, on the east side.

"Head east. Toward the Rio Grande." I gave him the remaining four dollars. "As far as this will take me."

He nodded and pulled away from the city.

"It's been hotter than hell. You surviving this heat?" *el chofer* asked, interrupting the quiet.

"Trying to."

"Why is a young girl like you traveling alone?" His dark eyes met mine in the rearview mirror.

Because my parents didn't come looking for me, I thought. Instead of admitting the ugly truth, I bit my tongue and lied. "My *familia* is expecting me."

"Are you a *gringa?*"

"No. *Mexicana.*"

He chuckled. "You're not Mexican. You're a white girl. *La gringa.*"

"I'm one hundred percent Mexican," I whispered, resting my head on the window.

El chofer turned up the radio, and soft Celia Cruz tunes soon filled the silence. I tried not to think about what would happen if we were going in the wrong direction. Without any money, I'd be as Apá would say, *mierda sin suerte*, shit out of luck.

But soon, familiar scenes started to come into view: the rundown town with the collapsing shacks, kids with spaghetti legs playing in the yard, and the mangy dogs.

I directed *el chofer* down unpaved, dusty roads as the landmarks spurred my memory. "Continue straight here. Take a left after the church with the purple jacaranda trees." At least we were on the right path.

Just a few minutes later, *el chofer* pulled to the shoulder of the road where the gravel met the thirsty desert. "Your four dollars gets you here," he said, looking at me in the rearview mirror.

"Uh . . ." My stomach clenched. How would I make it the rest of the way? The secretary dropping me off in the middle of Juárez was nothing compared to going up against the desert on a hot day.

I slowly opened the door. "Gracias."

"Good luck to you, *chica Americana*."

I stood there as his rusty yellow taxi faded into the horizon.

There was nothing ahead but the long open dirt road. Just me and the callous desert vastness. No cars. No trail of breadcrumbs to lead me home. No map I could follow or a compass to point me in the right direction.

I was totally alone.

23

I walked and walked and walked, the hostile sun burning my scalp while an eerie stillness surrounded me. Along the horizon, the fuzzy purple mountains that once looked peaceful now looked ominous. Covering the thirsty ground were wicked-looking scraggly bushes and dried-out cacti, their needles still attached. My mouth was drier than a cotton field in the summer, so I tightened my cheeks and sucked, trying to find any last saliva to swallow and quench my thirst.

My stomach snarled. That dollar burrito wasn't holding me over. The hunger made me dizzy, while the heat dazed me. Sweat trickled down my neck and forehead, soothing my burning skin. If I didn't find shelter soon, I'd fry like an egg. Either that, or when it got dark in a couple hours, I would be coyote food.

Suddenly, rattling and vrooming echoed in the distance. Headed right toward me was a cloud of dust. A truck. The first vehicle I'd seen since the taxi dropped me off. A chance! I stood off to the side of the road and put my thumb high in the air. I had seen hitchhiking in the movies and sometimes the situation ended badly, but I had no choice. The truck sped closer.

"C'mon, slow down," I whispered. "Slow down."

The truck grew closer and closer, but no sign of slowing down. He sped past me, leaving me tasting dust.

"Damn you!" I yelled.

By now, my slippers were dusty and frayed and the soles in pieces. Stones and pebbles stabbed into the bottoms of my raw feet. Worthless pieces of junk. I chucked them into the desert, letting out a roaring scream.

I only wished I were walking to a beautiful home where I was loved and wanted. With a mother who would smile big just to have me back, or a father who would scoop me up for a bear hug. Instead, my family didn't care about me. Apá didn't. Amá didn't. My sisters didn't. Julio didn't. No one did.

I collapsed to my knees, sobbing. My palms gripped the small stones that lay in the road while foggy tears dripped down like rain. Did I belong anywhere on this damned earth?

Nowhere, Minu. You belong nowhere, the voice in my head spoke back.

Bowing my head, I started to whisper the Bible verse I had recited all those Sundays we went to church: "For I know the plans I have for you, declares the Lord—"

I had forgotten the rest. I repeated the verse again, hoping the words would trickle off my tongue, but nothing.

For sure, I would die right there. The taste of salt and dirt leaked into my mouth. I cried until my tears were rung out, sitting on the side of the road for what could have been ten minutes or an hour. In that moment, I vowed to myself I would never rely on anyone else again. Ever. The only person I truly could count on was me. Only me. It had always been *only me*.

And then the rest of the verse came to me: "For I know the plans I have for you, declares the Lord, plans to prosper you and not to harm you, plans to give you hope and a future."

I brought myself to my feet, brushed off my filthy hands, and wiped my face. I took a step and then another and another. By now, the sun was beginning to dip below the horizon, taking the light and intense heat with it. My bare feet kept moving.

And then I saw it— the half-built adobe fence. I blinked hard. Could it be? Yes! The shack was close. I started to jog, my feet dragging across the stones, kicking up a trail of dust behind me. My arms dangled like ropes. My knotted hair bobbed on my heavy head. I ran faster, my heart pounding.

Soon a faint laugh reached me from the distance. Danny's high-pitched laugh. There it was again. It usually irritated me, but at that moment, it was music to my ears. My sunburned face hurt, my sweat-soaked shirt stunk, and my bare feet were numb. I wheezed through my mouth.

Ahead in the clearing, David, Danny, Ruben, and Sammy chased one another around the shack's yard. Danny laughed again. Ruben let out a yell. Sammy swayed a stick in the air as if it was a sword.

"Hey!" I huffed, running up the lawn with one hand raised. "David! Danny! Ruben! Sammy! I made it! I'm here. I'm here!"

The boys paused in their tracks, looking confused. As I grew closer, I spotted Apá sitting in a camping chair with a soda bottle in his hand.

"Minu!" my brothers yelled and ran into my arms.

The five of us hugged, laughing and falling to the ground.

"Where have you been, Minu?" Danny asked as I squeezed him.

"Yeah, we didn't know what happened to you," Ruben said.

I glanced in Apá's direction. He stared back at me blankly.

"Why didn't you come get me?" I called out to him.

He placed the soda to his lips and took a sip, keeping his eyes on me. "I knew you'd figure it out."

When the smuggled immigrants didn't have a secure place to stay, Apá offered our Cashion home as a temporary stop. They stayed in the puny wood shack he had built in our backyard. They were usually grown adult men with not much else to do but smoke and drink with the Cashion neighbors.

Having unfamiliar cologne-drenched macho men at the house made me uneasy, especially since my body was changing. My hips had expanded, giving me an hourglass figure. My breasts had swelled, stretching my shirts tighter and shorter. Boys went from barely looking in my direction to flashing winks and sneaking peeks from the corners of their skittish eyes.

On a hot Saturday night later that summer, the living room clock read just past ten. I had just gotten home from Lola's house. She and I shared a blunt to end the night, and unlike my first-time smoking with Five Minutes, I felt lightheaded, woozy—and hungry.

I went into the kitchen to make a turkey sandwich: two slices of stale bread, a tomato, mustard. Just as I positioned the knife over the tomato, the front door flung open. It was one of the men staying in the shack out back. Apá had smuggled him across the border the previous week. And since he'd been staying with us, I hadn't seen him sober.

It didn't look like anything had changed at that moment either. He walked in, swaying from side to side. His thin mustache and greasy hair shone through the dim kitchen lighting.

I continued to slice into the tomato, the knife meeting the counter, sensing the man's piercing stare on my back. I cut another slice while staying attentive to his next move. He came closer until he was directly behind me. He touched my halter top and slid his hands down to my hips. His tequila-drenched breath warmed the back of my neck.

On impulse, I pushed out of his grip and turned to face him, pointing the tomato-covered knife at his stomach. His eyes grew wide, and he put his hands up as if to surrender.

My hand shook with panic, but the rage boiling in my veins took over. "Touch me again, and I will cut your fucking balls off."

He jumped back. "¡Ah! *Lo siento.*" (I'm sorry.)

I nodded toward the back door while keeping the knife blade pointed in his direction. "Get the fuck out of here."

The man scurried out into the night.

I threw the sandwich away. My appetite was ruined.

The following morning, I approached Amá as she hung damp laundry on the line outside. She had clothespins in her mouth and hummed to herself. She wore a low-cut top and tight pale blue jeans that showed off her cleavage and curves. She loved flaunting her body and looking sexy—a new realization I had had since getting a body of my own.

"Amá, can I talk to you?"

Her humming stopped.

"That man staying with us . . ." I paused, searching for the right words. "He put his hands on me last night."

Amá took the clothespin out of her mouth and used it to hang one of the boys' T-shirts on the line. She took one long, drawn-out breath and said, "Not surprising. Do you see what you wear around the house? You brought this on yourself with those tight shirts you've been wearing."

"Really, Amá? Really? My clothes are tight because I've grown, and we don't have money to buy new clothes that actually fit me. Do you see what you wear? How can you say that to me?" I paused and took a breath. "Why can't you ever defend me?"

"That's ridiculous, Minu. Stop being so sensitive. *Muy delicada.*"

24

*A*pá brought his brother's son over to the United States from Mexico when I was about five years old. Alejandro was fourteen at the time, and since then, he had lived with us on and off, picking up English quickly. Every few months, he headed back to Mexico to see his family, but fit in naturally with our family when he stayed with us—like another brother.

Apá didn't hide his favoritism toward his nephew in front of my siblings and me. They bonded over projects, like building extra rooms onto the house or fixing up the chicken coop.

When Alejandro was around, Apá perked up, suddenly animated: grinning, cracking jokes, and cackling his belly laugh. That was what I wanted—what we all wanted, but my siblings and I stood on the sidelines only to catch glimpses of our rare, joyous father adoring our cousin. It had always irritated Julio the most. He wanted Apá's admiration more than anything. What son doesn't?

Julio would say to Amá, "Why doesn't Apá like me? He doesn't care about me."

It riled her up enough to say to Apá, "Quit acting like Alejandro is your oldest son. Julio is. *¡Ay, Dios mío!*"

"It's always something with that one," he would say.

During his teens, Alejandro was a devout Baptist, rarely missing a Sunday service and loyally reading the Bible at night—another activity that strengthened my father's relationship with him.

At the age of nineteen, Alejandro and Irma's friend, Carmen, began dating. Just three months later, they married. They had their first son shortly after. Alejandro and Carmen came over often, and Alejandro seemed genuinely happy. A year later, they filed for divorce with barely a reason.

More recently, Alejandro had been flirty with Lola. And when I hung with her, Cousin Alejandro came around more too—the three of us spent most evenings together.

"Let's stop here," Alejandro said as he parked his clunker car in the parking lot of the Cashion bar, Ray's Place. Bits of trash and snack wrappers covered the stained carpet and torn seat covers.

It was late afternoon on a Friday, and once again, Lola, Alejandro, and I were together, talking until we ran out of topics and then finally surrendering ourselves to a tightly rolled joint.

Except this time, it wasn't weed Alejandro was offering. On the center counsel in between Alejandro and Lola were two syringes, along with a teaspoon, a lighter, and a powdery yellow substance.

Alejandro concocted the substance while Lola watched closely. He rolled back his long sleeve t-shirt, revealing dark bruises and fresh reddened sores on his forearm. He tied a short strap around his elbow and pulled it tight. His veins awakened, bulging from his arm, and turning a vivid blue. He pierced one of the syringes into his forearm, doing it in a manner that looked as normal as tying a shoe. His jaw tightened, and he closed his eyes, taking in the feeling. Paleness spread across his caramel skin.

"Lola, you want a shoot?" he mumbled. He tightened his razor-sharp jawline, a feature of most of the Becerra men.

"Hell yeah," Lola said from the passenger's seat.

"Lola, don't do it," I said.

She rolled her eyes. "Don't be such a baby, Minu. Try it, it's not that bad."

"Not a chance in hell."

I craned my head from the back seat to see Alejandro concocting another dose in the teaspoon. Once it was ready, he flicked the syringe a few times with shaky hands and reached for Lola's arm. Alejandro searching for a thick, rich, purple vein. He lightly slapped it several times and then stabbed the syringe into her arm, the needle disappearing beneath her skin. Lola leaned her head back and closed her eyes, smiling.

"C'mon, Güera. Try it," Alejandro said through narrowed pupils, heavy with sheer evil. "One push of this and all your troubles melt away."

"It doesn't hurt. You'll like it," Lola slurred, sinking deeper into the seat.

"Nah, I'm good. I don't want to," I said. "I should probably head home anyway."

And then, in a fast instant, Alejandro grasped my arm from the driver's seat.

"Alejandro, I said no. Don't even—" I yanked my arm, but he gripped it tighter and flipped it so my forearm was facing up.

"Alejandro! No!" I yelled. "Lola, help!"

Lola said nothing. She was now asleep.

I held my other arm out as a shield, but his grip was too strong. He pinned my arm down tighter and stuck the syringe in my skin. I wanted to scream more, but I instantly felt weak. The blood seeping through my veins rushed to my head.

Alejandro whispered something, but I couldn't make it out. I melted into the back seat like ice cream thawing on a hot summer's day. Dizzy. Faint. Nauseated. My palms began to sweat. My stomach churned. I hunched over and vomited all over the floor. My eyes grew heavy. Darkness appeared around the edges of my vision. I tried to fight the sleep creeping in but slipped deeper into it.

Wake up, a voice in my head whispered.

I blinked a few times to force myself awake. Through the window the sky was dark. I was covered in sweat, and my head throbbed. I recognized the familiar padding underneath me: my bed. Somehow, I had made it home, though I had no idea how.

My head began to spin as images flashed in my mind: Alejandro. Lola. The syringe. The puking. I wore the same jean shorts and T-shirt from earlier that day. My body felt jolty and twitchy, and my arm ached where Alejandro had stuck the needle.

Something rustled across the room. I sat up, squinting, making out a silhouette over the bed across the room. Once my eyes adjusted, I knew the tall shape: Alejandro.

"Alejandro?" I called out. "Alejandro, what're you doing?"

"Shhh," his voice slowly rose through the dark. "Go back to sleep."

I heard Lola's sleepy groan.

"Lola?" I called out.

"Go back to sleep, Güera," Alejandro whispered.

"Lola?" I called out again.

No answer.

"Shut it, Minu. I said go back to sleep," Alejandro growled.

The rustling grew louder. Alejandro's silhouette moved in a fast motion over the bed.

"Alejandro. Stop it! Get off her! Get off her!" I screamed, hoping someone—anyone—in the house would hear.

"*¡Perra estúpida!*" Alejandro yelled as he darted out of the room.

25

*L*ater that summer, Lola was talking about boys with Esméralda and me in our bedroom when Esméralda let out a giggle and said, "Look at Apá's face."

Lola and I moved closer to her and peeked into the living room. Sitting on the weathered brown sofa, Apá stared at us, unblinking, his mouth pressed.

"What's wrong with your dad?" Lola asked. "He looks *loco*."

Esméralda and Lola laughed, but my stomach turned at his terrifying stare.

With a quick jolt, Apá roused from the sofa and charged us. His face fumed red, and his eyes bulged out of their sockets. Crazy Eyes. He pulled on his belt buckle, and the leather flew out of his pants. He raised it high and slashed it down, hitting Esméralda and then me, the loud snap echoing against the walls. When one of his swings struck Lola, she bolted out of the room. Esméralda followed.

I was cornered. Letting out a yell, Apá gripped my hair and yanked me off the bed. He slashed me with the belt and kicked me in the stomach again and again, knocking the breath out of me. He bundled his other hand into a fist, pulled back, and sent a punch to my face.

"What, Apá? What'd I do? What'd I do?"

"You fucking white girl!" he yelled.

His hits rammed me up against a metal shoe rack that pierced into my back. I almost made it to the door, but he caught me by the arm and threw me like a rag doll.

"I can't stand looking at this *güera*," Apá said with another kick to my thigh.

Just then, Amá stormed into the room, screaming for him to stop. She grabbed Apá's arm, keeping him from taking another swing. I army-crawled to the living room and shot to my feet. A quick look over my shoulder and I sprinted out the front door. Everything hurt, but I gathered all my strength and ran through the neighborhood. When I reached the end of the street, Esméralda and Lola stood waiting.

"What the hell was that?" Lola asked as I approached.

"Just run," I said in a full sprint.

The three of us ran and ran and ran and didn't stop to catch our breath until we made it to the next town east. We hitched a ride from Esméralda's air force boyfriend, who took us back to his apartment in Avondale.

Leaning over the bathroom sink, I squinted into the mirror. The cut under my eyebrow throbbed, as did the huge welt Apá's belt buckle had left a on my collarbone. Esméralda pressed ice packs to the purple bruises that covered my legs. She and I stayed silent, too afraid to talk about the monster we had just witnessed.

Two days after the beating, Esméralda, Lola, and I were still staying at the apartment. My sister and her boyfriend had gone to town but had kindly left money on the counter for Lola and me to get lunch and snacks at the Circle K gas station down the street.

The purple bruises on my legs were now black-and-blue splotches, so to hide the evidence and avoid any questioning, I covered the bruises on my legs with bandannas I had found in the bathroom drawers, though there was no hiding the cut above my left eye. It was so inflamed by then that I could only open my eye halfway.

I limped beside Lola to the gas station, both of use silent. I blamed the Arizona heat for making it too hot to talk, but the truth was, what had happened with Apá weighed heavily on my mind. It had only been forty-eight hours, but it felt like years of aches in my heart.

Why did Apá hate us? Why did he hate me? I wasn't good enough.

I would never be good enough as his daughter. I was the rottenest egg, the blackest sheep, the ugliest duckling.

Deep in thought, I almost walked into a police car parked in front of the Circle K. The officer inside leaned out his window. "You ladies, okay?" he asked, his eyes hidden behind large black aviator sunglasses.

"We're good, officer," I said, quickening my pace, trying to hide my limp.

"Mind explainin' why you have bandannas wrapped around your legs?"

Just as I was about to respond, Lola answered for me, "No, we're not okay, officer."

I shot her a don't-even-think-about-it look. Lola shrugged apologetically. "My friend here isn't okay."

Lola went on to explain to the officer what had happened two days before with my father. It was only a matter of minutes before we were in the policeman's car and on our way down to the Avondale Police Department.

"Sometimes he just loses it," I said. I sipped the ice-cold water in front of me on the wooden desk. The detective seated across the table wrote something on her notepad. Her glasses rested on the edge of her bulbous nose, and her hair was pulled back in a tight bun. She kept firing basic questions at me: How old was I? Where did I live? Where did I go to school? And then her questions turned to my relationship with Apá.

Yes, Apá had hurt me, but I didn't want anything to happen to him. I didn't want him to go to jail. What would the police do with him? To me? I wanted to ask but didn't.

Instead, I told them about the kicks to the stomach, the blows to the skull, the snaps of his belt; this angry-eyed stranger that was my father. The detective listened intently, nodding with kind eyes.

Once I was finished, she reached across the table to touch my hand. I winced and pulled back. "Thank you for sharing your story, Minu. We'll take it from here."

The officer from the gas station escorted Lola and me to his car. Without a word, we piled into the back seat and drove back to Cashion.

When we turned into the neighborhood, my stomach twisted into tiny knots. The streets felt familiar yet strange, as if I saw the rows of houses with a fresh pair of eyes. First, we dropped Lola off at her house. She stood at the end of the driveway, waving somberly, her face torn between uncertain, remorseful, and fearful of what was to come.

As the officer parked in front of my house, the knots in my stomach turned into a tight ball.

He opened the car door. "Stay here, please."

"What? Why? What's going to happen? Why can't I get out?"

Not answering, he slammed the door and walked to our door. When another police car pulled up and parked behind me, I thought I'd be sick. Backup? They had called for police backup?

The usual hectic neighborhood was quiet. The fathers of the households must have taken their drinking parties inside when they saw the cops strolling through. Across the street, I spotted nosy Mrs. Sanchez peeking through her living room blinds, only revealing a tiny curious eye.

The officer knocked hard on the door. No answer. He knocked again and waited. Suddenly, the door opened. It was Amá, her face somewhere between startled and confused. She and the officer exchanged a few words, and she opened the door wider, inviting him in. As the front door closed, my heart raced faster. I squeezed my hands together until the tips of my fingers were white. Had I said too much? Was I going to jail? Were they taking Apá to jail? Should I have lied?

After a few minutes, or what felt like an hour, the door opened. First out was Apá. I cringed when I saw him in handcuffs. The officer followed Apá with a hand on his shoulder, guiding him down the yard. Amá stood in front of the door, her arms crossed.

"Apá," I whispered helplessly.

As he passed me in the car, he spat on the window. I flinched and watched the glob of saliva trickle down the thick glass.

"¡María!" Apá yelled. "When I get back, I never want to see that white girl in my house again. ¡La pinche gringa!"

The officer steered Apá into the second police car, and within seconds, the vehicle skirted away. Then the officer opened the door and reached his hand out to mine. His eyes had gone from intense and focused to sympathetic and sad.

"I'm sorry you had to see that, little one," he said.

I took his hand, but I was angry at him for taking my father to jail. The officer had heard his wounding words. "Never want to see that white girl in my house again". Lola had made everything worse. I should have been braver. I should have sucked it up. Because I also did this. This was my fault. Apá was going to jail because of me.

As I made my way toward the house and Amá's twisted scowl, guilt's cousin, shame, crept in full and heavy. My mother's eyes softened when she noticed my swollen eye and the bandannas wrapped around my legs. Without a word, she led me into the kitchen and ripped a branch from the bright green aloe vera plant that sat on the dining table. I plopped myself on the kitchen counter while she squeezed out the gel from the leaf and dabbed my wounds.

"Why did you turn your father into *el policío, mija*?" she asked.

I winced at the cold salve that cooled my flushed face. "I didn't, Amá. The officer saw my bruises." I waited for her to respond, but nothing. I looked at her bleak brown eyes, cupped by heavy pouches, but she kept her attention on dabbing my wounds. "What's wrong with him? Why is he so angry? Why is he always angry with me?" I grabbed her wrist to listen to me. "And why does he call me a white girl?"

She stiffened at the question and gave a despairing shrug. "He's sick."

"What do you mean 'he's sick'?"

"His mind is sick . . . it's manic depression. He goes to the mental hospital sometimes when he isn't here. He never wanted any of you kids to know . . ." She trailed off. "He's been sick for years."

Young David's voice rang in my head, *He ain't right in the head, Minu. Don't you know that by now?* Julio's voice followed, *He's loco.*

That explained why he acted like two different people. And why he went from hot to cold in the snap of a finger. I'd heard about manic-depressive people before—but I'd never met anybody with it. And it turned out my own father had it?

"He's a good man," Amá said, setting the aloe vera pot back on the dining table.

"Well, I don't want to be here when he gets back."

She shook her head as if brushing off the whole thing. "When he gets out, he'll be better. He'll have forgotten all about this. *Para que te apuras*. Don't you worry."

But what about me? What if I couldn't forget this? While hideous, throbbing bruises dotted my legs, it was t my father's painful words that had embedded themselves in my heart forever. And now, discovering the illness my father suffered from added a whole other piece to the mess. Maybe Apá truly loved us, but the disease distorted it.

There were only two things I could make sense of that day. The first: that was my last whipping. No one was ever going to touch me that way again. And the second: I was through with Cashion. The minute I had my high school diploma, I'd get as far away from this stifling small town as possible. I'd make it happen, that I was sure of.

Apá spent the next few days in jail, followed by a two-week stay at the mental hospital in downtown Phoenix. I told my brothers about Apá's sickness, but they didn't seem surprised or interested in hearing the likely reason our father exploded the way he did. During those two weeks, Amá seemed extra reserved, her typical unreadable self. She carried on working long days at the tortilla factory and laundromat and stayed on top of chores. Nothing seemed to faze her.

On the day Apá was released from the mental hospital, Amá and I went together to pick him up. The building was white with a few scattered fluffy palm trees in the dirt yard. Even in the triple-digit temperature, the place gave off an ice-cold feeling. Apá walked out in the same clothes he wore when he was taken away in the cop car on that dreadful day. He scuffed his feet along the sidewalk, and his face looked drained and saggy.

"Hi, Güera," he said, climbing into the front passenger seat.

"Hi, Apá," I said, my voice shaky.

"How are you feeling?" Amá asked.

"Much better," he said, his voice calm.

"Good. The time you had in there has done you well. No need to take those pills anymore," Amá said, gently patting her husband of twenty years.

Apá nodded.

26

*L*ola, Esméralda, and I stood on the bypass of Highway US 85 with our thumbs raised.

"Here comes another one," Lola said as a car approached from the distance.

We all stuck our thumbs higher in the air, but the car sped past.

"Dammit," Esméralda yelled, stomping her foot into the gravel.

We each held a small bag packed with only a few days' worth of clothes and a few toiletries. The plan for our hitchhiking trip? Well, there wasn't one. For all we knew, this runaway expedition would be several days or a few months or maybe we would never come back.

We didn't consider school coming up or that none of us had a car or where we'd stay or our lack of money. We were teens from broken homes with adventure on our minds and blinders over our eyes. As for me, still choking on shame for Apá's arrest, I was running away from the tension that stayed thick between my father and me.

"Nobody's picking us up because there are three of us," Lola said. "We'd practically take up a whole damn car."

"I got it!" Esméralda clapped. "Minu, hide in those bushes over there." She pointed next to the highway. "We'll trick the cars to thinking it's just Lola and me."

"Why me?" I asked.

"Because you're the youngest," Esméralda snapped. "Now go. Some cars are coming."

I ran to hide. After a few more cars passed by, a white semitruck screeched on its brakes and pulled to the side of the road. Esméralda and Lola caught up to the truck's cab, and I followed.

The driver craned his head out the window. "Y'all need a ride?"

"Where ya headed?" Esméralda asked.

"Bakersfield," he yelled out. Clumps of oily gray hair peeked through the sides of his sweat-stained baseball cap.

"California sounds nice," Lola said with a shrug.

"Three of ya?" the driver asked. Esméralda nodded. He combed his snarly gray beard with his fingers. "Well, all right. It might be a tight squeeze, but we'll make it work. Hop in."

Lola climbed up and opened the passenger door. "Bakersfield it is."

The three of us sat snugly in the back, crunching Twinkie wrappers into the crevasse of the seat cushion.

"The name's Ed. Runnin' away, eh?" His tone was friendly, maybe even thrilled he had tagalongs for the ride.

"From all the problems in the world," Esméralda said.

Ed let out a husky laugh, revved the engine, and turned the truck onto the state highway. We were off.

From Phoenix we drove for eight hours, zigzagging through rugged mountain ranges and speeding past beater trucks, bohemian vans, and cheery motorcyclists who flashed us a peace sign. Ed told us story after story of his time on the road, sneaking in a few bad jokes here and there. He barely took a breath. That was probably what happened when someone spent months alone on the highway.

When we passed the Welcome to California sign, shivers went down my back. A fresh start. We drove through rolling rangeland of Joshua trees with bristly leaves and white flowers and continued on through Los Angeles, where the buildings reflected a glittery orange color from the late-afternoon sun. Every hour, we stopped to use the bathroom, stretch our legs, and take a break from Ed's tales. During the seventh hour on the road, he turned silent, and so did we. After a while, we drifted off to sleep.

I woke to Lola nudging my head off her shoulder. "We're here."

My blurry half-asleep vision focused, revealing a gas station. Ed opened the door, and we leapt out of the truck.

"You young ladies be careful out here," he said, bouncing his finger in the air. "Stick together and watch out for the loonies."

We saluted him, gave one last forced giggle at his awful joke, and turned to the city.

With nowhere to go and nowhere to be, the three of us wandered through the thriving town, passing hippies wearing bell-bottom jeans and platform shoes, preaching free love and flower power. The street was packed with Bohemian shops, motels, and fast-food restaurants. Tall palm trees lined the sidewalks, and white men on chopper bikes sped by us. Everywhere was something to tempt the eye.

We weren't there for twenty minutes when Esméralda started a conversation with a Mexican man. He was short with slicked, stiff hair and wore a deep V-neck shirt that showcased his hairy chest. He looked to be in his thirties. Esméralda told Slick about the long trip we had just endured. "We'll be sleeping on the streets if we don't find a place to stay."

"*Una pregunta*. No place to stay? You'll come back with me then," he said. I could tell by his accent that he was Chilango, which meant he was from Mexico City.

The next thing I knew, we were following him to his apartment. I wasn't a fan of staying at some strangers' place, but it was better than sleeping under a viaduct or a bench as I'd seen other homeless people do.

Slick lived in a small brick complex with a narrow staircase and dim green lighting. The hallway reeked of mildew and echoed with merengue music. He led us to a grungy apartment that smelled of aftershave mixed with dust and old beer. It was dark with one small window, a soiled couch, an overflowing trash can, and empty whiskey bottles scattered across the brown stained carpet.

"Make yourselves at home. Sofa's yours," Slick said, acting as if he had just taken us to the Ritz Carlton.

"Free stay," Lola whispered in my ear. She must have noticed the look of disgust on my face.

Esméralda fell into the sofa. "This is perfect."

"Well then, shall we celebrate?" Slick asked. He pulled three beer bottles out from a cardboard box in the kitchen and passed them out to us. He raised his bottle high in the air and said, "Welcome to Bakersfield."

We clanked our lukewarm beer bottles together, ready for our new beginning.

Life in Bakersfield was nothing but one big party. Packed houses, deafening music, thick haze from cigarettes or pot, Esméralda making out with sleazeball Slick, Lola snorting any drug she was offered and drinking until she barfed in the toilet. I joined in with the drinking but that was all. Early one morning a week later, I woke up to a hard knock on Slick's apartment door. I peeked through the peephole to see two Bakersfield policemen.

The neighbor across the hall had reported Slick to the cops for living with several young girls. After hardly asking any questions, the officers led us out of the apartment and drove us to the police department. Since Esméralda was older than eighteen, the officers drove her to the Arizona border, where she hitchhiked back to Cashion.

Lola and I took were escorted to the Kern County Juvenile Detention Center.

My second stint in juvenile hall was much different from my first. For starters, Lola and I were crammed into a prison cell barely six-foot square. The bed was a plank of wood with short legs, and we each had a thin blanket, although the place was so hot and stuffy we didn't use it. This time, the jail staff didn't try to get a hold of our families. Instead, they told us if our families cared enough, they'd come find us.

And unlike the El Paso Juvenile Center, we weren't the only ones there. Other teenage girls badmouthed each other and started fistfights in the hall. On the way to the shower, I watched four inmates jump another girl, beating her up pretty badly. And the food was disgusting.

"This food tastes like hot garbage," Lola said, sloshing around the gooey mixture on her Styrofoam plate. She smelled the mush on the end of her plastic fork and dry heaved. I ripped off a bite of the stale dinner roll. It was tough and sour, but I ate it all.

After a week of avoiding eye contact with the juvenile torments and choking down the slimy food, Lola received money in the prison mail to hop on a Greyhound back to Arizona. Esméralda had informed her mom of our whereabouts. She boarded the bus that day. A day later, my stomach churned when I received money in the mail from my parents for a ticket back home.

That day, I climbed aboard the bus, meeting the kind eyes of the bus driver. She smiled politely at me, but I couldn't return a smile. She didn't know she was driving me back to my troubles, my heartaches, my pain.

I walked past the rows of blue seats until I reached the last row and slid next to the window, taking one last look at the Kern County Juvie Hall. Was it wrong for wanting to stay there instead of going back to Cashion? Apá would be furious my sister and I had run away. Had Esméralda already received her whipping? Regardless, it was now my turn. Amá would let it happen. Maybe she'd snap a few whips on my behind too. I could feel the yank of my hair, the pull of my arm, the kick to my side.

After a three-hour bus ride, we approached the depot. I craned my neck over the rows of bus seats, scanning the parking lot for the family station wagon. There it was, in the back. The familiar twisted knots in my stomach returned.

I walked to the car, studying my parents through the dusty windshield. Amá stared straight ahead, her mouth slack, and from the passenger's seat, Apá had puffy eyes and a somber face. They looked . . . sad. Had they been crying? Had they missed me? Or maybe they'd been worried sick about me?

I opened the car door and climbed into the back seat. The three of us sat in silence. No one moved.

"I'm sorry," I muttered. No answer. The silence continued. I tried again, "I'm sorry. I'm sorry I ran away. I'm sorry, okay?"

Apá dropped his head and did something I'd never seen him do in my fifteen years: he cried. His shoulders bobbed up and down as his cry turned into a sob. I had broken my parents' hearts. They weren't going to beat me. How could I have thought such horrid things? They really did love me.

"Apá, I'm sorry—"

"No," he said. "It's not about you, Güera. It's something else. Mariá, tell her."

Amá reached over and cupped Apá's cheek. He cried harder. She leaned on the center counsel and looked at me. "Cousin Alejandro killed Agapito."

I gasped. "What?"

It took a minute for her words to sink in. Agapito—Esméralda's boyfriend, the young guy we had brought to the States from Mexico—dead because my cousin had killed him. Murdered him.

"Drugs," my mother said in a monotone. "It's all because of the damn drugs that came into *el barrio*. Alejandro stabbed Agapito to death. He showed up at our house after he did it, asking us for help . . . covered in blood."

"What will happen to him?"

Apá's voice cracked. "We don't know."

We rode back to Cashion in a thick fog of silence. My mind raced to the young, innocent Agapito in Mexico forced by Apá to leave his family. After he had left our house, Agapito had moved into a cheap apartment in Tolleson, a town east of Cashion, and worked a full-time job, sending some of his paychecks to Mexico to take care of his six siblings back home.

Now, he was dead. And my cousin was a murderer.

I believed Apá was so upset about the incident, not only because Agapito had lost his life, but also because he felt responsible for bring-ing both of them to the States. To Apá, it was like losing his own son, a maddening thought since he had barely batted an eye when Julio left.

Eventually, Alejandro turned himself in to the police. He received a five-year sentence.

My parents never mentioned juvenile hall.

27

*F*or years, I wished things were different. That my life would be different with different people in it. A different family, one that didn't mistreat one another. A family where the father wasn't a potential minefield and where the mother hugged and cared for her children. A different town that wasn't contaminated with alcoholics, druggies, and some sort of danger on every corner.

Soon after we returned from Bakersfield, Dolores and her baby girl moved out of the house and in with the baby's father, and Esméralda left to live with her boyfriend. Irma and Dolores stopped by regularly, and Julio visited more often after the horrible incident with Alejandro. And my younger brothers, David now twelve, Danny eleven, Ruben ten, and Sammy nine, constantly bickered, squabbled, and argued.

Since Amá came home from her long workdays too tired for barely a hello, and Apá was off doing God knows what, most days I took care of my brothers. I helped them with homework, reminded them to wash their face and brush their teeth, and cooked them *fideo y papas* for dinner. This was the only thing I knew how to cook. Irma had taught me how to make it before she moved out.

When I turned fifteen, I knew not to expect a *quinceañera* celebration. Normally, in a Hispanic household, the age of fifteen represents when a Mexican girl is said to be passing from girlhood to a señorita. I knew this because my cousins in Mexico had *quinceañeras*. I even attended a few. The decorations, the flowers, the big pretty dress, the gifts, and the fluffy cake—I wanted it all. What young girl doesn't want to feel like a princess for a day? But there would be no such thing in the Becerra house. We couldn't afford such a wasteful party, Amá told us. "Besides, it's become more of a 'permission party' to condone sex in a young Spanish girl's life. And we'll have none of that here."

When I confided in Lola about the *quinceañera* I always wanted but would never get, she sided with my mother. "Your mom's right. Shit's wasteful." Then she said with a shrug, "Plus, we don't need a party to give us consent. We can have sex whenever we want."

"Yeah, *you* can. I'm not into that." The way Esméralda described sex had stuck with me. I knew boys were dangerous. They would flirt, say "I love you," maybe hold your hand here and there, all the while after something else.

There was one exception. Lola's brother, Alberto, now twenty. He was different from guys my age with his mature, even-keeled, and gentle demeanor. His subtle side smile and spellbinding brown eyes—the color of pancake syrup—made my body warm. We exchanged flirty glances, and occasionally when speaking to me, he'd ever so lightly brush a curly strand from my face. Playful teasing turned to compliments, which turned into endless conversations, which turned into wanting more.

One night, while riding around town with him in the famed Pontiac GTO, he pulled to the side of the road and turned to me, his handsome face illuminated by the streetlight.

"I like you, Minu. A lot," he whispered softly.

I took one long, drawn-out breath to steady my nerves.

"I know you and I could be something great together."

You and me? Together? I wanted to grab his handsome face for a hard kiss. But then it dawned on me I hadn't kissed anyone before. I'd read all the Harlequin Romance novels, the intense kissing and sex scenes, but had never practiced on anyone. How do I do it? What did I do with my hands? Open mouth or closed? I panicked. What happened next?

"I'm fifteen, Alberto. Doesn't that scare you?" I was stalling.

He shook his head, a smile twitching at his lips. The flutter in my stomach rose to my chest. He leaned across the center console and his soft lips touched mine. He moved his mouth around a bit, and I moved my lips to follow, his eyes closed. Mine were slightly opened to see him.

"It scares the living shit out of me," he said, breathless. "But let's give us a try and find out for ourselves."

My heart thumped so loud I thought he'd hear it.

"Mmm," was all I could mumble, absolutely hypnotized.

After that, Alberto and I started the whole dating thing. At first, it bothered Lola. She was nervous I'd spend more time with him than her. She wasn't wrong. Alberto and I became inseparable. Occasionally, we strolled the park bewitched by one another, our hands clasped and fingers entwined. I did most of the talking in our relationship—gabbing about my chemistry homework, my dreams of being a stewardess, and to one day travel the world.

In a sincere voice, Alberto would say, "You can do whatever you want, Minu. You have the brains, the beauty, and the character to do it all."

I'd lean over and lay a wet smooch on him because I could. I was getting good at the whole kissing thing. No sex, I'd told him. I wasn't ready.

This new relationship meant everything to me. A fresh start, a clean slate, a radiance of the love and happiness I'd never had. I had a man to protect me, to comfort me, to warm me, to love me. He was everything I needed. When I was in his arms, I could do anything.

I finally found what I'd been missing for so long.

28

*F*ive months later, I received a call from Alberto's mother, Rosa, that changed everything. Through her cries and sobs, I could make out that Alberto had been arrested for armed robbery—before he and I had started dating. His two friends had raided a local bar at gunpoint while Alberto had been the getaway driver. Rosa called to tell me that the three of them had received a five-year prison sentence and were headed to Florence, Arizona.

Unbeknownst to me, Alberto had been out on bail the whole time we were together.

"It was the wrong place at the wrong time, Minu." These were the words he repeatedly told me any time he was allowed to call from prison. The shouts of inmates echoed through the phone.

"And it's costing you, Alberto! Five years. What am I supposed to do? Sit here and wait for you to get out?"

It was around this time when Amá found out about the relationship. "That boy is nothing but trouble. All those Espinosas are. And he's too old for you, *mija*. This must be a sign from God himself. Leave him."

I brushed her comments aside, too in love to listen. The first couple of months Alberto was locked up, we sent letters back and forth. In one note, he described his cold, lonely cell and the fights he witnessed between the other prisoners, but he'd always finish his letters ensuring me not to worry about him. I'd been to juvenile hall twice, but I knew my experiences didn't come close to his.

In another letter I received that winter, he asked me to send a photo so he wouldn't forget what I looked like. I sent a five-by-seven picture of myself from when I'd gone to the Arizona State Fair the month before with some friends. In the photograph, the colorful, glittery lights from the fair rides dotted the background, and my hair draped down to my chest as I smiled a bright, happy smile. Alberto addressed his following letter to "his beautiful *gringa.*"

A few weeks later, Rosa asked me if I'd ride along with her to visit him. I dreaded the thought. I pictured his handsome face behind metal bars, caged like an animal.

"Come on, Minu. Come with me," she said. "Alberto so badly wants to see you. Don't you want to see him?"

I agreed to go.

Rosa and I completed our required background checks and were on our way to the Florence Prison. During the car ride, Rosa talked mostly about her rich boyfriend who bought her expensive gold jewelry and swooped her away on luxurious beach trips.

Eventually, she shifted the conversation to Alberto and me. "Give my son another chance, Minu. He fucked up, but he's a good man. He'll be outta that hellhole soon enough." She tapped the butt of her cigarette on the top of the half-open window. "I know my son, and he won't disappoint you."

I wanted to tell her that her son had already disappointed me and that I felt abandoned once again. Instead, I nodded.

Ever since Alberto's sentence, I'd contemplated breaking it off. I didn't want the life of an inmates' girlfriend. The constant waiting for the letters to arrive, the fifteen-minute phone calls, me working in the real world while he sat in his cell. The years we had ahead. It felt like punishment for me too, as if I'd done something wrong. But this wasn't my mistake. Why did I have to pay for it?

Rosa and I pulled up to a tan brick building surrounded by a tall, barbed-wire fence. In the recreation yard, a few prisoners in bright orange suits moped around while others shot a basketball at a frayed hoop.

During the pat-down and the examining at the metal detector, a guard ran his clammy fingertips from the top of my head and palmed through my hair. He patted me down from my shoulders to my ankles. Across the room, Rosa experienced the same, although she looked used to it.

"Both clear," the guard said with a nod.

Rosa and I were escorted to a plain white room lined with tables of inmates sitting across from their families and friends of all ages and intentions: young kids seeing their dads or loved ones simply checking in. Some people laughed, while others had grim expressions. A few dabbed their eyes with a tissue.

I held my breath when I saw Alberto hunched over at a table in the back corner. His face lit up when he saw us. His hair was shorter, and he looked tanner wearing the orange suit—perhaps from the extra sun in the recreation yard. Still so handsome.

Rosa and I took a seat across from him. I studied the black number stamped on the left corner of his shirt—a reminder that he belonged to the prison. At first, we kept the conversation light. We mentioned the weather, Rosa yakked about her boyfriend, and I lied about how well-kept and pleasant the prison appeared. At one point, the conversation turned one-sided as Alberto told us about the tasty cafeteria food, the hour of recess the inmates were allowed each day, and the few friends he had made. I couldn't take my eyes off his gentle hands folded in the metal handcuffs.

"It's not that bad in here. Honestly," he said with an unconvincing smile.

Finally, I asked the question I believed Rosa was thinking too: "How are you, Alberto? Really?"

He shook his head. It looked like he was on the verge of tears, but he'd never allow me and his mother to see them.

"I'm good. Really. Don't you worry about me." He reached across the table, the chain hanging from handcuffs clanking across the surface, and cupped his hands in mine. Rosa turned her head to give us privacy. "I hate that I put you through this, Minu."

I stared at the table, counting the wood slivers to keep the tears from starting.

"Wait for me, baby. I'm working on myself in here. I'll come out a better man. I won't let you down. I prom—"

"Hands off at table twenty-two!"

A guard with bulging neck muscles glared directly at us. Alberto released my hands.

"It's hard to see you like this," I whispered. If my voice had gone any louder, I knew I'd burst into tears.

"Don't you dare worry for a second about me. Focus on yourself so when I get out, we can pick up right where we left off. I love you, Minu Becerra."

"Alberto, I—"

A guard approached the table. Our time was up. The unfinished conversation dangled in the air. When we said our goodbyes that day, Alberto snuck in a quick but gentle kiss on my cheek.

"Wait for me, Minu," he whispered in my ear.

Sometime later that week, I made two important decisions. First: I would break it off with Alberto. In a heartfelt letter. I told him I could no longer promise to wait for him. He wrote back, bitterness and anger flying off the pages.

Second: I would never pick in the fields again, not one more second. I asked the owner of Garcia's Market if he had any job openings.

"I might," he said. Can you count money?"

I nodded. "Yes. Yes, I can."

"Then you can be a cashier. Come in tomorrow after school."

No more chapped lips, no more filthy clothes, no more swollen fingers, no more sunburn.

I was done.

29

*O*ne afternoon while I was doing chores around the house, Apá yelled at me that I was in the way and hit me in the back with his belt. When I told Lola, she offered to let me live with her. I jumped at the opportunity to leave home.

Finally, it was my turn.

But Lola's house was a different type of chaos. Since Rosa was too busy spending time with her boyfriend and working long hours at the hotel, the Espinosa house came alive after school with high schoolers pressing for their next high. Still, I told myself, anything was better than living at home.

Most days, Lola's boyfriend, Henry, showed up after he finished working at the mill. And on the days Henry didn't show, she slept around with other guys at the house.

The following weekend, Lola received an invite to a party in the neighboring town. I told her I didn't want to go, but of course, she didn't listen—we were usually on Lola's schedule, anyway—and we left for the party. The teens there were just as troubled as those in Cashion. Lola didn't care.

When we arrived at the dirty trailer, a cluster of people swarmed the front yard and bottlenecked into the front door. I trailed Lola through the crowd until she met who I guessed was her drug dealer. The three of us weaved our way inside, where the air was hot and tight, seasoned with the skunky stench of pot. Lola followed the dealer into a bedroom, and I observed the mix of people throughout the room—everyone was either hanging out, making out, or passed out. Lola and I had come to Laveen a few times before, so I recognized a couple of faces. I wasn't sure they'd remember me, so I kept to myself.

In the corner of the room was a man concentrating on inking a star tattoo across a girl's upper thigh. A circle of people crowded around, watching him carefully sketch hues of ink, bringing to life the rickety shape on her skin. After finishing, he called out, "Who's next?"

I jolted in shock when someone said, "Give Minu one."

"What? Me?" I said.

"Yeah, you," said a guy leaning against the wall. I recognized him from the last party we attended. I couldn't remember his name. "Tattoo her wacky ass name so she doesn't have to spell it for us every fucking time."

I remembered he had asked me to repeat my name when I met him, so as I usually did, I spelled it for him. I couldn't remember his name. Javier? Juan?

"Yeah, do it!" someone else yelled.

I shook my head and let out a forced laugh. "Nah, I'll pass, guys, really." I searched the room for Lola but couldn't find her.

"She needs some ink on that precious white skin of hers, Jorge," someone else yelled. Jorge. Yes, that was his name.

In a fraction of a second, a tight grip took hold of my left wrist. It was Jorge.

"Funny one, guys," I said. Beads of sweat sprouted across my brow. "Really, I'm good on the body art."

"You're in good hands," Jorge whispered as he pressed my wrist harder into the table.

I pulled my wrist, but it was locked in his grip. The man with his ink pen pulled up a chair, situated himself close to me, and said in a croaky voice, "Let's make sure no one forgets your name ever again. Hold still. This shouldn't take long."

I panicked and screamed, "Lola!"

"How do you spell it?" the tatted man asked.

"M I N U," Jorge said, gripping my wrist through gritted teeth.

The needle buzzed as it pierced my skin, burning like a bee sting.

"Stop!" I screamed again. "Lola!"

The man gave me a little smile. The pricking sensation continued to my middle finger, then to my ring finger, and finally to my pinky. Just as I thought it was finished, he flipped my forearm and poke the pen in an erratic motion across my forearm with a sneering laugh.

"Stop it! Stop it!" I screamed louder.

He pulled the needle back, and I held my breath when I saw my name upside down in crooked black lettering. "M" on the pointer, "I" on the middle finger, "N" on the ring finger, and "U" on my pinky. The constellation of small, inked dots covered my forearm.

"There, there's better," the man said. His mouth twitched as if he were fighting a smile.

Lola suddenly stood over the table. I looked up to see her dilated, bloodshot eyes. "What'd I miss?"

"Where the hell have you been?"

"In the back bedroom. Where else would I be? Let me see your new ink." She grabbed my left hand and lifted it close to her face. My four fingers were stuck between tingling and burning. Lola let out her obnoxious laugh. "Now that's a stick and poke! This'll save so much time, Minu. You'll just have to flash people your hand when they ask you your name."

Everyone in the room hooted. I snatched my hand from her and stormed out of the trailer. Lola followed, calling my name.

When we were out in the front yard, I stopped in my tracks and turned to look her dead in her eyes, my blood now steaming. "You're a real shitty friend, you know that? Your only concern is getting as high as a damn kite. And while you're off sticking your nose where you shouldn't, some guy is carving me up!"

"Take a chill pill, Min—"

"No! I needed you! And you weren't there. Nobody's ever there for me!"

"Minu. Get over it. It's really not that bad. It's just a tattoo."

I didn't say a word to her for the rest of the night.

A week later, the ink settled in. My four fingers went from inflamed and oozing to inching and flaking, and now the crooked letters were nothing but a permanent reminder of the shitstorm of a universe that was my life. But I knew there was nothing I could do about it.

Like everything else, I learned to ignore it, forget it, or turn a blind eye. I hid the four tattoos by placing oversized plastic rings on my fingers.

While I lived with Lola, she and I grocery shopped every few days with the chunk of change her mom gave us to buy food. We'd get the usual: sourdough bread, a tub of mayonnaise, deli meat, cheddar cheese, and my favorite salty pickles—our typical fancied lunch and dinner.

One evening as we rounded the aisle to the bakery section, I nearly jumped out of my skin when I saw Amá. I should have known the risk of running into her—she usually shopped early weekday evenings. Her eyes locked onto mine, and she pushed her tortilla and meat-filled cart next to ours.

"Minu, you haven't called in over two weeks. You need to come home."

"Amá, don't worry about me," I murmured. "I've been busy." I covered my left hand with my right to conceal the tattoos.

"You need to come home," she said again.

"No. I'm better when I'm away."

Her face turned from wearied to distressed, her eyes barely blinking. "I went to the doctor and got some terrible news." She paused. "I have a tumor growing in my head. I need your help around the house. I need you home."

My bitterness toward my parents was loud, but my conscience was louder. Could I live with myself if something happened to Amá? The gut-wrenching feeling of guilt brought me home the following day.

A week later, while she was making salsa, I asked Amá how she was handling the tumor. She smashed a ripe red tomato so hard juice spattered on her shirt.

"Oh, *mija*. I never had a tumor. I just wanted you home."

30

I sat up on my bed, still wearing the previous night's T-shirt and jeans. I rubbed my heavy eyes and swallowed the leftover saliva in my dry mouth. My head pounded. It was the kind of ache that stopped all the other parts of my brain from working.

"Minu, Lola's on the phone," Amá called from the kitchen.

Oh, I had a bone to pick with that drug-obsessed burnout. The night before, I'd gone to a neighborhood party with her and someone had drugged my Coke. The worst part? I was confident Lola was the culprit. She'd been the one who had held my drink while I used the bathroom, and when I returned, she acted all giddy and asked me several times how my soda tasted. After a few sips, the hallucinations started. The guy I'd been talking to sprouted whiskers from his nose as fur grew around his face. Before my eyes, he morphed into a nasty beady-eyed rat.

By the time I got home, I was woozy and lightheaded. The hallucinations continued. The portrait of my younger self in the plush pink dress winked at me, and when I climbed into my bed, the room twirled and spun like a whirling merry-go-round.

I stumbled into the living room to the phone. "Lola?" My voice was croaky and hoarse, as if I hadn't talked in years. "We have to—"

"How was your first acid trip? You must have been stoney baloney." She laughed.

"I knew it, you bitch. What is *wrong* with you? How do you call yourself my friend when—"

"Oh, Minu. Don't be such a fucking baby. It's not that bad."

"No. No. I'm done with this. I'm done with you. I can't be around you, Lola. You're nothing but a low-life, strung-out junkie. Don't you ever come near me again."

Before she could spew a rebuttal, I hung up the phone.

As painful as it was, distancing myself from Lola was the right move—like dodging a red-hot, lethal bullet just before it heaved into me. On my way to school, I'd pass her house, reminded daily of the best friend I once had. After our phone call, she never apologized or tried to talk it through with me, turning from a friend to a foe in a night. At school, she trash-talked me, cussing me out and calling me loco.

If there was one thing I'd learned: it was up to me to protect myself and my own fragile heart.

Two months later, Rosa called me one afternoon, asking if I'd go with her to see Alberto. "They've moved him to the Fort Grant prison for good behavior, Minu. I told you he wouldn't let us down!"

"Rosa." I sighed. "I appreciate the offer, but I can't—"

"Minu, what will it take for you to realize he loves you? He misses you, and it would raise his spirits to see you. Please. Come with me."

I caved and told her yes.

A few days later, a letter from Alberto showed up in the mail. Seeing his scribbled handwriting on the crinkled lined notebook paper filled my stomach with butterflies.

> *Minu,*
> *Can't wait to see you.*
> *I have something to show you.*
> *Alberto*

So here we were once again, Rosa and I, on our way to visit Alberto. We picked up Kentucky Fried Chicken with a side of corn and mashed potatoes—his favorite meal—and met him at a wooden picnic table in the prison courtyard. The environment at Fort Grant overall was much more lenient: we breezed through security, the guards were actually welcoming, and prisoners weren't shackled.

The three of us ate our fried chicken and sides while Alberto filled us in on his new job working in the laundry room. He looked sexy in his denim short-sleeve shirt that perfectly squeezed his chest and biceps. I could tell he'd been lifting weights.

Rosa left for the restroom to give the two of us time alone. The moment turned awkward. The last time he'd heard from me was through my letter ending our relationship.

"Thank you for coming, Minu. You have no idea how much I missed you." From across the table, his eyes twinkled with what looked like hopefulness.

"What did you want to show me, Alberto?"

"Ahh, yes. You want to see?" He folded back his right sleeve, revealing a tattoo of a familiar face. My eyes. My smile. My nose. Me. It was my face from the photo I'd sent him several months before. I couldn't speak.

"What do you think?" he said, filling the silence.

"Why'd you do that?" I spat out.

His smile faded. "That's the face of the most beautiful woman in my life. *Mi gringa.*"

"But it doesn't wash off." I looked at the upside-down "M I N U" across my fingers.

He reached across the table to grab my hand. "Now I have you in my heart and on my arm. Forever."

I forced out a laugh. "Forever? I guess I didn't know you felt that way."

"What?" Alberto said, unfolding his shirt sleeve, my inked face slowly disappearing.

I fixed my face to hide my disappointment. I couldn't find the words. "Just . . . in shock, I guess. That's all."

"Minu, I love you. I want to be with you. I'll be out of this place in no time, and we can get on with our lives. Get married. Have babies. Live happily ever after in Cashion. You'll see."

Happily ever after in Cashion? I cringed at the thought.

31

*A*lberto reeled me in hook, line, and sinker. For heaven's sake, the man had tattooed my face on his arm.

I visited him once a month at the prison, and we sent letters every week. I sprinted to the phone whenever it rang in case it was him. We made it work. I just prayed it'd be worth it in the end.

But I wouldn't let Alberto distract me from school since I was finally succeeding. I loved my literature class and learning about mythology, especially about the phoenix, an immortal bird who had to burn to rise from its own ashes. I had even taken advantage of after-school tutoring, and Bs and Cs started replacing big fat Ds and Fs. Still, I often jumbled my letters, or would add extra letters to words, so I'd have to go back to writing slower and reading more carefully.

One afternoon, barely halfway through my junior year at Tolleson High, I flipped through the class ring brochure. An oval turquoise, a square azure, a round purple diamond, but it was the ruby diamond with the silver band that made my heart skip a beat. Ruby was my birthstone. I fanned out my hand to envision the shimmering ring on my finger and stuck the folded-up brochure in my pocket. I had to have it.

The entire walk home, I rehearsed how I would ask my parents for the money to buy the ring. I hadn't asked for anything like this before, I justified. We didn't receive Christmas presents or gifts on birthdays, and I had slaved away in the fields for years to earn Apá a buck. How could they say no?

The ring would represent my hardship years, the ones I wanted to forget, but strangely, still wanted to remember since my life would only go up from here. When I was a stewardess traveling from country to country, the ring would be a daily reminder of where I'd come from. Or maybe this ring could be something my parents and I could bond over, a way to wipe the slate clean, bury the hatchet, and allow bygones to be bygones.

When I arrived home, Apá was slouched on the couch watching the Spanish news. The anchor went on about the drought in Arizona as if the locals didn't already know. I took a seat on the other end, waiting for a commercial to pitch my spiel.

"Apá," I said softly. He didn't look away from the TV. I cleared my throat. "I'd like to ask you something." No answer. I carried on. "The school is selling class rings to the junior students." I pulled the brochure from my pocket and opened it to the page with the ruby red diamond. "I'd really like this one. The ruby is my birthstone. For July. Could I, Apá?"

He craned his head to get a good look at the ring on the page. He sighed with a disheartened look. "We can't, Güera."

"But Ap—"

He ripped the brochure from my grip and threw it to the floor. "You're stupid if you think we'd spend that kind of money !" His words fired out like bullets. "And besides, you're not going back to school. Your ma and I need you to work full days." I felt like he'd slapped me—a slap so hard it knocked the breath from my body.

"But Apá, *por favor*! I have one more year left! Let me graduate, and then I'll help you. I'll work two jobs. Anything you ne—"

"No! You're lucky because you're a *güera*. You're privileged. The ones who have lighter skin are always more successful. You can get a job easier—wherever you want. I've lost several jobs just because of my dark skin."

"Apá, plea—"

"*¡Bastante!*" he yelled. "You can finish school later."

My lip quivered, and I tightened my mouth to stop the tears from streaming down my face.

My mother appeared from the kitchen, wiping her hands on a towel. She'd been listening.

"Amá, please. Tell Apá how hard I've worked. Please don't make me quit."

"*Mija*, no. We need the money. Listen to your father."

Hot anger blazed through me like a crackling, flaming fire.

"This isn't fair! How can you do this to me? I can't wait to get out of this house for good!" I yelled, storming into my room. I buried my face into my pillow, soaking it with salty tears, crying myself to sleep.

I dropped out of school the following week and found a job working at a local manufacturing factory. All day long, I stood at a table, shaving off the edges of the metal material that didn't fully cut during production. I was the youngest there by thirty years. The women I worked with wore jean overalls and talked about the affairs they'd cooked up with the men in the warehouse.

"Honey, stay in school," one woman told me. "Otherwise, you'll end up like us when you're our age—cutting metal and jumping the blue-collar handymen."

I didn't waste my breath explaining that my family was stuck in a cycle of poverty and that if it were my choice, I'd be sitting at a school desk taking a chemistry test right that second.

At the end of the work week, I handed my parents my paycheck. I continued to dream of the days when I would be grown and able to buy any ring—any piece of jewelry—for myself alone.

32

I did exactly what I told myself not to do: I waited for Alberto. After three years of incarceration, he called me with the news of his early release date for good behavior.

"You mean it?" I cried through the phone.

"I mean it, baby. The wait is over." I could tell he was beaming on the other end of the phone. "I can't wait to see your pretty face as a free man today, Minu. You're all mine. All mine."

That day was perfectly sunny. I wore a butterscotch-yellow sundress with tan buckled sandals I had bought from the local thrift store for seventy-fifty cents. As he walked out of prison, a free man, and more handsome than ever, I sprinted into his arms. He twirled me around and around.

"It's the start to the rest of our lives, baby," he whispered in my ear. "We made it."

I gazed into his syrupy eyes as we danced around the parking lot, knowing I had found my match, my partner, my forever. I thanked myself for sticking it out when the times were tough and for setting myself up for that happy life I craved so badly. We were two kids madly in love who wanted nothing more than a secluded room and time alone to make up for what had been lost.

Rosa gifted me a silky mauve nightie along with see-through matching panties, and she surprised Alberto with a '72 blue Ford Pinto. And even though Amá didn't fully approve of Alberto, she showed up with a gift: a used stock pot.

"You can make Minu's favorite—*nopalitos* with red chile rice and beans," she said, handing Alberto the unwrapped pot. Rust spots lined the handle, and hardened charcoal stuck to the inside of the pan. It looked like it had seen over a thousand meals.

So, in Alberto's new Pinto, with our used pot, the two of us drove to our grungy white trailer with the cheap rent we'd soon call home. It was in the south side of Phoenix on Van Buren Street, a road dubbed "hooker street" for obvious reasons.

That night, I lay on Alberto's bare chest. I loved the way strands of his tousled dark hair hung over his forehead, and his coffee and cream skin was as smooth as marbles. I loved when his hands followed the curves of my body and the way his lips danced with mine in harmony, like a tango, elegant yet sensual and roaring with passion.

"I can't wait for this life with you, Minu Becerra," Alberto whispered, kissing the top of my head.

I whispered ever so softly in his ear, "This is the happiest I've ever been."

Rosa's boyfriend had a job lined up for Alberto working at a warehouse driving the forklift. It was a good job, offering him more than minimum wage and overtime pay on the weekends. But he didn't seem to care much about making that extra money, instead, spending his weekends drinking, smoking, and playing poker with his friends. When he'd crawl into bed with me in the early morning, his breath reeked of rum and cigarettes.

After a month of living with him, I was already at my breaking point. I kept thinking things would change, but they didn't.

"Dammit, Alberto. Quit this! I didn't wait three years for you to get out of prison to be irresponsible and throw your second chance away," I yelled.

I called Amá to confide in her since she had dealt with Apá's uncontrollable behavior for twenty-plus years. But she preferred the I-told-you-so route.

"I knew this was going to happen, Minu. How could you not see this coming? Those Espinosas were trouble from the start. You've gotten yourself into quite a mess, *mija*. You're so stupid. You'll probably end up pregnant and stuck with this man for the rest of your life."

To make the entire matter worse, Alberto talked about marriage and babies. I couldn't fathom the thought. There we were, eating ham, cheese, and crackers each night for dinner, and he wanted a house full of kids. I shot his fantasy down immediately, making it clear I didn't want a repeat of how I grew up. My future kids would have the class rings they wanted, attend the summer camps I could never go to, and, dammit, open presents on Christmas morning. I ordered birth control and hid the pill cases under the bed, making sure Alberto would never see them.

After two months of living with him, Alberto was on his way out the door to play poker on another Friday night. I reminded him he was scheduled to work the following morning. "You should stay in, get sleep, and be ready for that extra money tomorrow."

"Don't you worry, baby. I'll be there. Just a quick game with the guys."

Later that night, I received a phone call from Alberto's younger sister, Yolanda. She wailed through the phone, "He crashed that beautiful Pinto into a ditch, Minu! He's fled the damn scene. Is he home? Is he there? Oh, God, tell me he's there!"

I told her he wasn't and that I'd seen no sign of him. When I hung up, I started to panic. Here we were again, stuck in the Cashion cycle. He'd be arrested, and once again, he'd be back in a jail cell. I couldn't do it again. I couldn't change this man.

In that moment, I knew what to do. After two phone calls, I finally had a plan—a plan to leave Cashion for good.

33

*A*t five o'clock, just as we planned, Dolores pulled into the trailer's driveway. I climbed into the passenger's seat with a small garbage bag. I took three shirts, a pair of jeans, a toothbrush, a tube of mascara, and four ten-dollar bills from the previous week's paycheck. No other items were worth taking. The light from the car ceiling lit up Dolores' slim face, the toughness I remember from our childhood still in her eyes.

"You sure you want to do this?" she asked.

"I've got to. For me, Dee."

The corners of her mouth raised faintly. She understood.

The early morning sky was dotted with silver stars when we pulled into the Greyhound bus station. Several cars spread across the parking lot while a small line of people waited under the awning. I gripped my bag.

In the past, Greyhound buses had symbolized the ride back to Cashion. This time was different. This time, it would take me to a place full of new promises. Dolores parked and turned to me with a tender yet sincere face. "Go make something of yourself, sis."

"Thank you, Dee . . . for everything."

I found a pay phone at the bus station, dropped a quarter in the slot, and dialed my parents' landline. My mother answered. She'd be awake—on Saturdays she worked the fields or at the tortilla factory.

"Amá, it's me," I said. "I left Alberto. I'm at the bus station and heading to California."

"What? Now?" her morning voice croaked.

"Yes. I'm catching the six o'clock bus in fifteen minutes. Keep my whereabouts quiet, please. I don't need everyone knowing, especially Alberto. Tell them all I went to Mexico to live with family."

"Did you pack the pot I gave you?"

I sneered at her response. This was the question she chose? "No, I left it at the trailer."

"Dammit, Minu."

"I'll get a new one." I let out a heavy sigh. "How's Apá?"

"He's been okay. Still has moments. *Está malo.*"

"Don't tell him about me leaving yet."

"I won't. And Minu—" Amá's voice was gradual and warm. "I always knew you were different. You know, I never had to worry about you."

Those words gave me a once-in-a-lifetime validation I never thought I needed to hear.

"Goodbye, Amá."

With my shoulders drawn back and standing taller than I had in years, I boarded the Greyhound bus. I picked a window seat toward the back, stuck my small bag between my legs, and propped my head against the dusty glass. I blew out a slow breath of relief. One step closer to freedom.

The bus soon pushed into motion, and we were off. It was as if I were drifting out into an open sea, into uncharted waters with no map, only momentum.

As the bus sped onto the highway, a compass view of Cashion stretched across the distance, looking as peaceful as the eye of the storm, though it was anything but. Far off, an onion field, where we picked and plucked until our fingers bled. I kept my eyes on the brown patch until it became a small blur. I thought of my younger brothers who still had years of picking ahead. And of Julio, wherever he was.

Behind the mountains that lined the sky, the morning sun rose, glowing orange across the land. I tenderly whispered to the home I'd lived in since I was born, "*Adiós.*"

Who would I become? Who would I meet? What places would I

see? What things would I do? The liberation I'd feel meeting people who didn't know where I'd come from, or know the Becerra family, or know me as the white girl. Maybe I'd cut my hair, embrace my curls, perhaps even flaunt my skin. Whatever lay ahead might be a great struggle or a wondrous adventure. There could be tears or oh so many laughs. Would I look back with regret or with gratitude for the best decision I ever made?

There was only one way to find out.

Twelve hours later, the Greyhound pulled into the depot. I stepped off the bus, breathing in the fresh, crisp air, my new life looming large on the horizon. I scanned the crowd and spotted Esméralda. Her honey-brown skin had that warm California glow. She beamed when she saw me and waved her arm high above her head. Standing next to her were her two young sons, four-year-old Mateo and five-year-old Leo. They both looked exactly like their father, who had left them a few months before.

Esméralda was the first person I called the night I was crafting my escape plan. She had moved to Lompoc after her husband split, living with Uncle Chalio until she found a place of her own. We made a deal that I'd live with her until I could afford a place of my own, all the while helping with Leo and Mateo.

"Welcome to Lompoc," she said with a soft embrace. I squeezed her back.

Like a bird caged her whole life, I craved to spread my wings and fly. So like a phoenix rising above her own ashes, I soared with the breeze.

PART TWO

Left to right: my sisters Irma and Esméralda, me, and
my sister Dolores. 1983.

34

*M*y first time at the beach, I pushed my toes into the soft sand and breathed in the salty crisp air. Miles and miles of waves rose and fell before me. I had read about the ocean in books and seen it on TV, but I needed to see it with my own two eyes to fully grasp its enormity and beauty.

I took off running down the shore, letting the brisk water splash my feet and ankles. The waves sang a song that soothed me. The tension in my body began to fade.

My new life in Lompoc was everything I had hoped for. I'd found work at Kenny's Shoe Store, working off the commission. I pushed Chuck Taylors, Reebok Pumps, and the Vans Classic slip-ons to the Lompoc locals, often able to make a sale.

One of the best parts was being near Uncle Chalio. He owned a bar called Michael's, a lively, bustling place filled with upbeat rhythm of traditional Mexican music and sounds of laughter.

Uncle Chalio was a stark contrast to my mother. Every time Esméralda, the boys, and I visited, he greeted us with welcoming hugs, and we'd spend hours playing together, eating his delicious food, and listening to him strumming his guitar. When we left, he'd tell us how much he loved us. No question, he was Abuelito Rosalio's son.

Esméralda's small two-bedroom apartment had cracked walls so thin you could hear the neighbor's conversations. The galley kitchen sink spat out only scalding hot water, and loaves of bread, dried milk, pasta, and canned food took up most of the counter space.

But I didn't care. The four of us danced and sang while we made the usual spaghetti and meat sauce for dinner. Mateo and Leo entertained us with story after story, licking their lips when they had another one to tell. We talked about everything: why the sky was blue, how rocks formed, what superhero power we would be. Mine was Wonder Woman's—strength, speed, and the ability to combat any enemy.

After dinner cleanup, bath time, and teeth brushing, Esméralda and the boys went to bed, while I camped out in the puny living room, where the candy-striped sofa served as my bed.

That was when Alberto usually snuck into my thoughts. What happened after he crashed the car? Was he still working at the warehouse? Did he wonder where I was? Or did he grimace at my name, never wanting to see me again?

Two or so weeks later, David called. "There you are! Alberto's devastated, Minu. How could you do this to him? Without even saying goodbye? He came to the house looking for you the day after you left. Hell, I didn't know where you were. Amá finally told me."

I was expecting this. "I had no choice, David. Like you and I said, there's nothing good about that damned town. I needed to make this move for me."

I begged him not to tell Alberto where I was. "I found a job. It's wonderful living with Esméralda and the boys. The ocean is like nothing I've ever seen. I'm happy. Please don't even hint that I'm here."

David agreed.

Three months later, just after my nineteenth birthday, I graduated from the candy-striped sofa to a bed of my own when we moved to a bigger apartment down the street. Soon after, I quit Kenny's Shoe Store after the pervert manager whispered lewd comments to me. It was a sign for me to get my GED. So the following week, I started evening classes. During the day, Esméralda paid me to watch Mateo and Leo while she worked in nearby California fields picking and plucking almonds, walnuts, celery, and grapes for fourteen dollars an hour.

"Tía Minu, look at all the colors!" Leo shouted, running down the sidewalk of downtown Lompoc, the leaves crunching beneath his feet. It was late October, six months after I had left Cashion, and the cool California autumn had crept in like a storm overnight.

Mateo jumped up to grab a handful of leaves from a low branch. "Tía Minu, do the trees change where you're from?"

Speckles of orange, red, and yellow sporadically floated to the ground. The boys collected the vibrant colors from the cement, organizing the stacks like a book, seeing the world through innocent eyes. I envied it.

"The trees don't change in Arizona. The desert's a special place because it has cacti, which have needles instead of leaves. It's a little . . ."—I paused to come up with the most perfect word to describe my roots—"prickly there."

On a Saturday morning soon after the Christmas holidays, Esméralda came out to the kitchen beaming. "You missed all the fun last night. I met some sexy Filipino guys at the bar."

Over eggs and coffee, she told me that she had invited them over later. "But stay away from the one named Ernesto, aka Ernie. He's mine."

"Go for it. I'm not looking,"

That evening when the doorbell rang, Esméralda was finishing up her makeup, so I answered the door. Five tan men dressed in fancy dress shirts, all with shiny white smiles. The one who introduced himself as Ernie resembled a young Bruce Lee, with a full head of hair, sweet teardrop eyes, and thick lips.

Esméralda kept her eye on him all night, but he talked to me instead. Through his choppy accent, he told me he was in the air force and wanted to make a career of it. After a few more drinks, he revealed he was the father of a little baby boy.

"His mother and I split last year. Wasn't meant to be," he said, taking a sip of his Manhattan with such confidence and composure. His mouth twitched as if he were fighting a smile.

I was attracted to his athletic build and genteel manners, and he loved my determination and grit. After a few dates of Ernie showing off his cooking skills and a couple of nights at the bowling alley, where we both had horrible scores, our relationship began to feel real.

I rarely called back home, but a month later, I called to tell my mother. "He's great, Amá. Successful in the military, self-reliant, handsome, religious, and he comes from a great Filipino family."

"This is your chance to make something of yourself," she said. "This is the life you want. He's better than that foolish Espinosa. This man will take care of you. Marry him."

I laughed at the irony of Amá's words since she'd married and stayed with Apá after he dragged her through the thickest and deepest mud. But she was right: life looked safe, secure, and easy with Ernie. Yet, Alberto still lingered in my mind. It had been just over a year since I left him. Why was it so difficult to move on?

"Everyone goes through that with their first love, Minu," Ernie said, swarming me with his thick arms and kissing my cheek. "But Alberto won't make you happy. I will. I have enough love for the both of us."

He was right. My mother was right. This was my chance to do something, to be someone.

One afternoon in January 1979, as I sat on the candy-striped sofa, Ernie crunched down to one knee and opened a small box. A silver ring sparkled.

"Minu Becerra," Ernie said, his voice shaky, "I can't imagine this life without you. Be with me forever, and I'll make you the happiest woman." He took a deep breath. "Will you marry me?"

Too stunned to scream or cry or jump for joy, I sat there frozen. Why was it, at that moment, I could only think of Alberto? I rocked back on the sofa, hoping by the time I leaned forward, Alberto's face would disappear from my mind.

"It's my mother's ring," Ernie said.

"Wow," I finally breathed out. I looked back at the elegant ring. "It's stunning. I-I . . . Sure. Yes. Yes, I will. I'll marry you."

Ernie let out a long, drawn-out sigh—I think he'd been holding his breath. He stretched to kiss me. Then with trembling hands, he slipped the twinkling piece of jewelry onto my finger.

That night, we popped open a cheap bottle of wine, clinked glasses, and listened to Aretha Franklin on the stereo to celebrate. I lifted the glass with my left hand rather than my right to admire the new sparkly weight on my finger. Esméralda, Mateo, and Leo congratulated us with hugs and laughter.

After the boys went to bed, and in between sips from our commemorative bottle, there was a knock at the door. Esméralda, Ernie, and I looked at one another confused. We weren't expecting anyone.

I opened the door to see David standing there with a smug smile. I almost collapsed when I noticed who was standing behind him.

Alberto.

35

*M*y eyes darted back and forth between my younger brother and my ex-boyfriend. They both wore leather jackets and jeans, their eyes filled with expectation. David now had a thin, patchy mustache, making him look like the younger version of our father, the one I'd only seen in sepia photos.

Alberto gave me a warm smile. His handsome face was exactly how I remembered it. My knees weakened, and my head felt so light I thought it would detach from my neck and float away.

"Al-Alberto? David? Wh-what are you doing here?" I asked.

David reached his arms out and hugged me tight. "We're here to see you, of course, big sis." He poked his head inside. "I hope we aren't interrupting."

"No, no. Please. Not at all. Come in out of the cold." I waved them through the door and into the kitchen where Esméralda and Ernie were uncorking another bottle of wine.

"You guys look like you're celebrating," David said. "Can we join in?"

Esméralda's jaw dropped. "David? Alberto? What the—!" She hurried over to the two of them for a hug. "Welcome!" she shouted. "Ernie and Minu just got engaged!"

Alberto flinched.

An uneasy smile spread across David's face. "Well, what timing we have! Congrats to you both." He reached out to shake Ernie's hand. "So you're the lucky guy? I'm David, Minu's most handsome younger brother."

Ernie looked stiff and dazed, realizing now that this was the Alberto I had mentioned to him. "H—hi. Hello." He was just as tongue-tied as I was. "Pleasure to meet you both."

We poured another round of wine and drank as fast as everyone's heart raced that night. I didn't think it could get more awkward, but then Alberto asked me, "Can I talk to you?" He looked at Ernie. "Please? It won't take long."

Ernie threw his hands in the air. "I guess it's over."

"What? No, Ernie—" I said.

Before I could finish, he was out the front door, letting it slam and shake the walls. Within minutes, the tires from his car screeched into the distance.

I panicked. "What have I done?"

Alberto cupped my arms and turned me around. "Ten minutes, Minu. I just want to talk to you. Come here."

I followed him into the living room, and we both sat on the sofa, the exact spot where Ernie and I had gotten engaged only a short time before. I looked up at Alberto and took a deep breath, inhaling his familiar smell: cigarettes and cheap cologne. It took me back to Cashion.

"I can't believe it's been almost two years, Minu," he said, his voice soft and tender, like I remembered. "You look beautiful."

I stared down at my hands in my lap. Alberto situated himself more comfortably beside me, dipping me further into the sofa as he scooted closer to me, his knee grazing mine.

"Minu, I've turned my life around," he said, his strong jaw tightened. "I'm better than the last time you saw me. I got a new job. My drinking is under control. I'm even learning how to cook." He took hold of my clammy hands, grazing the letter tattoos across the top of my fingers. God, how I had missed his touch. "Give me another chance, Minu, and I'll be the man you've always wanted me to be. I'll be the man you des—."

"Alberto," I interrupted him, "I can't do this. I'm marrying Ernie."

"No, you can't, Minu. I think about you every day. Shit, do you know what it was like the morning I found out you left?" He gently caressed my cheek with the back of his hand. "I know deep in your heart you still feel it too, baby. Don't fight it. Come back to Cashion with me."

Later that night, we went out to Michael's. David, Esméralda, Alberto, and I listened to a Beatles cover band live and ordered pitchers of lime margaritas. I drank too much.

"Another round, please," Esméralda said, twirling her finger in a circle at the waitress. The waitress nodded and headed to the bar. "It's not every day almost one-third of the Becerra siblings are together. Cheers."

Alberto, David, and I followed suit, lifting our glasses to hers. She looked me in the eye. "For making the right choice."

"Cheers to that," David said.

"Aye," Alberto said. "Cheers to *mi gringa*."

We clinked our glasses together and sipped the sour drink.

That night, the four of us didn't get back to the apartment until after midnight. Esméralda went to bed, David made his bed on the couch, and Alberto followed me to my bedroom, kissing my neck and stripping off my clothes.

The clock next to my bed read five thirty a.m. I turned over to see Alberto lying next to me. Strains of his tangled hair matted to his forehead, his tan skin glimmering from the early morning sunrise shining through the window. On his arm, the tattoo of my face stared back at me. I sat up, holding the bed covers tightly under my arms to keep my naked body covered. Flung around the room was Alberto's leather jacket, my blouse, his jeans.

The outlandish turn of events from the previous day slowly caught up with me, like a ball of yarn unraveling, revealing a mass of knots. I glanced at my ringless left hand—I'd left Ernie's engagement ring in a bedroom drawer after he'd stormed out. Blood rushed to my head, and my stomach churned. I thought I'd be sick. Too much tequila? Yes, that, but mostly it was the deplorable mistake I'd made. I looked at Alberto with a fresh pair of eyes, seeing only Cashion—the life I worked so hard to outrun.

What had I done?

Caught in the moment and drowned by lust and desire, I'd fallen back into the hex—mesmerized, charmed, captivated by him once again. I was stuck between what I was in the past and what I could become in the future.

I scooted out of bed quietly, careful not to wake him. I dressed in yesterday's jeans and threw a T-shirt over my head.

In the kitchen, the typical California sun gleamed through the front window—I wished the day was dark and rainy to match my mood. Esméralda leaned over the table, sipping steaming coffee and flipping through the newspaper. I peeked into the living room to see David still asleep on the couch.

"You're up early," Esméralda said, taking a cautious sip. "Weird day yesterday, huh?"

I grabbed a mug from the cupboard and filled it with lukewarm water from the faucet, chugging the entire glass without a breath.

Esméralda and I both jumped when the phone rang. She answered and mouthed to me, "It's John." Ernie's best friend and roommate. I took another gulp of water and placed the phone to my ear.

"John?"

"Minu, what the hell? Ernie's a mess. How could—"

"I know, I know." I leaned over the counter, resting my forehead on my palm. "I screwed up. I need to see him."

"He doesn't wanna see you, Minu." John's angry voice vibrated through the phone. "How could you? And on the day of the fucking engagement?"

"I'm going to fix this, I swear."

In my head, I repeated those words over and over until I convinced myself I could actually repair the botched situation. When I hung up, I slipped on Ernie's engagement ring, scrambled for my purse, and snagged my car keys from the counter.

"Don't you dare tell me you're going to Ernie's right now?" Esméralda spat out.

"I have to." I threw on my shoes at the front door.

Esméralda slammed her coffee mug on the countertop. "You're just going to leave him here? You cold-blooded bitch!"

"What do you want from me, Es? I have to fix this."

"Minu, you're a fu—"

I shot out of the apartment before I could hear the rest.

Maybe I was a cold-blooded bitch, but I'd be a cold-blooded bitch who made it right.

Through shameful sobs, I delivered a waterfall of apologies to Ernie. He sat across from me with tears dripping onto his lap. I didn't realize I could hurt someone I loved like this. I wanted nothing more than to heal his heart. Why is it that we so often have to lose someone to realize how important they are? That they're worth fighting for? Worth suiting up in metal armor, lining up your cavalry, and storming into battle to save.

Ernie forgave me that day. We agreed to put the previous night behind us and focus on our engagement and marriage ahead.

Later that evening, when I returned to the apartment, an envelope lay on the kitchen table with the words "*Mi Gringa*" written across the front. I tore it open to find a letter in Alberto's handwriting. He said he understood why I left for Ernie that morning and that he only hoped for me to have a wonderful, beautiful life. "I'll always have you in my heart, as well as on my arm."

I let go of Alberto without looking back.

36

Six months later, June 30, 1979, was a picture-perfect day for a wedding in Lompoc. White, puffy clouds floated across the pale blue sky while a gentle breeze eased the summer's heat. Antonia, Ernie's psychic-palm-reader mother, flew in from Louisiana. As she stepped off the plane, we embraced, officially soon to be family.

"*Maganda*. Beautiful. My son is lucky," she said through her thick accent. "Now give me your hand. I want to see if you give me grandbabies." Her eyes buzzed with curiosity as she examined my palm in her tiny fingers. "Aha, there it is. Two babies."

"What, really?" She didn't know that a couple of years before, I'd had abdominal pain and discovered I had ovarian cysts. The doctors warned me it'd be difficult to conceive.

"And," she continued, "you have them overseas."

What nonsense. Ernie and I had just talked about how much we loved Lompoc and had no desire to leave.

"And what's this?" Antonia asked as she held my palm closer to her face. "Your mother wins the lottery?"

I tried to stifle my laugh. "Well, wouldn't that be nice . . ."

Antonia was surely a fake. Amá didn't even play the lottery.

The rest of the guests trickled in, a few friends and some family members. Dolores, Esméralda, David, Ruben, Danny, and Sammy all came.

Irma didn't. Her husband was in the air force, and they were stationed in England. And Julio was still estranged from the family.

The entire wedding weekend, Amá glowed with a rare bliss. "I can't believe it—my youngest daughter is getting married," she said. "Your father can't wait to walk his *güera* down the aisle."

All my sisters had been married by a justice of the peace, and I'd made my wedding a big event to please my parents. Amá loved weddings, and Apá wanted his moment to give me away. But while they were basking in all of it, I had a billion questions running through my mind. Was marrying Ernie the right decision—was he *the one*? Was I in love with him? In love with him enough for a happily ever after? I was almost twenty-one and not someone who had ever fantasized about weddings.

I couldn't think of a single marriage I admired and wanted to copy. When the doubting part of me—or the cold feet as most people would say—took over, I focused on the comfortable, safe, and happy life away from Cashion that I longed for.

Just before the ceremony, Apá and I met in the back of the air force base chapel. I wore a quarter-sleeved, ivory satin dress with a ruffle that covered the bottom. A long, tulle veil hung from my hair to the floor, trailing behind me. Apá was dressed in a black tuxedo with a bolo tie, looking so handsome. The sweetest smile—hung on his face—a smile I hadn't seen in years, maybe decades.

"Ahh, my Güera," he whispered in a brittle voice. "Look at you. You look beautiful, *muy hermosa*."

He took my hand and twirled me in a circle. My dress swayed with the motion. "I'm so proud of you, Güera." His words warmed my heart. I wanted to replay them over and over again.

Just then, the piano started a light tune. I linked my arm with my father's, and he walked me down the aisle. Ernie and I recited our vows, kissed, and turned to the crowd of familiar faces to present our union.

For the reception, the thirty wedding attendees all meandered to Uncle Chalio's bar, where we ate a mixture of Filipino and Mexican food and took advantage of the bottomless drinks. Amá found her way onto the small stage that stood off to the side. She adjusted the microphone to her five-foot height and positioned it a few inches from her mouth. Uncle Chalio joined her on stage with his guitar. He nodded to Amá, and in her melodious voice, she sang "*Volver, Volver*" (Return, Return).

> *Este amore aspasionado*
> *Me trae todo alborotado, por volver . . .*

She tapped her foot to the beat, her magenta dress swaying left and right. Uncle Chalio chimed in with the next verse:

> *Voy camino a la locura*
> *Y aunque todo me tortura*
> *Se querer . . .*

We laughed and danced and sang the night away.

Shortly after our wedding, Ernie and I honeymooned in Biloxi, Mississippi, where we met Ernie's three-year-old son, Little Ernie. He charmed me from the beginning with his big smile and two cheek dimples. "Miiuu," he called me.

It was even more heartening to witness Ernie as a father—his attentiveness, his caution, his playfulness, and the two of them laughing together. Between Ernie, his ex-wife, and me, we agreed Little Ernie would visit us for summers and holidays and stay in Biloxi the rest of the time.

Overnight, I had earned the new titles of wife and stepmom.

37

"*A*re you sitting down?" Ernie asked me over the phone.

I was at my new job, where I inspected computer chips all day, a lot different than working at a grocery market or selling shoes or babysitting.

"Yes, what is it?"

"We're going to Europe, baby."

"What? What are you talking about?"

"I just found out that I'm assigned to the air force base in Turkey. We're leaving next month."

"Turkey?" I couldn't keep the disappointment out of my voice.

"What's the matter? You said you always wanted to travel. Here's our chance."

"Well, I was thinking more like Paris or Italy or London. Spain even."

Ernie laughed. "Turkey, here we come."

The timing felt off. I was doing well at my job and still wanted to pursue my GED. But marriage called, and a month later, we moved to downtown Adana, a small Turkish town twenty minutes from the Incirlik Air Force Base.

We lived in an apartment on the tenth floor overlooking a constellation of buildings and the glass-like Seyhan River. The downtown was filled with candy stores, bakeries, and butcher stands with fresh slabs of meat. Some things about Turkey felt familiar: the dust, the desert, the dryness. Other things were a complete and utter culture shock—like the soupy food, the armed Jandarma patrolling the streets, the language, and, most of all, the clothing. Women wore burkas, only revealing the color of their eyes, while Turkish men wore baggy trousers that hung like a saggy diaper and tightened around the ankle—I called them "seven-day shitters." Most people there also didn't wear deodorant, so when the elevator doors closed, no amount of *parfüm* could hide the smell.

Ernie worked as an administrator for the satellite division, spending time at the base and neighboring countries, like Spain, Germany, and England, leaving me alone for long periods of time. I stayed busy by volunteering at the Red Cross and taking classes at the base for my GED. In a year's time, I finally received it.

I also befriended one of the other military wives, Judy, who lived in my apartment complex. We got together a couple of times a week and sat at her cherrywood dining table with a plate of artichokes, cheese, salami, crackers, and fig jam, sipping Turkish coffee from small porcelain cups. Pretty and thin with shiny golden-brown hair, she sat primly, like a bird on a tree branch.

"Well, that's just it, Minu," she said one afternoon, sipping her coffee, her pinky finger floating daintily in the air. I found myself mirroring her etiquette. "We military wives must unequivocally band together. It can get so diplomatic in this lifestyle."

Unequivocally? Diplomatic? I vowed to look up half the words this woman dropped. I had never been around someone with such eloquence and poise.

"Take it from me, darling," she said. "I've been doing it for over a decade. Sometimes substantial validation from other DWs is just what we need."

Dependent wives. I nodded in agreement, taking a sip of the bold yet bitter, steamy coffee.

"So, anyway, tell me, Minu"—she crossed her legs gracefully—"I've met Ernie, but what's your family like?"

"Oh . . . um."

There were many ways I could answer such a question. I went the modest route. "Well, born and raised in Arizona. Both parents are Mexican." I looked to the ceiling, thinking of my next line. "I have eight siblings. Three older sisters and five brothers."

Judy almost spit out her coffee. "Your mother popped out nine of you?"

"And we only had one bathroom."

"A whole baseball team." Judy laughed. "How fun that must have been, though, growing up with such a big family. I'm sure birthdays and holidays and summer vacations were always such a riot."

I smiled and nodded. "You have no idea."

Irma and I wrote to each other every few months, and I'd write Amá letters in Spanish around the holidays, but other than that, I barely talked to anyone in the family. Ernie and I didn't go back to the States since I discovered I suffered from claustrophobia on the twenty-two-hour flight from California to New York to Turkey.

When the plane's cabin lights went off, the dark, tight area robbed me of the present and brought me to the scene of my eight-year-old self being locked in the backyard refrigerator until I passed out. For most of the flight, I gripped my seat and huffed into a paper bag.

It was an easy decision to stay in Turkey.

On the verge of my twenty-third birthday, I discovered I was pregnant. Having resigned myself to not having kids, I was shocked when the test came back positive. Ernie and I were both excited. At my thirteenth-week checkup, the doctor instructed me to fill out my family's medical history, so I called Amá on Ernie's work phone at the base.

"It's Minu."

"Who? I don't know a Minu."

"Amá . . ."

"Well, it's about damn time you called. To what do we owe the pleasure?"

"Amá . . ." Static filled the silence.

"Well, if you didn't think so highly of yourself, *sabelotodo*, maybe you'd call more."

I hunched over and placed my forehead in my hand.

The house burned down, Minu."

"What? How?"

"Someone left the gasoline in a plastic jug after filling the lawn mower, and it got pushed up against the water heater. Most everything was lost, but we were able to save a few things—some pictures, boxes, insurance documents, and an armful of clothes."

"Did everyone make it out? Is everyone okay?"

"Yes. We all got out just fine."

"I'm so sorry, Amá."

"We're staying with the next-door neighbors. Everyone has been very helpful. There were a few walls still standing, and with the insurance money, we're building back with brick. And adding an extra bathroom. Should have it up and sturdy soon enough."

And then came the typical pause that snuck into our conversations, so I shifted to my news. "I'm pregnant."

"Ah, that's the reason for the call. How far along are you? When's the baby due? That's good. That's good."

"Amá, the doctor wants me to fill out my family's medical history. I want to make sure the information is correct. What does Apá have again? Schizophrenia?" I cradled the phone between my ear and shoulder to get my notepad and pen ready.

"Oh," she said as if thinking out loud, "you're the only one who doesn't have to worry about that."

"What? What does that mean?"

"You don't need to check any of those boxes on the medical form. Just leave that section blank."

"What're you saying?"

She let out a sheepish breath. "Never mind. Never mind. I'm just joking. It was a joke."

"Huh? Why would you kid about something like that? Is there something you need to tell me?" My heart started thumping.

"No. Forget it." She quickly changed the subject. "The neighbor boys always have the police at their house. And you know that Lola is still doing those drugs. Saw her the other day and she's missing some of her damn teeth."

She went on and on about the latest neighborhood drama, talking fast and loud.

But I was hardly listening.

In January 1982, after a year in Turkey, Jeremy was born. I fell in love with his beautiful muddy-brown eyes and his full head of jet-black hair. He filled me with a brightness I never knew existed.

When I called to tell my mother about Jeremy, I asked again about what she had said to me, as I had every time we talked. "Is Apá not my real father? Is that why I don't look like anyone else in the family?"

"Don't be ridiculous, Minu," she'd say through the static. "Of course, he's your father. And you take after your grandmother. Enough already."

38

I shot up in bed, gasping for air, my nightgown drenched with sweat, clinging to me. I looked at Ernie sleeping peacefully next to me. Another Cashion nightmare. They'd been happening more and more lately. I stooped over and rubbed my eyes, freeing any last haunting image that might still be lingering.

So often the same thing: I'd be lying in my childhood bed, the scratchy blanket tickling my chin like it always had. From the window, the bright moon illuminated the room, allowing me to distinguish the shapes of my brothers sleeping in the bunks.

Just as I was about to doze off, the bedroom door would jerk open and thrash into the wall. A dark silhouette entered the room. I'd recognize that stocky, muscular black outline from anywhere. I couldn't see his eyes, but I knew they were crazy. And then, his roaring yells. I stretched the blanket over my head, shaking. My brothers screamed. They called for me to help them, but I couldn't. I lay there, scared, stunned, stuck. I wasn't strong enough to confront my father. I couldn't save my brothers.

Other times I dreamed of the night the letters of my name were tattooed on my fingers. I had the ink surgically removed by a military doctor at the base. Stitches covered the four fingers on my left hand. He removed most of the ink, but a few dots remained to remind me of that horrifying incident.

"You, okay?" Ernie asked sleepily.

"Yes. Just another nightmare."

I flipped off the covers and walked to Jeremy's room. We were now stationed at the San Miguel Island Air Force base in the Philippines, and if there was one thing that brought me peace, it was the little bundle of joy down the hall.

In his room, the half-open window allowed the warm ocean breeze to whisper through the screen. I peeked over the bar of the crib to see him asleep—my miracle baby we had been blessed with for a year now. I still couldn't believe he was mine.

Soon after he was born, the doctor found a tumor on my uterus, and I had emergency surgery to remove it. My doctor warned me it was too risky to conceive another baby, so I accepted the thought of being the mother of one beautiful boy.

I continued to keep my family at arm's length. Yet I thought about them often. Where was Julio now? Had David bought the motorcycle he always wanted? Would Danny, Ruben, and Sammy graduate from high school? In one of Irma's recent letters, she'd mentioned that all three of them had been in and out of juvie.

The familiar feeling of profound guilt once again overcame me. Guilt for distancing myself, for not calling or writing more often. Even with all the bitterness I felt toward Amá and Apá, they were growing older, and I was afraid something would happen to them. Would I regret not visiting?

I soon discovered that my fear had been on the mark—except it had nothing to do with my parents.

That June, my mother called me, and I knew right away that something bad had happened.

"What's wrong, Amá?" I could barely breathe.

"It's David. He had an aneurysm that burst."

"How's that possible? He's only twenty-two."

"They've put him in a coma, Minu," Amá said in a throaty voice. "There isn't much time."

The next day, I booked the first flight back to Arizona. I would fly

Space-A on an eight-seater bomber plane, with layovers in Hawaii and San Francisco, a three-day trip.

God wouldn't take David, I kept telling myself. He couldn't. David had just gotten engaged. With so much life ahead, God had to keep him here.

Through the small oval window, the sun rose over the tarmac as I buckled into the net seat. The pilot spoke over the intercom, reminding us of the long jaunt ahead, and the claustrophobia crept in. *Dammit, David, you started this panic of mine. Your little fridge trick—it wasn't funny then, and it isn't funny now.* His childish laughter, so free and pure, rang through my ears.

Hold on, David. Hold on just a bit longer, little brother. I'll be there soon.

Twenty-two hours later, I landed at the San Francisco airport.

"Dolores, it's Minu. I'm in San Fran," I called from a pay phone. "I'll be in Phoenix in twelve hours. How is—"

"Oh, Minu . . . he's already gone."

I crumpled to the floor and wept.

I made it to Cashion just in time for David's wake. Amá was heartbroken, and Apá cried the day away. He kept saying over and over that David always wanted a baby blue car, but instead, he got a baby blue casket. He didn't have a headstone yet—my family couldn't afford it. All my siblings showed up, even Julio, who had stayed by David's bedside the whole time.

After the wake, I pulled into what used to be my childhood home. The brick was a light blue, and the house stood more like an L-shape, but other than that, it looked as if a day hadn't passed since I left seven years before. Freshly hung laundry swayed on the clothesline. Apá's pickup truck was parked in the driveway. The random pine tree we had planted for Christmas in 1963 was still in the front yard. Sawdust spread across the lawn from one of Apá's projects. Even the neighborhood looked identical, although Amá told me Alberto and Lola had both moved to Minnesota.

The house smelled like roasted green chiles, bringing back a kalei-doscope of memories. Amá busied herself chopping a head of lettuce while she hummed softly, a fabled scene.

A new fireplace sat in the corner of the living room. Above was the portrait of me as a baby, wearing that plush pink dress, the lace socks, and that puzzled look on my face.

"My baby photo made it through the fire?" I asked Amá

"Yes," she said. "But the frame was a bit burned."

Funny, it was a priority to grab that and not any of the damn pots she obsessed over.

On a shelf in the living room were portraits of deceased family members, one of them Abuelito Rosalio—my dearest love. A wave of sadness washed over me when I realized David's photograph would soon join Abuelito's on the shelf.

Through the window to the backyard, I saw Apá tinkering with the chicken coop, finessing the barbed-wire fencing. How many times would he fix that thing?

"Your father's been good," Amá said, wiping the counter with a dish-rag. "Except I'm worried about your brother now—Danny. He might be sick like your father. He's showing the signs."

"Have you taken him to the doctor?"

"No." She looked at me and shrugged. "What can you do? If he's sick, he's sick."

I opened my mouth to press her yet again about Apá not being my real father, but I stopped. I let it go for that day.

39

I jogged across the sand. Foamy waves from the Philippine Sea softly soused the beach, swashing my bare feet and splashing my calves. Long curls hung from my ponytail that bounced along my back—I hadn't cut my hair since moving overseas. I ran past sunbathers, picnickers, and elated kids building sandcastles that the high tide would eventually sweep away.

With each running stride, my mind listed off my itinerary for the rest of my day: teach aerobics class at eight thirty at the base; work my six-hour shift at the Military Commissary and Exchange; stop by the market for eggs, bread, and fresh fruit; and, finally, relieve the nanny watching Jeremy.

Nannies were oddly affordable in the Philippines. As little as we made, we could afford to hire one while Ernie and I were at the base working.

I slowed down to a walk. Seagulls screeched, and I could taste the salty air on my lips. I stretched my arms down to cup the round bump that took over my stomach. I was pregnant again—another surprise and delight.

Three months prior, I had been filling out the nanny's paperwork at the base. The building had no air conditioning, and it was so hot and stuffy standing at the counter. The next thing I knew, I woke up on the floor and was rushed to the doctor's office. After a few blood tests and the typical checkup procedures, low and behold, I was pregnant.

"But that can't be," I said to the doctor. "I was told I couldn't have any more kids. I got rid of the crib and the bottles and all the baby clothes."

The doctor smiled. "Believe it."

When I told Ernie the good news of yet another miracle, he leapt across the kitchen the second the words left my mouth. He hugged me tight, his smile like an unexpected ray of sunlight peeking through on a cloudy day.

We had been struggling. Over the years, Ernie had become controlling, bad-tempered, even jealous. I could barely talk to the man without upsetting him. Admittedly, I'd become defensive and easily irritated. We still had good times together, but they happened much less often, and I believed this second baby would give our relationship the boost we desperately needed.

"We're having a baby?" he kept asking over and over, his face glowing. "There will be four of us? Four of us, Minu? Can you believe it?"

I laughed along with him and hugged him tighter. His happiness was infectious. "It's a girl," I whispered in his ear. "I can feel it."

Ernie and I practically danced in the kitchen that night, allowing our joy to light up the darkest corners of the room.

But it all changed six months later, like a storm rolling through the night.

Ernie had returned from a weeklong temporary duty assignment and was acting strangely. Our conversations were short and abrupt, and he barely looked at me. While on his brief assignment the week before, he had asked me to come see him with Jeremy. I said no. I didn't want to drive three hours through the mountains with our stick-shift car.

"Ernie, I hate driving that thing, you know that," I told him over the phone. "I'll just stay here with Jeremy. You'll be back in a few days."

I figured he was angry with me for not making the trek. But when his odd behavior lasted through the week, I knew it was something more.

"What's wrong, Ernie?" I finally asked him after he arrived home from his men's softball game one night.

"What? Nothing?" He looked away.

"Ernie—" I stepped between him and the counter, forcing him to look at me. "Talk to me. Something's off."

As I stood there, hands resting on my protruding belly, a surge of desire coursed through me. The truth was this pregnancy had made me hornier than a pig in heat. All I wanted was my husband to go shower so we could meet in the bedroom for a steamy rendezvous. But instead, after several back-and-forth exchanges with him trying to convince me he wasn't upset, he finally blurted out, "Fine. Yes. Something has been weighing on me."

At first, I thought it was a minor issue. But when Ernie sucked in a deep breath and closed his eyes, I knew something much more serious was going on.

"While on my assignment last week," he began, his voice shaking, "my roommate—"

"Yes, Paul," I interrupted. "You traveled with Paul. What happened?"

"He had been whoring around the entire trip . . ." Ernie continued. He looked down at his twiddling fingers. "I used the same towel he used after he had showered, and . . . now I have an STD."

My heart dropped. I could feel my face flushing, through my cheeks, up my temples, and in my head. "What? You can't—is that even possible?"

"Yes, it's possible," Ernie said, his eyes avoiding mine. "It's what happened to me."

"W-what—where—how," I stammered, searching for the right words. Any words. "H-how can that be?" I managed to spit out.

Ernie shrugged and shook his head. "It just happened, Minu," he whispered.

That night, I lay awake in bed, consumed by thoughts of what this meant for our relationship. Perhaps it could be transferred. It was either possible, or the hard truth was that Ernie had cheated. Regardless, the trust we had built over the years was shattered.

The next day, I sat outside with my friend Jan, trying to distract myself with a late lunch. As a nurse at the base, Jan tended to the airmen and their families, and she often worked long hours, leaving her ravenous when she finally had time to eat. Across from me, she dove into her leftover lamb kebab.

I thought back to Ernie. His work trip. The towel. The STD.

"Minu," Jan said, "you've barely touched your lunch."

I looked down at my soup bowl. "Can I ask you something?"

Jan tilted the kebab to bite a chunk of lamb and pull it off the skewer. "Shoot," she said midchew.

"Can someone . . ." I paused, scared to know the answer. "Can someone get an STD from using an infected person's towel?"

She stopped chewing and looked at me with narrowed eyes. "No, of course not. Where did you hear such nonsense?"

As I stepped into the house that night, the air was thick with tension. Ernie finally mustered up the courage to confess his infidelity. It happened on the work trip when he was drunk. My world crumbled beneath my feet as I tried to comprehend how the man I had loved so deeply could betray me so callously.

I screamed at him, asking him how he could do such a thing. He begged for forgiveness, but I couldn't fathom how we could ever get past it. I was seven months pregnant, exhausted, vulnerable, and in a flick of a second, my husband had turned into a stranger.

In the weeks that followed, I tried to make sense of the senseless. But just as I felt like I was losing hope, my saving grace sparkled into the world. My daughter, Jacqueline, named after the graceful and poised Jacqueline Kennedy, her beautiful skin like porcelain. She was a beacon of light, reminding me that love could overcome even the darkest of days. As I watched her delicate face, I felt a renewed sense of purpose. Everything was going to be okay.

Jeremy met his little sister for the first time that hot June day. He watched her with a look of love and awe. Ernie was there, but my eyes remained on my two kids, who seemed to fix my brokenness.

After settling in with Jacqueline, I told Ernie I needed time away to clear my head. Still whiplashed with the pain of betrayal, I took off with a few-month-old baby and a lively toddler and wound up at my parents back in the States. I left out why Ernie hadn't joined me on the trip.

Yet the minute I arrived, I was reminded why I had stayed away after all these years, once again questioning if I belonged anywhere.

40

"*Güera*," Apá called out to me the next morning.

His voice tugged at my memory, bringing to the forefront so many mixed emotions I had stowed away.

"Güera," Apá called again.

In my parents' spare bedroom, I rolled over to see Jeremy sleeping, his chest rising and falling peacefully. I peeked into the old rickety crib my brothers used to sleep in to see baby Jacqueline, asleep as well. The alarm clock on the dresser read six eleven, so it would just be getting dark in the Philippines, past their bedtime. I got up before Apá called again and woke them.

I jumped into jean shorts, threw on the only black tank I had packed, and wrapped my hair in a high ponytail—anything to air out my neck, the house was so damn hot. I ventured out of the room, the scents of my childhood swirling around me.

My father was sitting at the dining room table with a steaming cup of coffee and a burning cigarette in his hand—the smell of Apá. I could hear Amá doing dishes in the kitchen, the clanging of pots and pans and glasses and bowls as she washed, dried, and put them away. Apá looked up at me, the lines around his dark eyes deeper than I remembered. "*Buenos días*, Güera," he said, patting the empty chair to his left. "Come sit with me for a minute."

I sat across from him, and just as I had done as a child, I scanned his face, attempting to predict his mood. He seemed soft today, composed. He slurped from the cup with one hand and tapped his cigarette on the ashtray with the other.

"Listen," he said, turning in his chair to face me. "There's something you should know, Güera."

"Yes, Apá. What is it?"

"Your father died."

I paused, then cocked my head, unsure of his meaning. "W-What?" I stumbled. "What're you saying?"

"Your father died."

"My fath—"

"Yes, Güera, your white dad."

"My whi—"

"*Sí*. Your white father. The dry-cleaning guy from when you were little. Don't you remember?" Apá burst into a belly laugh.

"What? That's not funny."

Apá continued laughing. I heard Amá chuckle from the kitchen. I stood up from the table, but Apá grabbed my hand. "No, don't leave. I'm only joking."

"I never liked that joke, Apá."

"I know, I know. But you know what, Güera? You're going to make it. The one with the lighter skin always lives a well-off life. *Privilegiada.* Privileged."

"I hate when you talk like that—"

"No. No. It's true. It's true." He looked at me with a gentle face. "You know I'm proud of you, right?"

It was the same old madness at my parents' house, but this time I was dragging my kids into it. Each night at eight o'clock, just like during my childhood, my father commanded we turn off the lights and swamp cooler.

"Can we keep the swamp cooler on for the kids tonight?" I asked my mother. "We'll roast in the heat. Just this once?"

She shrugged. "Wet their sheets with water like we used to."

Like old times. But now Apá was suffering from insomnia. For all the nights we stayed there, just as Jeremy, Jacqueline, and I had finally fallen asleep, music would blare from the garage and continue into the late hours of the night. Then around three in the morning, Apá would rush into the room, yelling it was time to get up, as he had done on the early mornings we worked the fields. He'd wake up a startled Jeremy and a fussy Jacqueline, and I'd have to rock back to sleep until sunrise.

After the fourth night, I left for Irma's. She and her husband had moved back to Cashion from England into a small house down the street from our parents. I continued to hop from her place and Dolores's over the next three months.

It wasn't until Jeremy cried for his daddy that I knew it was time to go back to Ernie.

41

*E*rnie's next deployment, New Mexico, was colorless compared to the Philippines. No taupe sandy beaches, no shining blue ocean, just dust, desert, and red and green chiles around every corner. Ernie worked at the White Sands Air Force Base while the kids and I lived in Albuquerque, three hours away. We saw Ernie only on the weekends.

During the week, I worked as a candy striper at the Red Cross, took prerequisites for dental hygiene at the Kirtland Air Force Base, raced to get Jeremy to the private air base school on time, juggled Jacqueline on my hip while cooking tacos four nights a week, and studied for my anatomy classes during their bath time. And through it all, Ernie and I tried to repair our relationship.

In the spring of 1989, now almost twenty-nine, I received my dental assistant certification. A baby step, I told myself. And as I was about to start applying for jobs in the dental industry, Ernie volunteered for an assignment to go to the Osan Air Force Base in South Korea. In the air force branch, airmen are encouraged to take an assignment for a long period without their families. If they complete it, they can get their choice of the top three states.

Ernie would go to South Korea. I wanted to stay in New Mexico since I had just been accepted into the University of New Mexico's dental hygiene program, but Ernie and I both knew I needed help with the kids.

Going back to Cashion was out of the question. So I went with the next best thing and drove myself and the kids to stay with my mother-in-law in Bossier City, Louisiana. Antonia lived across from the Barksdale Air Force Base, where my father-in-law had been stationed. He had become a truck driver after his military career, spending month after month on the open road. While he was gone, Antonia lived alone in an antique house with the most crooked white picket fence I'd ever seen. She was still her critical, feisty Filipino self.

I discovered that she cooked enormous meals, the kind of meals that could feed an army, but there wasn't an army to feed. Once, when Jacqueline, now five, said she wanted a snack, Antonia went to work in the kitchen, making *lumpias, pancit,* and *adobo* chicken. Hours later, when Antonio served Jacqueline the meal, she refused to eat it. Antonia inhaled, pressed her crinkled lips together, and mumbled, "Ungrateful child."

Later that evening, after the kids had gone to bed, Antonia and I sat silently watching the late-night news. Without moving her gaze from the TV, she said, "Ignore my crankiness. I'm going through menopause. Wouldn't wish it on my worst enemy."

I'd gone to Louisiana for help with my two young kids, but I ended up taking care of them and my emotional, menopausal mother-in-law. Her mood swings were hot, cold, left, right, low, and high. She set the house thermostat at sixty-one degrees to calm her hot flashes, and if Jeremy or Jacqueline laughed, cried, or even looked at her funny, she got irritated.

One night, with a glass of her favorite white wine in hand, she said, "Why doesn't my son give you more money to buy some clothes? Get rid of the damn scrubs."

I guzzled my glass of wine as if it were water.

A few weeks later, I moved the kids and myself into a cheap apartment two blocks away, telling Antonia we needed more space and that it had nothing to do with her—a trivial lie that saved face.

In our new neighborhood, I found a job working as a dental assistant at Dr. Brown's Dentistry. One day at lunch, a dental staff member said, "Another damned Mexican came in today. Nasty degenerates with no manners." She scrunched up her face. "And my God, they smell."

The rest of the staff chuckled. A few others broke in with offensive comments: "spics," "wetbacks," "beaners." My jaw clenched, biting at the lashing words stuck on my tongue. Did they not see me sitting right here? Finally, on impulse and a bit of fury, I butted in, "Excuse me, but I'm Mexican, and I don't appreciate those comments."

They all looked at me with wide, rapid-blinking eyes. One gal laughed uneasily. "What do you mean? You're white."

I looked her dead in her puzzled face and answered, "I can assure you I'm a full-blooded Mexican."

The room turned awkward, and the topic was instantly changed.

The next day, the office let me go—apparently, I wasn't qualified enough for my position.

Once the summer of 1991 ended, Ernie received his last assignment: Luke Air Force Base in Arizona. We packed our bags and bought a house in north Phoenix—as far away from Cashion as possible.

The neighborhood was quaint. Matching adobe houses with an assortment of plush green bushes and cacti decorated the front yards. The house had three bedrooms, two bathrooms, a bright, and spacious kitchen perfect for every cooking venture. The neighbor kids sped up and down the roads on their bikes, skateboards, and scooters, and soon enough, they invited Jeremy and Jacqueline into their posse. It was the stable ground our family needed.

When I told Amá we closed on a house an hour from Cashion, she wasn't happy. "It's so far from here. It's too long of a drive."

That was exactly the point. I didn't want Jeremy and Jacqueline around the Cashion craziness that I had worked so hard to escape. Even though I hated going there, when my mother asked for help cleaning her house or assisting her with groceries, I'd make the trip.

Other than some holidays and short visits, we didn't see my sisters and brothers much. And when we did, we talked mostly about the latest and greatest Cashion gossip, which I'd listen to with little to no interest.

But then, Amá became the talk of the town. To our huge surprise, she won the lottery. Half a million dollars. Esméralda called me, hooting and hollering from the other end of the phone. In the background,

I could hear her son Mateo howling, "My grandma won the lottery! We're rich! We're rich!"

I laughed. Antonia, that sassy Filipino psychic, had been right.

With the winnings, Amá bought a new car, vacationed in Mexico a couple of times, took various trips to the Laughlin casinos, and sponsored *quinceañeras* for two neighbor kids (which I thought was bullshit since she wouldn't spend a dime on mine or my sisters' growing up). She also purchased a desolate plot of land south of Cashion along the Estrella Mountain range, where she built a cemented awning and an outhouse to spice up the place. It became the perfect new party spot for the family to spend their weekends.

Ernie and I fought on and off for four more years. On our fifteenth wedding anniversary, I knew I couldn't continue. My heavy heart told me it had reached the end. That evening, I confronted Ernie after the kids had gone to bed.

"I'm leaving you, Ernie," I said softly, unsuccessfully fighting back tears. "I can't do this anymore."

He tilted his head to the side, his eyes showing the sorrow of the years. "Fine. Leave me. But nobody is going to want you—you're almost forty and a mother of two kids."

My tears dried up at his comment, and my voice grew as big as the sea. "It's not about somebody else wanting me, Ernie." I gritted my teeth so hard I thought they would break. "This is about my own damn happiness."

That night we agreed to separate, making space for a different kind of future. After our impending new normal sunk in, we broke the news to Jeremy and Jacqueline. Jeremy, at age fourteen, was focused on practicing for the school talent show and excelling in his honor classes. Meanwhile, Jacqueline, now eleven and much more reserved than her brother, preferred staying at home.

"Why can't you just love Dad?" Jeremy said through pooled-up tears. "We know he's not perfect, but why can't you just stay with him? Keep our family together, Mom."

His words pierced my heart. There was something harrowing in deliberately breaking up my family—to sign up voluntarily for separate holidays and birthday celebrations. To knowingly choose to share my kids with a once-beloved stranger. Yet amid the pain and suffering that came with divorce, there also came a reawakening—an understanding that I, too, was human and deserved happiness. For me to be the best mother and person I could be, I had made the right choice. Of course, I had done it for my children, but at the same time, I wasn't afraid to admit that I had also made the decision for myself.

I was working as a part-time dental assistant, earning twelve dollars an hour, but it wasn't enough. I could barely pay the kids' expenses and put food on the dinner table. Something had to give. So I set my sights on becoming a full-time dental hygienist, and to get that, I needed to finish my dental hygienist education. I pushed full steam ahead to fulfill all the requirements.

One night after my biochemistry class, the professor stopped me in the hall. "Have you ever heard of dyslexia?" he asked.

I shook my head.

"I notice that you transpose numbers, letters, and words in your assignments. These patterns can often mean you have this condition."

"Dyslexia," I said as if it were a deadly disease.

"It's a lifelong difficulty, but with the right educational techniques, many people can overcome it."

The reading. The writing. The struggle to articulate the jumbled words in my head through my mouth and into language. It all made sense now. And here was a word that described it all.

I thanked him. "Nothing has stopped me so far, and I'll be damned if any reading and writing disability does."

42

One Friday evening, I sat propped up on the sofa flipping through the channels: *Seinfeld, Home Improvement,* and *I Love Lucy* reruns. Tapping the remote turned into a rhythm. I was the only one in the house. Both kids were spending the night with friends.

I was slowly getting a grasp on single motherhood. Rebecca, one of the other dental hygienists at work, had been a solo parent for some time, so I often leaned on her for support. When her eleven-year-old son was with his dad and Jeremy and Jacqueline were spending time with Ernie, she and I hung out together at her house eating tortilla chips and salsa and washing it all down with fresh margaritas.

Earlier that day she had pulled me aside. "If you aren't doing anything tonight, come to Bobby McGee's BBQ for my brother-in-law's thirtieth birthday."

"Sure, I'll think about it," I told her. "I'm getting used to spending my weekend nights watching TV."

Rebecca smiled. "Six thirty. See you there."

I checked the time. Almost eight o'clock. I tipped my wine glass into the air, finishing the last swig. Should I pour another? I thought about Bobby McGee's. They were all probably about to leave. It'd be pointless to show up now. I should just stay in. Save money.

Pretty Woman. Click. *Dateline.* Click. The local news.

"Screw it," I said out loud. I threw on a denim jacket, sprinkled my hair with moose, and arrived at Bobby McGee's twenty minutes later. I'd peek around the corner to see if they were still there, and if not, I'd simply go back home and continue flipping through channels as if I hadn't even left.

I craned my neck to the bar area, scanning through the faces, looking for Rebecca's teased blond hair. She was mid-conversation, her back to me. Before I could even count the people there, the man Rebecca had been talking to called out, "Is that her?"

Rebecca turned around and waved her arms over her head as if she were landing a plane. I smiled and approached the leftover crew from the celebration.

"Sorry, I'm late," I said.

"No worries at all," Rebecca said, pouring a margarita from the pitcher and handing it to me. "Party's just getting started. This here's the birth-day boy, Steve." She pointed to the tall man sitting next to her at the bar. He had dark curly hair and a mustache to match, reminding me of Tom Selleck.

I lifted my glass to him. "Happy birthday. And welcome to the thirty club."

Steve laughed, revealing a small dimple on his left cheek. "Tell me it gets better."

"No luck there," I said. "Been in the thirties for six years, but I'll al-ways try to be young at heart."

After a few more margaritas, my head started to buzz. And here we were at the bar getting another pitcher.

Rebecca turned to me. "Minu, ask Steve to dance."

"Oh, please. No."

"C'mon, Minu, I think he's lonely. Just look at him."

I glanced over at Steve, who had moved to a booth by himself to watch the band. He tapped his foot to the music, both hands wrapped tightly around his drink.

"He's going through a divorce, and he might need a little fun in his life. Plus, it's his birthday."

I thought about my own situation: Ernie and I were stuck in a sep-arated-but-still-married mode. I looked down at the silver wedding ring I'd had for sixteen years—a reminder of the calamity that had yet to be healed.

"You're right. What's the harm." I slurped the top of my margarita for some liquid courage and strolled over to Steve.

"What are you doing over here all by yourself?" I asked over the roaring guitar solo of JukeBox Hero. "Would you like to dance?"

His warm brown eyes lit up, and he nodded.

We both felt the chemistry in the first twirl on the dance floor that night. His dark curls bounced as he pulled me close, our hands intertwining, his gentle touch giving me the comfort I forgot existed. As I moved in next to him, I caught a whiff of his cologne. He smiled through each twist and turn, and so did I.

As the night progressed, we confided in one another about our failed marriages. I told him about my dream of becoming a licensed dental hygienist, and he opened up about his passion for finance and his scholarship start-up business.

Near midnight, when I left for home, the scent of his cologne lingered on my skin, a reminder of the night I'd just had. And to think I had almost stayed home.

The following Monday afternoon, I received a call at work.

"Minu, it's for you. It's a man. And it's not Ernie's voice," said the receptionist. The other hygienists and I had access to a vacant office if we needed to have private conversations. I stepped inside and shut the door.

"Hello, this is Minu."

"Minu, hi, it's Steve,"

"Steve, you can't call me here! This is—"

"I know. I know. But it's a beautiful day outside. Would you like to join me for a picnic?" His voice was even calmer than I remembered.

"You shouldn't be calling me at work," I said again.

"I understand, but I found tons of information on dental and college scholarships you might qualify for. I can bring them to you."

"Can you leave the information with Rebecca?"

"No, no. I have to go over it with you in-person."

Of course he did. I remained silent, wondering if I was charmed by this man or completely creeped out.

"I'm close to your office," he said.

"What are you doing? Stalking me?"

"No, I asked Rebecca where—"

"You know what, no. I can't do this." I hung up and shook my head.

"Is everything okay?" the receptionist asked. "Who was it?"

I shrugged. "Some sales guy trying to help me with a scholarship."

On my way home early that afternoon, I sat in my scrubs at a stoplight when a tattered white truck pulled up next to me. Pressed to the window was a white piece of paper with large black letters:

> *It's a beautiful day for a picnic, and I hate to eat alone.*
> *Please have lunch with me!*
> *Steve*

Steve's eyes peeped out from behind the paper along with a tight smile. I seesawed between sneering and laughing. When the light turned green, Steve sped ahead of me and turned into Thunderbird Park. I followed. He stepped out of the truck in a crisp button-up shirt with a picnic basket, a bottle of wine, and a single rose.

He flashed a big grin. "Funny seeing you here."

I shook my head at him in disbelief.

"Over here," he said, leading me to a picnic table under a short palm tree. "Would you prefer a tuna or turkey sandwich?"

I sat across from him. "Tuna is wonderful."

"Glass of white wine?" He started to uncork the bottle.

"Steve, it's the middle of the day, and I have to go home and take care of my kids. My mother-in-law is actually in town."

It was true. Antonia had arrived from Louisiana to help me. Ernie had told her that we were going through a rough patch and he'd be staying at the base until we sorted things out. "Rough patch"—separation was more accurate.

"Sweet of you," I said, "but I can't."

"Okay." He put his hands up as if to surrender and smiled. There was that dimple again. "This is for you." He set the red rose in front of me. "I really enjoyed getting to know you the other night."

Sticking to his word, he showed me the scholarships I most likely qualified for, specifically for dental hygiene school. Impressed, I munched on my tuna sandwich while he went through the documents and eventually caved and had a glass of wine with him.

When I checked the time and saw an hour had passed, I jumped up to leave. Antonia would be suspicious.

"Steve, thank you for walking me through all this." I wrapped up my half-eaten tuna sandwich. "This turned into a really nice afternoon."

He smiled. "Before you leave, can I get one thing?"

I looked at him cautiously.

"Can I get a hug?" He stood up with his arms open. "C'mon, you've hugged me before."

He was right. But Friday night after a few margaritas was different than broad daylight on a Monday afternoon in my dental scrubs. I went in for a side hug, but Steve maneuvered himself so we faced each other. His cologne flooded my nostrils.

When I finally made it home—giddier about the spontaneous afternoon than I wanted to admit—I threw the rose into the garbage bin in the garage to avoid raising any questions from my mother-in-law.

As I walked into the kitchen, the smell of *pancit* and *lumpia* enveloped me, taking me back to the Louisiana days. Jeremy and Jacqueline sat at the dining table doing homework.

Turning from the stove, Antonia stared at me with her head tilted and lips pursed. "You smell like you been outside."

"Of course. I've been out running errands." I walked over to Jeremy and Jacqueline, kissing them both on the tops of their heads.

"No. Smell like you been sitting outside. For a long time."

Guilt flooded me. She wiped her hands on her pants and walked toward me. "Let me see your hand." She cuffed it with both of hers. For a minute or so, she studied my palm with squinted eyes and lightly touching my fingertips. Then she gasped and shoved my hand down.

"What, Grandma?" Jeremy asked. "Is Mommy going to die?"

"No, she not going to die." Antonia glared at me. " I tell you later."

After Jeremy and Jacqueline were off to bed and it was just Antonia and me in the kitchen, I asked her what she had seen. She stopped wiping the counter and looked up at me. "You met someone," she said.

"No, I haven't. I want to be clear—I am not leaving your son for someone else."

Antonia ignored me. "This . . . this man not successful now, but he'll be very successful one day."

Was she referring to Steve? It couldn't be. He lived with his brother and couldn't afford to get the air-conditioning fixed in his beat-up truck. There was no way she was talking about him.

Right?

Wrong. Antonia struck again. A couple of months later, once Ernie and I were officially divorced, Steve and I started to get serious. He was a hopeless romantic who wrote poems and planned picnics in the park with tuna sandwiches and wine. I was a recently divorced mother of two just trying to get back on her feet. But together we'd laugh so hard tears would pour from our eyes. Three months into our relationship, I introduced him to Jeremy and Jacqueline, who soon adored him just as much as I did.

In 1996, I was accepted to Northern Arizona University, but kindly declined after I realized I wouldn't be able to see Jacqueline and Jeremy as much if I went to school there. Instead, I attended Rio Salado Dental Hygiene School. I'd officially earn my dental hygiene license from there three years later.

Steve and I married in 1998. No wedding. No honeymoon. Only Jeremy, Jacqueline, Steve's brother, and his parents were invited to dinner at a nearby restaurant.

Life was good. For the moment.

43

I raced down the freeway, weaving in and out of five o'clock traffic. Amá had called me in a panic, telling me Apá had lit the bedsheets on fire.

"I'd been napping, Minu, and I woke up smelling the damn smoke!" my mother yelled over the phone. "You need to get your father. Come get him now!"

I told her that Apá needed to go to a mental hospital, that I couldn't manage him in his manic state. Her voice rose. "Minu, you know damn well he won't agree to that. He went to your sister's house last time he had an episode. It's your turn. I've calmed him down. Now please just come get him for a few days. He'll be fine by next week."

What was up with my family and fire? Parts of their house had recently burned down for the second time when Ruben left the fireplace unattended and a nearby stack of newspaper caught fire. Once again, my parents were able to save sentimental boxes, insurance documents, some clothes, and, oddly enough, the portrait of me as a baby that hung in the living room.

When I got there, Apá was standing at the end of the driveway fidgeting with his duffel bag. He waved as I parked the car. His eyes were bloodshot, and he squinted as if he were sensitive to the sunlight.

"Hey, Apá. You're going to stay with me for a few weeks. You okay with that?"

"Oh yes," he said, tossing his bag into the trunk. "I've never stayed at my *güera*'s before. I can't wait to see your new house."

Amá stood in her bathrobe and waved from the porch. "Have fun, you two."

On the drive back to Phoenix, Apá went on and on about the scrap material he'd found at the dump the day before, saying nothing about what had just happened with Amá.

"I'm going to make so much money from it, Minu. We'll all be rich. You'll see. You'll see."

"That's great, Apá. What kind of material is it?

"Oh, I can't tell you. You'll have to wait and see." He cocked his head as if deep in thought. "But you know what we should do, Güera?"

"What?"

"We should take a trip to Mexico. You and me. Just like we used to." A wide smile spread across his face, a smile so rare. "C'mon. What do you say?"

"I can't. You know that. I have Jeremy and Jacqueline, school, and I have to work."

"What? Your job? Where?" he asked, as if I hadn't told him many times before.

"I'm a dental hygienist, Apá. Remember?"

"Ah, wow. A dentist. I would love to see where my Güera works."

From the start, we were bombarded with the usual commotion that followed Apá wherever he went. On the first day, I came home to a mess in the garage. He had been trying to create a fishing trap to set up in the lake across the way, some type of metal contraption with netting and a spear at the end.

"This is just what we need to make a fish dinner," he said. "Doesn't that sound nice, Güera? A nice seafood dinner."

And at night, Apá still didn't sleep. At three in the morning, like clockwork, he'd ring the doorbell over and over.

"Time to wake up! Time to wake up!" he'd yell through the house.

"Apá, you can't keep doing this," I'd say, steering him back to the couch where he was sleeping. "The kids have school, and Steve and I have to go to work."

Sometimes, for brief moments, his craziness left him. He'd shower, dress in his best clothes, and even spray on his nice-smelling cologne. I'd find him listening to the radio while smoking his Winston cigarettes, letting the music take him back to what he referred to as the good ole days.

And then, like an inevitable force of nature, he'd act out again.

After a week, I admitted him to a rehab and recovery center. He stayed for close to a month, and then Amá picked him up and brought him home.

44

*I*n March 2004, my mother called me with a toothache.

"Since you're a dentist now, can you help me out?" she asked.

"Amá, I'm a dental hygienist. Not a dentist." It wasn't the first time I'd corrected her, and it wouldn't be the last. "But, yes, I'll schedule you an appointment. How's Thursday at three?"

After I finished up with a patient that day, I walked into an adjacent room to see Amá sitting upright in the dental chair, her hands nicely folded in her lap. She was waiting for Dr. Price, the lead dentist, to come check her out.

"How's the toothache?"

She smiled. "Oh, there you are. It'll be better after this. Just got my X-rays taken. Thank you again for making this happen."

"Of course. Happy to help."

Just then, Dr. Price knocked on the door. "Minu, can I see you in my office?"

I followed him to his office, where he took a seat behind his desk.

"What is this?" He folded his hands as if he didn't know what to do with them. "You can't just be taking people off the streets and giving them your dental discount."

"What do you mean?" I asked, confused.

"Who's that woman in room two?" he stared at me, unblinking.

"My mother."

"Okay, so are you going to tell me that's your father in the waiting room? You pick him up off the corner too?"

"What? My father's here?"

Dr. Price scratched his head.

Was he serious? I didn't need *him* questioning my family too.

"If you don't mind, Dr. Price, I'm going to go say hello to my father."

In the waiting room, Apá sat next to Esméralda, who had moved back to Cashion and was now regularly accompanying my parents as a translator. She flipped through a *People* magazine, bright pink curlers in her hair. When Apá saw me, his face lit up. His hands and head shook—he had been recently diagnosed with Parkinson's disease.

"Güera," he said, sweeping his arm around the room. "Look at you. Look at this. ¡Estupendo! I had to ride along with your ma to see where my Güera worked."

He stumbled to his feet and hugged me. "There's something else I wanted to tell you." He leaned in close to my face. "Please take care of your mother's teeth. She loves her smile."

A couple of weeks later, in early April, Apá and I had sat in my childhood home eating Burger King Whoppers and fries for his birthday lunch—his favorite. He had turned seventy-six the day before. Despite the sunspots that decorated his face, he was still handsome: his big brown eyes, his sharp face, his thick, dark hair. He seemed fragile, as delicate as Spanish porcelain. His shoulders and arms were shakier than the last time I saw him—his Parkinson's tremors were getting worse.

"You okay, Apá?"

"Oh yes. I'm good." He smiled. "You don't worry about me, Güera. You just take care of your mother."

His body relaxed, and his blinking slowed. He was getting tired. The Whoppers had been eaten and the conversation dwindled. It was simply a father and daughter soaking in each other's presence. We sat for a while.

It would be the last time.

PART THREE

Left to right: My daughter, Jacqueline; my son, Jeremy; and me. 2008.

45

At Apá's funeral, I hid in the church's bathroom stall, avoiding the strained sympathetic conversations. "Sorry for your loss" . . . "He was a good man." Yada. Yada.

It was hard saying goodbye, even to a father like him. I'd spent most of my life painfully angry at someone I was now grieving for. Despite what he did, I still loved him—my father was a part of me, and I couldn't turn away from that.

I sat on the toilet, a wadded-up tissue in hand, drifting deeper into a sea of contradictions. Two women talking at the sinks broke through my thoughts.

"Did you know that one of his daughters wasn't his?" one woman asked.

"Yes, I'd heard that, actually," the other woman said. "Do you know which daughter?"

Leaning to the side, I peeped through the stall crack. I didn't recognize them.

The first one muttered, "Not sure, but let's see if we can spot her."

On impulse, I flushed the toilet, warning them that they weren't alone, and opened the stall door. As I approached the sink, they both acted startled. One woman fidgeted with her hair, pushing a few out-of-place strands back into her donut bun. The second woman grazed a tube of red lipstick across her lips. She looked at me in the mirror and asked, "Did you know Mr. Becerra?"

I pressed the soak dispenser. "I did."

The first woman said, "He was such a nice man."

I nodded with a slight smile, running my hands under the faucet. They both awkwardly turned for the bathroom door and left.

Once the door closed, I braced myself against the sink counter.

Their words made me dizzy. Had I been a topic of gossip in this entire damn, godforsaken town?

Words—heavy baggage—from my past flooded my mind:

"You're not Mexican."

"My Güera!"

"Look at yourself, *mija*. You're a white girl. *Una chica blanca*."

"Minu, your white dad is at the door!"

"A white girl living with a Mexican family?"

"I never want to see this white girl again!"

I tossed water gently on my face, trying to wash it all away. In the mirror, my delicate features reflected at me. I studied them once more, searching for the truth: my curly strands surrounding my pale face and high cheekbones. It pained me that no one ever saw me as a part of the family.

Back in the church, I walked down the aisle, passing neighbors and the Cashion locals dressed in black. My family and their spouses, along with my nieces and nephews, took up the first five pews: my three older sisters sat primly in their black dresses, like birds. Julio, Danny, Ruben, and Sammy slouched behind them. Amá sat on the end, dried tears on her cheeks.

Then I made eye contact with the gossipers from the bathroom who sat a few rows behind my family. Their eyes widened when they saw me stop at the seats reserved for the Becerra family. I scooched in next to Steve.

The funeral began with a loud organ, and after a few prayers and blessings, the priest gestured to Apá's wife of fifty-eight years and his eight kids. "Would any of Julio Becerra's sons or daughters like to say a few words?" he asked.

Silenced swept through the church. I kept my gaze on my lap until I heard someone rustling through the row. Esméralda approached the podium, lined the mic to her mouth, and cleared her throat. In Spanish, she said, "Thank you all for coming. I'm Esméralda, Julio's third eldest daughter." She paused, her breath trembling in the microphone. "My father was a wonderful man. We were so blessed to have him in our lives. He taught us so much." She let out a soft chortle. "Like how to find the good in every situation. And he continually encouraged us to get a good education. And one time—"

Did I hear that right? I almost choked at the hogwash she was gabbing. Dolores and I made eye contact, reading each other's minds. I thought I had left my resentment and bitterness at the door, but there I was, seething in it. Steve grabbed my hand and squeezed it, bringing me back to the moment.

"We'll miss you, Apá," Esméralda said, her voice cracking. "Until we see you again."

In my own way, I said goodbye to my father that day. I couldn't fester in the spiraling, resentful, and angry thoughts forever. I had to do one of the hardest things I'd ever done—I forgave him. I forgave him for the pain, tears, and hurt he had caused. I forgave myself for the guilt I carried for keeping him at arm's length after all those years.

Forgiveness brought the liberation to heal my heart and find peace. It was a chance to push off the heavy bricks from my shoulders and break the shackles that had bonded me for so many years.

Letting go of all the anger and resentment opened up a new space for me. In came a feeling I hadn't felt before. *Resolve.*

I was now hell-bent on finding the truth.

And there was only one person who could give it to me.

46

It was early May, two weeks after Apá's funeral, and the warm air had cooled down for the night. I poured a glass of Amá's favorite sweet red wine, and we sat on my back patio under the pink and orange sky. Her red lipstick was faint on her lips, and her silver-gray hair was lightly curled around her smooth face.

I had invited her over to my house for an enchilada dinner and to spend the night. This time I wouldn't let her change the subject.

No matter what you find out, you're still you, I kept telling myself.

We talked about Jeremy and Jacqueline, the weather, and pointless feuds between my sisters. As the conversation dwindled, I knew the moment had come.

"Amá, there's something I'd like to talk to you about." I swirled the red wine around in the glass.

She eyed me suspiciously. "Well, what is it?"

I breathed in deep until I could feel the air in the back of my throat. "I—I need you to tell me who my real father is."

Amá stared at me. Just as I expected, she said, "What're you talking about? Julio was your father!"

"C'mon. Apá's gone now. You can tell me the truth."

"That's the truth. I don't know what else you want, Minu."

"Do you remember when I took Apá for those few days after he set fire to the sheets?"

She nodded, pursing her lips, her face wary.

"Well, I took him to the doctor and he had blood work done. I also had blood work done." I was lying. This was my plan to get her to reveal the secret I was so confident she was hiding. "We weren't the same blood type, Amá. And the doctor told me it was impossible he was my father."

Alarmed, she sat forward. "Yes, he *was*. They are wrong. He's your father. And he was a good father."

She never realized how much she betrayed me every time she made that statement.

"He was *not* a good father. Sure, he may have been a good man in some people's eyes, but he was not a good father. He was aggressive and angry my entire childhood. We were beaten. Julio—" I stopped, careful not to steer us off track.

"That's because he was sick, Minu," she said softly, practically in a whisper.

I suddenly felt guilty for bringing it up. Was it best not to press her for the truth? Was it better not knowing? *No, don't let up*, I told myself. "Please, Amá. Who was my real father?"

Her voice rose. "Julio is your father."

"Okay. If you say that he was my father and you're my mother, then something must have happened in the hospital. Maybe there was a mix-up there. Back then, hospitals weren't as strict about putting bracelets on newborns. Maybe I was switched. Maybe your daughter is out there somewhere. Wouldn't you want to know that? I have gone almost forty-six years knowing things made little sense, questioning my appearance, my identity, my belonging. Please. I deserve to know the truth."

A long pause. Taking a deep breath, she said, "No, he wasn't your father."

My heart dropped to my stomach and then to the floor. There they were, floating in the air before me, the words I'd been waiting for. I wanted to grasp them, replay them over and over and over—to know, to understand, to recollect that they were real. Five words and a lifetime.

"Thank you for telling me, Amá. So who is my father? You can tell me. I can take it."

She looked into her lap for a moment, her gaze somber. "Cash. His last name was Cash."

"Johnny Cash?" were the two words out of my mouth before I could drag them back in.

"No, no, no. *Mauricio.* Maurice."

I echoed his name in a whisper. "Who was he?"

"He owned the cotton farm your father and I worked for when we first came to Arizona. The Anderson Clayton Cotton Farm."

The farm where I'd spent so many of my childhood days picking and plucking. The early mornings. The jarring truck ride over. The long, frothy rows of cotton plants. Those long, hot, steamy days, picking and plucking.

"Julio and I worked as cotton pickers." Her eyes wandered as if questioning if she'd already said too much. "Then he had one of his crazy episodes and disappeared for months, leaving me alone with your sisters and brother. Mauricio helped me. He gave me food and a comfortable home."

A thousand vexing questions, but one specific question took priority. "Did he know about me?"

"He did. He wanted a professional photograph of you, so we took you to downtown Phoenix. He always said you'd look beautiful in a pink dress, and he gave me money to find you the most perfect one."

She let out a weak chuckle. "But I couldn't find one, so I bought you a yellow one with lace around the edges instead." She looked off into the distance, deep in thought, ions away. "I liked you better in yellow anyway. But Mauricio liked pink. When the photo was printed, he had the photographer paint the dress pink."

The framed picture that hung on the plain white living room wall my entire childhood. A clue right before my eyes. I had overlooked it all those years. A yellow dress painted pink, requested by my real father.

"Mauricio helped me with money. That's why you had the birthday parties. And he gave me the money for a down payment for the Cashion house."

"Did Apá—did Julio know?" I asked. Amá flinched when I called him by his real name.

"A few times he suspected something, but, no, he never knew."

"How did he not know? When he returned, you were pregnant? He also went his whole life calling me the white girl, Güera."

"He thought we conceived you before he left." Her voice turned gentle. "Either way, he was sick, Minu. And despite it all, he was excited to have you. He loved you so much. All you kids."

I shook off her unconvincing words. "So what happened to Mauricio?" I was afraid of her answer. "Where is he now?"

"He died. When you were three and a half."

My heart skipped a beat. I could hardly breathe. This secret man—my birth father—was gone. I'd never have the chance to see him, touch him, know he was real. I blinked hard, letting the tragic words sink in. I felt woozy.

Off the tip of my tongue, I blurted back-to-back questions. "Did he have other children? Were you in love with him? What did he look like? Was he married?"

She shrugged. I knew I had pushed my mother to her limit. I studied her face—a face that had seen a plethora of heartbreaks. Did she finally feel relieved for telling me? Or would she wake up tomorrow with a pit in her stomach for divulging the truth?

"So that's it?" I asked. "That's all you're going to tell me after all this time?" My voice rose. My muscles felt stiff. I shifted in my chair.

"That's it." She wave her hand, dismissing me. "Julio is the father that raised you. Just accept it."

She fell quiet. After several long minutes of silence, I understood that our talk was over. The pink and orange that filled the sky at the start of our conversation had now twisted into a dark blue. I thanked her again for telling me. We finished our wine and went to bed.

But I didn't sleep. I tossed and turned all night, knowing this was only the beginning of discovering another part of me.

My mother had carried a deep, dark secret her entire life, and that secret was me. Had it been out of shame, denial, self-protectiveness? Out of love? I doubted if it kept her up at night. In fact, she probably did everything in her power to forget about it.

I thought back to the ugly duckling story I had read as a little girl. I now knew what the little fellow felt when he discovered where he'd come from. All my life, I had fielded questions about not looking Mexican, and I finally had the missing piece.

No, I hadn't been adopted or switched at birth, nor was I the daughter of the dry-cleaning man. I was the daughter of an American cotton farm owner. I had heard my real father's name—Maurice Cash, and I couldn't unhear it.

47

Over two cups of steaming black coffee, Amá and I sat in the living room watching the Saturday morning news in silence. I wrapped both my hands around the mug, feeling the warmth transfer to my skin.

"How'd you sleep, Amá?" I finally asked.

Her frail hands lifted the coffee mug to her lips. "Fine," she said, keeping her eyes on the TV. The weather woman reported the blue skies the Phoenix Valley would experience for the rest of the weekend.

Of course, Amá didn't have anything to say. How typical. Her refusal to say more the night before was infuriating enough—her silence this morning was even worse.

Had she woken with regret?

Was she sorry for saying his name to me?

From the recliner, Amá said just above a whisper, "I don't want your sisters or brothers to know about Mauricio. They won't understand." She set her coffee mug on the side table and folded her arms across her chest. "I don't want to cause a divide between you and them."

I absorbed her request, feeling sympathy and anger at the same time. "Okay, Amá. I won't say anything. But I plan to tell Jeremy and Jacqueline."

She shifted her eyes from the TV to the floor and back to the TV. "Fine." Then she switched the conversation to the hot temperatures we'd be having over the next few days.

The discussion was over.

Later that day, after Amá went home, I sent her a bouquet of plush red roses with a note:

> *Thank you for sharing. I love you.*
> *Minu*

My head spun with the news. What did you do with the information of a long-lost father? When I told Steve, he responded with the umph I didn't know I needed. "Oh, for Christ's sake! She kept this from you this whole time?" he blurted out. "C'mon," he said, booting up the computer at the office desk. "We've got work to do."

Steve typed "Maurice Cash" in the Google search bar. No obituary, no newspaper articles, no photos, yet at the top of the page was the blue hyperlink "Maurice C. Cash Elementary School." The link led us to a photo of the brick school with an American flag waving. We scrolled down the page to a photo of young students smiling and another of the school's roadrunner mascot at a young boys' basketball game.

"Where is this?" I asked Steve over his shoulder.

He scrolled fast to the bottom of the page and squinted at the computer screen. "Laveen."

The town just west of Cashion.

On Monday, I called the school that bore my father's name and asked the receptionist if she had any information about the history. Unfortunately, the only thing she knew was that the school's land had been donated by a man named Maurice C. Cash more than forty years before.

Over the next week, I called Amá a few times, careful not to reveal my desperation for more information. I dropped questions gingerly. "Hey, about the other night. Was he married? Did he have kids? Where had he died? How did he die? Were you in love with him?"

In her typical hardheaded manner, she would deflect the questions with loud sighs. "I don't know, Minu." She didn't divulge a single fact. "Enough with this," she'd say. "I don't remember. It was so long ago."

The irritation in her voice increased with every question. I suspected that Amá saw my eagerness to know more about Maurice as a deep betrayal of her and the family she had raised.

After a moment of silence, she'd predictably change the subject or say she had to run an errand, leaving me hanging on a cliff with no next move. But I wasn't deterred. I'd artfully bring it up every time it was just the two of us—when I talked with her over the phone or helped her shop for groceries or cleaned her house.

And then one day, after another conversation that led to more questions, she blurted out, "Enough of this! I made it all up. It's not true. None of it."

"What? You don't mean that!"

"I did it to appease you. To finally get you to quit asking about not fitting in."

"It is the truth! It's the only thing that makes sense of this mess."

"I made it all up. None of its true," she snapped back.

Was my mother capable of rigging such a story to shut me up? No. I didn't believe it for one minute. How selfish she was, moving through life unaware of how her actions affected others.

Okay, no more questions.

But the genie was out of the bottle—and Amá couldn't put it back.

48

*O*ver the years, the news about Maurice never left my mind. Even in 2008, nine years into my marriage to Steve, when his student loan business took off.

What had once been a simple business idea had turned into a three-million-dollar campus build-out with leftover buckets of money. The company hired hundreds of employees, added a gym, bought a private jet, and paid the five owners handsomely.

When Steve and I sold our shares in the company, it was as if money did indeed grow on trees. For the first time in my life, I experienced financial freedom. I no longer had to worry about how to pay the electric or water bill or groceries. Steve and I both bought new cars and moved into a two-story adobe house with a pool and hot tub. We bought a charming cottage nestled in La Jolla with a view of the endless ocean. Steve even started a trust allowance for Jeremy and Jacqueline each month.

Antonia had struck yet again.

With the extra money we had pouring into our bank accounts, we played. I bought a new wardrobe from Nordstrom, a Louis Vuitton purse with a matching wallet, a top-notch Piaget watch, a thousand-dollar dress for a charity ball, a white gold four-carat marquee titanium ring, and a pair of Jimmy Choo shoes I could barely walk in. Once, for a celebratory gift, Steve bought me a guitar signed by Jewel.

On some weekends, we'd take out the silver yacht we kept at the Lake Pleasant marina. On other weekends, Steve and I, the four other owners, and their lots-of-Gucci-wearing wives flew to Vegas on the private jet. We would stay in the presidential suite at the Mandalay Bay and gamble at the blackjack tables, drinking expensive bottles of Dom Pérignon and sipping tequila on the rocks, followed with Bloody Marys the next morning.

Occasionally, during this luxurious season of my life, my childhood imaginary rich aunt would cross my mind. Here I was, over forty years later, living in her life. But I was still flipping our shampoo bottles upside down to use every drop while Steve would tell me to "just throw them out."

This was when my brother Julio and I started getting together regularly. He had a new love in his life, Ruth, who brought him the happiness I always hoped he would find. The four of us—Steve, Ruth, Julio, and I—would sit along our backyard pool with wine as the laughs we missed out on over the years echoed through the air.

Early one evening, the golden hour, the sky spoiled us with another brilliant display of oranges, pinks, and purples.

"Refills?" Steve asked, getting up from the pool.

I raised my empty glass.

"I'll do another, please," Julio said with his sweet smile.

"I'll help you, Steve," Ruth said.

She followed him into the house, leaving just Julio and me. I studied my brother. He looked just like our mother, even a bit like Uncle Chalio in his dark eyes, yet I could still make out that innocent little hooligan from our childhood.

"It's good to see you, Julio," I whispered with a nudge to his arm. "You don't know how much I've missed you."

He swished his feet in the pool. "It feels good to be back." He looked up to the night sky. "I hope you understand why I stayed away from the family all those years."

"I do. I just wish things had been different."

"Trust me—me too. I didn't like my life, Minu . . ." he trailed off. "Apá mistreated all of us."

I nodded, trying not to let the painful childhood memories that haunted me for years creep in.

"And look at the boys now," Julio went on. "David's gone, and the rest are into drugs. Some things never change."

"*Las cosas malas nunca mueren*. Some things never die," I said, quoting Amá's eminent adage. I put a hand on my brother's shoulder. "But you must let it go, Julio. Let it go for your own peace."

"I try," he whispered. I hated the grip my father had always had on Julio's life. It wasn't fair. We had lived in the same house, wished on the same stars, breathed the same air, and were hurt by the same father. "By the way, I must say, you did good, Güera." He waved his hand to the view before us. "Look how far you've come."

"The house next door is for sale," I nudged his arm and laughed. "If you're interested in being our neighbors."

Julio smiled. "Ruth and I would love that."

Through the kitchen window, I could see Steve talking to Ruth while opening another bottle of wine. Ruth was an accountant, and she and Steve could speak knowledgeably on a range of topics from formulas to international politics to the stock market.

"You have a good one," I said.

He shifted his gaze to the kitchen window. Ruth was now smiling her bright smile while nodding at Steve.

"She's the salt of the earth, really," Julio whispered. "She makes me the happiest man. I've loved no one like I love her."

His face glowed with a happiness I had never seen on him before. And that made me the happiest little sister.

49

*A*s parents, we watch with angst as our children test out their wings. As they grow older and find their own way, we let them know their home is still their home should they ever need it, full of home-cooked enchiladas, clean sheets, and hugs.

Jacqueline, at twenty-three, had just graduated from Arizona State University with a degree in communications and was now on the hunt to start her career. Jeremy, at twenty-six, was working in real estate.

But he was also battling an acute drug addiction.

Drugs had been readily available and copiously consumed by his friends. What started as peer pressure became a constant craving. Happy moments became painful.

We admitted him into a treatment center in Wickenburg, Arizona, but his progress was slow, and we had to try something else. A treatment center in Newport Beach, California, was our next hope. Steve and I moved full time into our cottage in La Jolla, where I could bring Jeremy home on the weekends. Every Friday, Steve and I drove to the rehab center to pick him up, and the entire way there, I'd tell myself that this week would be the turning point.

At the center, we would accompany Jeremy for group therapy with his psychiatrist. After the last session, when Jeremy had left the room to gather his things for the weekend, the psychiatrist spoke to us.

"You both must prepare for the worst," he said, unmoving.

His words shot a numbness through my body, through my soul. The only thing I could feel was the egg-sized lump in my throat, clogging my airway. I swallowed hard and managed to murmur, "How does someone prepare for the worst?"

Steve grabbed my hand.

The psychiatrist frowned as if debating what to say. "You do the best you can."

Holding a small bag, Jeremy walked out of the center in a baggy T-shirt and jeans with his favorite gold chain draped around his neck. Steve opened the car door for him while I beamed at my perfect son. He half smiled back, his face fatigued and shoulders bowed. Steve patted his shoulder and Jeremy climbed into the car.

"There he is," I said, as cheerful as I had in me. "C'mon. Let's have ourselves a weekend."

On the way home, I thought back to four-year-old Jeremy. Such a smart, well-behaved young boy. I remembered the first time I took him to a grocery store in New Mexico. Until that time, he had only ever gone to the base commissaries, where they sold the bare minimum. So before we went in, I told him, "Now Jeremy, you are about to see tons and tons of candy. Especially when we get to the checkout line." He looked up at me with his innocent wide eyes. "Now Mommy's asking you to not beg for any candy when we are there, okay? Otherwise, Mommy can't bring you along on grocery trips anymore."

Jeremy nodded and gave me the thumbs up. "Okay, Mommy."

During the grocery trip, Jeremy was, as usual, well-mannered and had listened to my instructions to not beg for candy. When we made our way to the cash register, dozens of shelves held candies of all kinds: the gummies, the chocolates, the lollipops, the list went on and on. But Jeremy didn't ask.

At the next cash register over, a little boy—around Jeremy's age—cried and screamed, "I want candy! I want candy! I want candy!" The little boy's mother yelled no, but he continued with the tantrum.

Jeremy looked up at me. "Well, he's never coming back to the grocery store with his mommy . . ."

I smiled and said, "Nope."

�֍

Back at the La Jolla cottage, Jeremy and I sipped iced coffee on the back porch, soaking in the warm summer sun. We talked about everything and nothing. The only thing more beautiful than the blooming hydrangeas and banana trees surrounding us was the sight of my son at my side. That afternoon, we aimlessly strolled Windansea Beach. I could feel the weight of the world on his broad shoulders.

"How ya doing, honey?" I asked him.

He looked out at the ocean and then down at the waves hitting his feet. "I'm good, Mom. Don't worry about me."

How could I not worry? Our children don't understand the meaning of worry. I pulled him in for a side hug while we kept our pace. "You are so strong, Jeremy," I whispered to him. "You can get through anything. Together, we can get through anything. This is just a small bump in the road."

He kept quiet, the sound of the waves filling the silence. He used to be so confident and full of life, but now he seemed tired and defeated. I wanted to see that spark in him once more, and I was willing to do anything to help him find it. How I wanted that Jeremy back. Not only for me, but for himself.

"Jeremy, what's it going to take for you to fight for this . . . to fight for this life?" I circled my arms to our surroundings. The bushes along the bank rustled in the breeze as if cheering me on. "Here we are, in this gorgeous place, getting the best help for you for a strong recovery. Jacqueline, your dad, Steve—we all love you more than anything else."

He rubbed the back of his neck with one hand. I studied his face, looking for an answer. He finally said, "I'm not comfortable in my own skin, Mom. I never have been." He blinked hard and kicked some sand as we walked. "Opioids make me feel normal. I just can't do it."

"Yes, yes, you can," I said, my voice cracking. I wanted to scream, but instead, I kept my voice as calm as I could manage. This was his addicted brain talking, this wasn't my Jeremy. "This isn't a way to live. Please, you must come out of this. You will. You will."

He looked at me with defeated eyes. "I'll try for you, Mom."

As I reflected on the past several years, it seemed that tragedy had become a constant companion. My family had gone through the unimaginable. Irma's oldest son had been killed in a drive-by shooting. Dolores's youngest son was accidentally shot dead in a shootout in Cashion. Ruben's son died in a car accident. Esméralda's daughter, a troubled yet brilliant young woman, died of HIV, and her oldest son hung himself from the Agua Fria Bridge.

And then the cruelest blow of all: my beloved Julio was diagnosed with pancreatic cancer. He died from a massive heart attack during exploratory surgery.

It felt as though tragedy was a specter haunting our family, a curse we couldn't shake off. I stood by my family through the sobs, tears, and dreadful funerals. I'd cry the entire way home, telling myself I wouldn't return. "I can't handle it anymore," I'd say through built-up tears. "That was it. That was the last time."

It was guilt or another tragedy or casualty that pulled me back.

Whenever the phone rang, my heartbeat pumped through my ears, and I held my breath as fear overtook me. What horrific event would it be this time? Someone in the hospital? Prison? Another death?

It was all too much.

Jeremy spent eight months at the Newport Beach Recovery Center before relapsing and being placed in a nearby home. A little over a month later, he ran away and went missing, finally calling me after two weeks. Then he moved to Tucson and lived with some friends.

We kept in touch during that phase. He and I talked often on the phone, and he claimed he was sober. He worked odd jobs for his friend's father, and when that fizzled out, he moved back to Phoenix into Ernie's apartment, about ten minutes away from Steve and me.

But it wasn't long before Jeremy relapsed again. Over the next two years, he continued with more rehab and recovery work.

And then early one morning in May 2010, Ernie called me. "Jeremy isn't breathing!" he screamed.

I raced over to his apartment, never driving so fast in my life. Through every yellow light I ran, I prayed to God, asking him to keep my son here, to not take him from me yet.

When I arrived, Jeremy lay on the bedroom floor while Ernie gave him CPR. I tried calling 911, but I couldn't get a good signal. Outside, the call finally went through. Crucial seconds to save my son.

Back inside, I took over giving CPR—never in a million years anticipating this very moment, trying to save our son's life.

It all seemed to happen in slow motion, as if we were underwater, muffled words, blurry vision. We held our breaths. The paramedics arrived and loaded my sweet boy into the ambulance. Ernie and I rode in back as they continued to try to resuscitate him.

At the hospital, the doctor put a hand on my shoulder. "He didn't make it."

I clutched my chest as tears poured down my face. Sobs and yells escaped my mouth. My mind and body went into shock.

There are no words to explain what it's like losing a child. None. Bleary-eyed and shattered, I slogged through the long hours. I was worn down, drained, and conquered, all the energy and motivation sucked out of me.

My life had gone from finally feeling full to being demolished beyond recognition. I was in an all-out war with my emotions: one minute, trying to stay strong, and the next, letting the feelings take over.

My family didn't attend Jeremy's wake or funeral because they didn't know about it. I didn't tell them. I didn't tell my mother or my sisters or brothers that he had passed away until two years after the funeral. Looking back, I'm not sure why I did that. Maybe I didn't want to burden them with another heartbreak. Maybe I knew I wouldn't find the comfort I longed for from them. Maybe I didn't know how to handle the agonizing, crushing pain. Maybe I was caught in a daze, sleepwalking through a nightmare I wanted so badly to forget. Maybe I was drowning in my own tears.

Months passed, and more followed. My grief set in. The voices in my head were ruthless, and by the day, they only grew louder. I tried to fix myself the same way I fixed a torn dress with a safety pin or how I put Band-Aids on Jacqueline and Jeremy when they were young. I resorted to glasses of wine to numb the pain of the darkest days of my life.

Most days, I didn't want to get out of bed, but I forced myself. Do it for Jacqueline, I'd tell myself. And then I'd pour myself a tall glass of red wine to dull the pain and sorrow. I would end up with a splitting headache the next day and then drink off the headache with more wine.

One time in the backyard, after a day of several glasses, I lost my balance and fell backward, hitting my head against a rock pillar and scraping my elbow. I clutched my head while blood soaked my shirt sleeve. Tears blurred my vision, and I cried hard, gulping for air. Weighted in guilt, blame, and shame, I had lost my way.

I couldn't live like this.

In the months to follow, I threw out the bottles of wine and started therapy. I turned to listening to Joyce Meyers videos and attending a local Christian church to find some guidance. Truth is, any mother who has to bury a child knows the emptiness that remains in her heart, and she has no choice but to live with it.

To this day, when people ask me how many kids I have, I tell them two. When they ask how old they are, I answer with Jacqueline's age and follow with Jeremy's as if he were still alive. Because they are our children for life, and our love for them is as infinite as the stars.

50

"Have you looked in the Arizona archives?" Ruth asked me while we were at one of our favorite restaurants in Phoenix—dinners out had become our Friday night thing.

Over the years after Julio's death, she and I had grown even closer. Being around her bright smile brought him back into my life. She was the one who reignited my search into Maurice Cash.

I hadn't tried the Arizona Archives. So the two of us went to downtown Phoenix and scrolled through black-and-white newspaper articles and columns from the '40s, '50s, and '60s. Old football scores, politics and elections, business openings and closings filled the fine print. We look for hours at the endless clippings.

Finally, in the *Phoenix Gazette*, just above a large toastmaster frying pan advertisement, were the obituaries dated December 1961, and Maurice C. Cash's name stood out in bold black letters.

I read fast, catching words that stood out: "Member of La Jolla Beach and Tennis Club," "attended the Episcopal Church," and "associated with the Anderson Clayton Cotton Farm for many years."

Then I read:

Semi-retired, he and his wife, Alice E., made frequent trips to La Jolla, Calif., where the couple's daughter, Elizabeth, attends school.

My heart stopped. I read the sentence again. And again. And then a fourth time. A wife. A daughter. I kept reading:

Besides his wife and daughter, survivors include a sister, Mrs. J. G. Oldman, and a nephew, W. D. Oldman.

Oldman.

I scrolled down, hoping for a photo, but nothing. I wanted a picture of him more than anything else. But having his death month and year, helped us find his death certificate.

Date of birth: July 11, 1901, in Oklahoma
Date of death: December 13, 1961

I was three, just as Amá had told me.

Father's Name: Henry Clay Cash
Mother's Name: Martha Hanna
Occupation: Rancher and Cotton Gin
Race: White

Soon after, I signed up to Ancestry.com for a DNA test. I spit into a vial and placed it back in the mail. Two months later, an email floated to the top of my inbox with "Your results are in!" Right there, the words before me told a different story than what I'd thought for decades.

According to Ancestry.com, my DNA was thirty-four percent Scandinavian and Norwegian, twenty-four percent Spanish and Portuguese, and eight percent British, Irish, and United Kingdom. In addition, I had a bit of French and German and a small percentage of West African.

A damn Heinz 57. Indeed, I wasn't one hundred percent Mexican.

A month later, I confirmed my identity even further with a second DNA test through 23andMe. On the last page of the results was a family tree of people who shared DNA with me. Two people with the last name Trejo—Abuelita Ángela's maiden name—and the rest of the pages filled with the last names Cash, Hanna, and Oldman.

I wanted more answers.

I thought back to Maurice's obituary. Reaching out to his daughter, Elizabeth Cash, was the next step. So I downloaded the Facebook app and searched her name. Several women appeared. I scrolled through the list, looking for any clue.

Elizabeth Cash from Whitefish, Montana, was as a full-time mom. Elizabeth Cash from Lansing, Michigan, worked in insurance. The Elizabeth Cash who went to Idaho University now lived in Lynnwood, Washington.

And then an Elizabeth Cash from La Jolla, California. I clicked on the image of a middle-aged woman with light skin and lank blond hair dressed in a flowing black dress. Most of Elizabeth's Facebook information was private, except her current location—Corolla, North Carolina.

I scrolled through her photos. Elizabeth's big, bold smile brightened each one. There was zero resemblance between the two of us. In most photos, another woman who looked like a younger Elizabeth stood next to her—I assumed it was her daughter.

I clicked the Message button and stared at the blinking cursor. What should I say? How did I let a complete stranger know we might be sisters? That we came from the same father? I took the simple approach, introducing my name and mentioning briefly that I believed she and I both had a connection to Maurice Cash. I hit Send.

After a month of no response from Elizabeth, I contacted the woman I assumed was her daughter. I messaged her with the same pitch. Another month went by—still no answer from either of them.

51

A year and a half later, on a crisp December evening, I stood over the bed, folding a load of laundry and forming neat mountains of clothes. My cell phone rang and I jumped. The incoming call was from North Carolina.

Spam, I thought, and silenced it. As I matched another pair of socks, it suddenly smacked me like a freight train—North Carolina? No. It couldn't be.

Just as I picked up the phone, a voicemail notification appeared on the locked screen. It was, indeed, Elizabeth Cash. In the message, she apologized for not responding to the Facebook message I had sent so long ago and mentioned she had received Steve's letter.

Letter? What letter? She wanted to connect, she said, suggesting that I call her back. Within seconds, I did, and she answered right away.

"Elizabeth, I'm so sorry I missed your call." I hoped she couldn't hear the desperation in my voice.

"I had no idea,"Minu, she said with a laugh. "When I received your message, I was so confused. I didn't know what to think of it."

"I can only imagine."

"You should know"—she cleared her throat—"I was adopted. Maurice and Alice took me in when I was just two years old. They officially adopted me when I was eight. So, yes, Maurice raised me, but I wasn't biologically his."

My brain stuttered for a moment as I let her words sink in. Not my biological sister. My heart sank, but I wasn't sure why. It's not like I didn't have plenty of sisters.

"When Steve's letter arrived in the mail," Elizabeth said, "I knew I needed to connect with you. Ironically, I received his letter on December thirteenth—Maurice's death anniversary." She paused. "To be frank, Minu, the whole thing has been quite a shock."

She continued with firsthand details about Maurice:

In the late 1920s, he had graduated from the University of Nebraska, earning a degree in business. A decade later, he and Alice married and settled in La Jolla, where Elizabeth would grow up. Coming out of the Great Depression in 1934, Maurice took advantage of Arizona's affordable ranchland and purchased a portion of property in Laveen, turning it into a cotton farm—the Anderson Clayton Cotton Farm. Anderson was his partner, and Clayton was Maurice's middle name.

For the next three decades, he traveled back and forth between Arizona and southern California, spending the weekdays on the farm and his weekends in La Jolla with Alice and Elizabeth.

In early 1960, Maurice and Alice donated the ranch land to the Laveen School District #59.

"Do you know why he did that?" I asked.

"No. Tax right-off? Maybe a business decision."

Had it been strictly a business decision? Perhaps Alice somehow found out about me and my mother and forced Maurice to sell the property.

"The district built an elementary school on the land and named it after my father. And then . . . a year later, in a town just over from the farm, Daddy died of carbon monoxide poisoning. The pilot light had gone out. . . . I was only fifteen."

"I'm so sorry," I whispered. I was sorry for both of us—sad for the both of us. That she didn't get more time with him, and I didn't get any.

"The rest of his property was sold after his death. My mother, Alice, later died in '87 of natural causes."

Elizabeth went to say that Steve had asked for a photo in his letter. She promised to send one.

"Oh, I would love that. Thank you," I paused for the pressing question sitting on the tip of my tongue. "Might I ask . . . what was he like?"

She didn't hesitate. "He was swarthy. Handsome. Patient. A wonderful man all around and a brilliant father. And so incredibly smart. He enjoyed the finer things in life—traveling overseas to Europe, Norway, Spain, whether for business or a vacation. Theology. Oh, and he loved to read. He'd read three or four books at a time."

I thought of my beloved Jeremy, who'd always had many books going, from biographies to mysteries to fantasies. He hadn't gotten it from Ernie's side of the family, and he certainly hadn't gotten it from the Becerras.

"In fact," Elizabeth said, her face lit by the memory, "when I got into trouble, his punishment would be to memorize Shakespeare. Can you believe that?"

How opposite two lives could be. I smiled. "He sounds incredible."

Every bit I learned helped me piece myself together. I couldn't help but imagine a world where Maurice didn't die from carbon monoxide poisoning. A world where he had sensed the poisonous gas, set down his poetry book and neat whiskey—or perhaps he liked wine like me—walked over to turn it off, and lived. Where one day, he would reach out to me through a phone call or email or letter. He'd introduce himself as my real father and ask if I'd like to meet for lunch, and he would tell me the truth my mother could never admit. We'd go on to have a wonderful father-daughter relationship, making up for the time we missed.

After about a half hour, my weighty, whirlwind of a conversation with Elizabeth began to slow. I thanked her for the call. We agreed to stay in touch and said our goodbyes.

On the other side of the wall, I heard Steve rattling pots and pans for dinner in the kitchen. I cornered him, gripping the kitchen counter and taking a long exhale. "You sneaky son of a gun," I mumbled.

"What?" He looked perplexed. "What'd I do?"

"I just got off the phone with Elizabeth Cash."

He shot me his devilish smirk. "And?"

It turned out that Steve hired a private investigator to find Elizabeth's address so he could send a two-page letter summing up my circumstances and explaining the connection between Elizabeth, Maurice, and me. Steve assured Elizabeth that we didn't want any money from her or the family, simply a photograph of Maurice. At the end, he included my phone number, encouraging her to reach out to me.

"And how are you with all this?" Steve asked.

I told him I was okay.

He pressed me again, "No, really. How are you?"

"Relieved, I think. Probably stunned. Maybe a mix of both. I mean, all of it is surreal. After all this time, I'm discovering that my biological father was a successful businessman who owned a farm and two homes, traveled the world, and read hundreds of books in his spare time."

I caught my breath and spoke slowly. "I wasn't just my mother's secret. I was his too."

A few weeks later, on Christmas Eve, a twinkling tree full of white lights, red wooden beads, and burgundy bows dominated the corner of our living room. Presents were piled underneath. Steve loved the holidays. On the other hand, I had little Christmas spirit, a repercussion from my childhood—the gypped gifts, the scrubby pine tree in our front yard with broken bulbs, and the disappointment every year.

Jacqueline and my seven-year-old grandson Hudson were there. Steve walked into the living room with a steaming mug of hot cocoa, cinnamon, and soaking marshmallows. "Shall we open one present?" He had started that Christmas Eve tradition.

"Yes!" Hudson said, jumping up and down. "Mimi first! Mimi first!"

"Okay, fine," I said, glancing under the tree for something with my name on it. "I'll take the sparkly one with the gold bow."

"No, not that one," Steve said. "I was going to save it for tomorrow." I raised my eyebrows in a question. "Okay, fine, you can open it. I'll just have to record it."

He reached for his iPhone on the end table.

"Oh no, you aren't recording this." I waved my hand. I was just getting over a cold and looked awful.

Steve smiled and nodded for me to open the present.

"Open it, Mimi! Open it!" Hudson shouted.

As I untied the bow and peeled back the wrapping paper, a framed sepia portrait of a man appeared. Stuck to the glass frame was a note that read, "Merry Christmas, Maurice C. Cash."

Time screeched to a halt. My eyes met soft almond-shaped eyes that stared back at me. He had a pale complexion with light-colored wavy hair combed around a defined part. A thin pointed-tip nose, just like mine, and a spitting image of my cheekbones. His ears looked like my son's. The photograph captured only the top of his shoulders and face, but I could see his suit and tie and how well-groomed he was. I smiled back at his warm, delicate smile and grazed my fingertips over his handsome face—the other half of me. He was exactly what I had expected.

My eyes filled with tears, but I didn't realize I was crying until my ribs and stomach began to heave. The cry continued up my body, through my throat, and burst into a sob.

What a comfort to finally know the answers. Where my almond eyes and high cheekbones originated, or why I have curly ringlets the color of the desert sand. For my entire life, I questioned this otherness I felt within my family. Now, for the first time, the part of me that felt excluded was gone. I held the missing puzzle piece of the story in my hands—the answer, the explanation, and the truth I had been searching for.

After seeing my real father's face, life turned into "before" and "after." His framed photo now stood on the mantel in my living room, and every now and then, when I'd walk into the living room, I'd catch a glimpse of him, returning the warm smile.

I thought about this handsome man with my mother way back when she was a young twenty-seven-year-old and he was almost sixty. Had it been true love between them? Had he thought she was the most beautiful woman he'd ever seen? Had he been stunned by her dark skin and red lips? Had she sung to him under the stars? Or had he run around with all the young, beautiful immigrant women?

The last time I had talked to Amá about Maurice, she recanted the story. Now, I wanted to confront her with the solid evidence I had discovered. She'd have no choice but to admit it was all true.

The Saturday after Christmas, I asked her to lunch. We went to Pete's Fish & Chips in Tolleson—her favorite. We sat outside on the patio, under a red umbrella and over baskets of greasy fish tenders and fries. There wasn't much to talk about except the weather and the latest movies.

"Amá, do you remember when we talked about Maurice?" I asked slowly. She bit a fry and fluttered a nervous chortle. "Well, we need to talk about him again. I took two DNA tests, and they both point to him."

My mother looked baffled, as if the answer were obvious, and she was annoyed she had to explain it once more. "Why are you bringing this up again? Your father, Julio, loved you. Enough of this."

"That's not what I'm getting at. I have proof he was my father. I've been asking you for such a long time. Why continue to deny it?"

She sat there, her eyes on her plate.

"He helped me out financially, Minu. With the house, with you kids, with a job, that's it. I'm eighty-seven years old. My memories are so distant now. There isn't much more I can remember about him."

On the way home from lunch, she and I rode in what seemed to be the foundation of our relationship: silence.

"There's something I want to show you, Amá." I reached over into the glove compartment and pulled out the photograph of Maurice. I held it in front of my mother.

She studied it, hardly blinking. "That's Mauricio," she whispered. "You look just like him." She turned to me. "I was going to take the secret to my grave, *mija.*"

52

*S*hortly after Christmas, I called Elizabeth to thank her for sending the portrait of Maurice. The conversation turned to our meeting in person. I offered to make the trip to North Carolina.

"How about sometime this spring?" I asked cautiously. "I could get a hotel and we could meet for dinner a night or two."

"Oh, don't be silly. You'll stay with me," Elizabeth said in a honeyed voice.

So I booked the flight, anxious to meet my long-lost sister, someone who had grown up with Maurice, eaten dinner with him, listened to his stories, and laughed at his jokes. Someone who had heard his voice, felt his goodnight hugs, and watched the way he hung his coat after a long day's work. Elizabeth's fifteen years with Maurice were the closest I would ever get to him.

At first, Steve was hesitant about the visit. "What if she resents you?" he asked one night at dinner. "What if you wreck her thoughts of the great man she knows as her father?"

"But what if we hit it off?"

Of course, I didn't tell my mother about Elizabeth or the trip to North Carolina. She wouldn't have supported me venturing out to learn more about her child's father she had tried so hard to forget. Not to mention, I was still angry with her. How could she not tell me the truth sooner? After all these years? I could have learned about Maurice earlier and met Elizabeth years before.

In mid-May, Steve took me to the airport. I'd been so frazzled and anxious about the trip that I forgot my driver's license, only realizing when I arrived at the airport. By the time Steve and I drove all the way home and then back to the airport, I missed my flight. I jumped on a later plane to Philadelphia, only to land and find out my connection to Norfolk had been canceled. I started questioning if I'd made a huge mistake making the trip. Maybe this was God's way of saying I shouldn't have dug so deep to find Maurice. Maybe things were meant to stay the way they were prior to discovering him. Perhaps Steve had been right.

After I found six other passengers stranded in the Philadelphia airport, all trying to get to Norfolk, we decided to rent a car together and drive the seven-hour jaunt throughout the night. Early the next morning, almost twenty-four hours from when the trip had first started, the six strangers and I arrived at Norfolk and returned the rental car.

I stood on the airport sidewalk with my luggage, tired eyes, and a gurgling stomach waiting for Elizabeth. A flurry of cars pulled over to drop off a traveler, and others picked up family members, greeting them with a hoot, a hug, and even a few tears.

What must Elizabeth be feeling, a woman in her seventies, to have a stranger reach out, claiming that we shared the same father? I suddenly grew nervous. My stomach started to heave like the damn ocean itself.

Should I greet her with a handshake? Would a hug be too much?

Finally, a dark car pulled up, and a tall, heavyset, short-haired blond woman got out. "Minu?" she asked.

"Yes!" I nodded.

Her jewel-blue eyes were as comely as the sky. I recognized her face from the Facebook photos. She held out her arms for an embrace. "Welcome, Minu."

On the long drive from Norfolk to the outer banks of Corolla, we covered the typical small talk: the grueling flight, the lovely North Carolina weather, dinner for the evening, and the five days ahead. Both of us avoided the beast of a topic that wove us together.

We drove through Corolla, gliding by three- and four-story beach houses with lush green lawns and wraparound porches overlooking the crimped seashores. Piers and lighthouses stretched out into the water, all the while standing sturdy against crashing waves. Soon, Elizabeth turned down a rocky driveway to a massive four-story dark green house with a wide balcony. When I stepped out of the car, the smell of rich salt cloaked me, reminding me I wasn't in the desert anymore.

Inside, I took in the front room of the house—well, it was more like a mansion. The ceilings soared high, and the walls were decorated with beachy wicker seashells and white framed photos of the ocean, as if straight out of a Tommy Bahama ad. I scanned the room for a picture of Maurice, a family photo, but saw nothing.

Elizabeth took one of my bags. "Please follow me. I'll show you to your room."

She led me down a long hallway to a small bedroom with blue floral wallpaper, a white bedspread, and a window cranked half open, allowing fresh, crisp air to envelope the room.

"Oh, Elizabeth, this is perfect. Thank you."

"Of course. Make yourself at home. Happy to have you."

Later, after a simple dinner of soup, salad, and bread, we sat on the sofa in her living room sipping dry dirty martinis.

"Tell me again—how many siblings do you have?" Elizabeth asked, plopping the olive into her mouth.

"Eight." I sipped the martini, the chill of the vodka running down my throat "Three sisters. Five brothers."

"Oh, how nice. I would have loved to have that many."

"It was . . . interesting," I let out a laugh and shook my head at the dysfunction she didn't have a clue about. "So what was your mother like? Alice."

Elizabeth's eyes sparkled. "She was wonderful. Everything you want in a mother. Kind. Smart. The most beautiful smile. She was lovely."

How I wished I could say those words about my own mother.

"They were both wonderful—Maurice and Alice. They had taken me in from my mother's older brother when I was just two years old. My biological mother had died in a car accident, and my real father was apparently incapable of raising me." She shrugged. "I guessed I lucked out."

"Dealt a good hand." I paused. "Do you think your mother knew about me?" A martini is the key to liquid courage.

Elizabeth took her time before answering, gazing out the window. "Not sure. She never mentioned anything."

"If you don't mind me asking, how was it growing up with him as a father?"

She went on to mention the dozens of countries she traveled to flying first class, the pretty dresses Alice would buy her from the department store, and the private-school education. She and I came from totally different worlds.

And then she smiled slightly as if lost in a warm, cozy memory. "My father and I read books: Shakespeare, Mark Twain, Harper Lee. He loved the historical stories." She paused. "You have his curly hair. You even look a bit like my grandmother—his mother—Martha."

I nodded slowly, letting the validation sink through me, hoping she would continue talking about him or his mother.

Elizabeth set her martini glass on the table before us. "Wait here. I have something for you."

When she came back into the room, she held out a fist and dropped a tiny burgundy pin into my hand. Printed in gold were Delta Tao Delta symbols.

"It was my father's—*our* father's," she whispered. "From his University of Nebraska fraternity. I want you to have it."

I studied the worn edges and the way it gleamed in the lamp's light. Something so small holding sentimental value as large as the sea. He had been here. He had held this. A piece of him right here in my hands. I pictured him pinning it onto the collar of his varsity jacket or maybe a sports coat or even his book bag.

"Oh, thank you, Elizabeth. This means the world to me."

53

*I*n 2018, my marriage of almost two decades began to unravel. Perhaps sometimes people simply fall out of love, turning into oil and water, ceasing to exist together.

Steven and I were still living the luxury life—expensive clothes, cars, jewelry—but I had an empty heart. I blamed the money for getting between us. He blamed me for letting our love die.

"Isn't this everything you ever wanted?" Steve asked me.

But it wasn't. He was comfortable with the extravagant spending, and I wasn't. I didn't want it, any of it. So we sold it all. The cottage in La Jolla and the yacht on Lake Pleasant, beginning the dreadful process of separating from each other.

Ringing in my ears was a conversation I'd had with my son before he passed away. We were in La Jolla drinking coffee together early one Sunday, watching the oranges and yellows from the sun brighten the horizon and listening to the city wake up.

"Mom, are you happy?"

"Of course, I'm happy," I said, an exaggerated chirp in my voice to rest my case. "What do you mean?"

"You and Steve have all this money . . . but I know you—you're not happy."

His words stung.

Although 2018 was tumultuous for Steve and me, it also marked the fiftieth anniversary of the Maurice C. Cash Elementary School. Elizabeth and I agreed to donate an enlarged portrait of Maurice, along with a brief history of him, to the school to honor his name and commend yet another successful decade.

"He'd be so proud his name lives on through a school," Elizabeth told me during one of our phone calls. "It was always so important to him to have the best education."

In mid-September, Elizabeth flew in from North Carolina. She, Jacqueline, and I met the school's principal and superintendent to present our gift. They thanked us again and again, hanging the portrait in the school hallway for all students and teachers to see.

I didn't tell my mother about the donation or even mention Elizabeth being in town—I'd accepted she wouldn't have cared. This was a part of her life she clearly didn't want to be reminded of. My siblings wanted nothing to do with it either. One time, when Irma stopped at my house to pick up some of my homemade tomatillo salsa, she asked me who the white man was in the picture on my mantel.

"Well, Irma . . ." I paused to search for the right words. "This might come as a shock." I paused again, examining her gentle face. "That man is actually my biological father. I took a DNA test that led me to him, and Amá admitted it."

Her face remained blank, unemotional, an expression my mother so often wore.

"Oh," was all she said to a secret so deep and tender. She didn't press me, and I offered nothing else on the matter.

A day after the donation of Maurice's portrait, Elizabeth and I road-tripped the five-hour drive to Glendale, California. It had been decades since she had visited Maurice's grave, and she wanted me to join her.

"Let's go see our dad together," she said with a kind smile.

The trip was just the sister bonding I had hoped for. The conversation flowed nonstop as we listened to eighties hits.

"Oh my gosh, Minu, our father was so intelligent," Elizabeth said. "He was on the brink of patenting a machine that thinned out the cotton. You and I would have been so rich."

When we made it to Los Angeles, we stopped to have dinner with two of Elizabeth's cousins on Alice's side of the family. Over delicious sushi rolls, they told me how I resembled Maurice.

"You even have his mannerisms," one cousin said.

Although hearing those words was wonderful, I only thought of Elizabeth and how those words might have stung. The next day, I asked her if the comment about me looking like Maurice bothered her.

"No, not at all. It's true. You look just like him."

We pulled through the arching metal sign that welcomed us into the Glendale cemetery. Hundreds upon hundreds of headstones stretched out before us, some complimented with colorful flowers blossoming new life into the soft soil. Some gravestones lay bare. We followed the cemetery dirt road to a massive white mausoleum with stained-glass windows and a pointed steeple reaching to the sky. Inside the building were breathtaking marble replicas of Michelangelo's sculptures.

Elizabeth led me to a grave site embedded in the wall, our father's name engraved on the stone plate and Alice Cash's next to his. I grazed my hand around his name, the closest I would ever get to him physically.

I bowed my head for a prayer with my dad, *Psalms* 139:13–16:

Oh yes, you shaped me first inside then out; you formed me in my mother's womb. I thank you, High God—you're breathtaking! Body and soul, I am marvelously made! I worship in adoration— what a creation!

You know me inside and out, you know every bone in my body; you know exactly how I was made, bit by bit, how I was sculpted from nothing into something.

Like an open book, you watched me grow from conception to birth; all the stages of my life were spread out before you. The days of my life all prepared before I'd even lived one day.

54

*I*n May 2020, Amá was rushed to the hospital with chest pains and shortness of breath. The doctors concluded she was suffering from water retention and a leaky valve in her heart.

When I made it to the hospital, I raced to her room in a panic. She was dressed in a blush pink nightgown, her hair somehow perfect and hardly a wrinkle on her pretty face. Her lovely dark skin had turned a grayish pale, and she looked smaller, more delicate and feeble. The food tray was untouched.

I stretched down to hug her. "Amá, are you all right? How are you feeling?" She smelled like antiseptic soap mixed with a leftover hint of bargain perfume. Our cheeks touched. I could feel the heat radiating from her soft skin.

"*No te apudas.* I'm f-fine," she wheezed. The doctors warned us it was difficult for her to breathe. "Why . . ."—she let out a breath—"why are you fighting w-with Steve?"

I hadn't had the chance to tell her Steve and I were officially separated—it had been a rocky two years divvying up assets and finances, a long-drawn-out separation. Clearly, one of my siblings had gotten to her first. But right then, it wasn't worth getting into the details with her.

"What're you talking about, Amá?" I whispered, cupping her icy hands. "I'm not fighting with Steve."

"Not w-worth it," she huffed. "Stop fighting."

In a way, I found comfort in my mother's cross words.

Over the next two days, my siblings and I took turns staying in the hospice room with her. Somberness filled the air as we waited silently. It seemed as if we all knew what we were about to lose but still pondered if we were ready for it.

And then Uncle Chalio arrived. He had driven from California to be with his only sister one last time.

He rushed into her room. "María, María, wake up. It's your brother. I've made it."

Amá lifted her head from the pillow. "Chalio," she murmured. A weak smile spread across her face. "*Mi hermano*, thank you for coming."

Uncle Chalio bent down next to her, holding her brittle hand in his palms.

"I wouldn't miss being here, *hermana*," Uncle Chalio whispered ever so softly.

Amá took her last breath that night.

I stood shoulder to shoulder with my six siblings under a black canopy, trying to escape the scorching Arizona sun. As the men of the family pulled the casket from the polished hearse, a heavy silence fell over the crowd. The ivory casket was adorned with elegant gold handles that glittered in the bright afternoon light. At least Amá was going out in style.

The pallbearers made their way across the cemetery and carefully set the coffin on the raised bier that looked over a dark, gaping hole in the ground. The priest began the service with an angelic Spanish hymn, bringing a fresh wave of tears to the mourners. A sob crept up my throat, and I swallowed hard to force it down.

As stoic as she was, a part of me went with my mother that day—a sliver of my heart. I closed my eyes and pictured her in the tiny kitchen from my childhood, tending to a sizzling pan that cooked her famed homemade tortillas. A hint of leftover cherry red lipstick stuck on her lips, and her dark hair parted delicately around her beautiful face. As she sang, she tapped her palm on her hip to keep rhythm, her beautiful voice filling the house.

When the funeral hymn ended, the priest motioned to my siblings and me with his tattered Bible. "If any of the daughters or sons of María would like to say a few words, now is the time."

The seven of us swayed from side to side, waiting for someone to speak up, until on impulse, I stepped forward. Scanning the familiar faces, from old to young, I took a deep, shaky breath.

"All of us here mourn for Amá, the matriarch of our family." I spoke in Spanish, my voice echoing through the solemn air. My three older sisters, Irma, Dolores, and Esméralda, stood in their dark dresses, their eyes red and puffy. My younger brothers, Danny, Ruben, and Sammy, gazed back with hollow stares.

"Our family has had countless heartbreaks over the years. It's been tough. Horrible at times." I paused, and with a deep breath, my voice strengthened. "But now is when Amá would want us to examine our lives and consider taking a better direction."

I raised my hand to the icy blue sky to reach for my mother one last time. "Amá, take care of our loved ones up there."

As I stepped back under the awning, a hand gently squeezed my shoulder. Uncle Chalio, his worn face full of sadness.

The priest finished with a blessing, and the crowd turned toward the road lined with cars. One by one, my siblings followed without a word, scattering into the sea of people.

"Walk with me, Minu," Uncle Chalio said. He limped toward Amá's grave site, leaning into his wooden cane. I followed him, keeping his slow pace, staring at the coffin topped with plush red roses—Amá's favorite. She'd be buried next to Apá, just as they had planned.

A few feet from the casket, Uncle Chalio braced himself against his cane and took hold of my hand, giving it a weak squeeze. His bottom lip quivered. "I know she wanted to take it to her grave," he whispered, "but there's something you should know."

His eyes searched mine. "I've been wanting to tell you this for a long time, *mija*. You are the daughter of Maurice Cash. You are a Cash." He held my hand next to his chest. "I worked as Mr. Cash's chauffeur back in the day—in the '50's—driving him all around town. He was an elegant and well-liked man—you would've liked him."

"Amá told me about him. But then she said she was making it all up."

"She *told* you?"

I explained about the conversation I had overheard at Apá's funeral, the DNA tests, and how I had confronted Amá.

"Every time I saw you, I could see Maurice," he said. "But I swore to your mother that I wouldn't say anything. I'm so sorry, Minu."

Here was the validation I had wanted for so long.

Uncle Chalio looked off into the distance. "When your mama got pregnant with you, your papa, Julio, wasn't around. The day you were born, I drove her to the hospital. She told me how scared she was, but I assured her the secret was safe with me, and I'd do everything in my power to help her." His voice shook. "When you were born, she was stunned when you came out light-skinned with curly blond hair." He let out a chuckle. "She thought her Mexican genes would override Mr. Cash's."

Uncle Chalio sighed. "Yet when your papa came back to town, he never said a thing—he was so excited to see a new baby girl—his Güera. That's when Mr. Cash helped your mama and the family move to Cashion. And around this time is when I moved to California. Mr. Cash helped me get on my feet with money and a job—I couldn't have done it without him. For the last sixty years, every time I saw you, it's all I could think about. I tried, Minu. I tried to get her to tell you. She wouldn't budge. But you deserve to know the truth, and that's it."

Hot tears streamed down my face. I leaned into my uncle, breathing in his words, and he pulled me closer. In the cloudless blue sky, three doves perched on a telephone pole caught my attention. Their bold cap of white feathers glistened in the desert sun. Three little angels watching down from heaven. I like to believe it was Amá, my son, and my father.

"Oh, and one more thing," Uncle Chalio said. "Maurice named you. He was so proud of your name."

A gift from my father that was mine, and mine alone.

Epilogue

*S*ix months after Amá's passing, Steve and I made our divorce final. The end of my mother's life overlapped with a new beginning in my own.

My phone rang. My attorney. "Did you receive the papers?" he asked.

The early sun was beginning to rise, filtering through the windows of my quiet new home. "No, not yet." I started flipping through the stack of unopened mail on my kitchen counter.

"Well, I'll deliver the good news to you directly then. You are now officially Ms. Minu Cash."

I froze. "Just like that?"

"Yes, just like that. Congratulations, Minu."

I thanked him and hung up, swirling with emotions. *Minu Cash.* I whispered my new name. It sounded . . . destined, like an undoing, a clean slate, and a new awakening all at the same time. Maurice C. Cash smiled at me from his portrait on the living room mantel.

In that moment, the world seemed different, more alive. The pink hibiscus bush in my backyard stood taller and stronger, the blossoms more vibrant than I'd ever noticed. The cloudless sky was brighter and more vivid, as if it had been painted with a fresh coat of blue.

Over the years, so many people had reminded me of the popular adage "Time heals all wounds." Perhaps there was some truth to that. Maybe time didn't heal all the wounds we endure in a lifetime, but perhaps its constant ticking mended some and at least eased the rest.

Time allowed me to accept that this indeed was my life. The passing hours, days, and years helped me recognize that I was made up of three people.

I'd recently hung a picture of my mother and me on my refrigerator, the first one of us I had displayed in decades. Though restrained, neglectful, and apathetic for most of her life, she possessed a strength I inherited. Over her almost ninety-one years, she faced hardships and tragedies yet never wavered, no matter what mayhem she had to navigate, making her a true survivor. Fortunately, I'm not defined by my moments of failure and trepidation, but on the days I must muster the strength to keep fighting, I can only thank my mother for the resilience.

The second person is the father I grew up with, Apá. It's true that I struggled with him for most of my life. I blame a mental sickness that went untreated. Still, a part of me will always be a Becerra—the daughter of María and Julio.

And the third person is my biological father, Maurice C. Cash, who provided me with not only my curly hair and high cheekbones, but the urge to read, travel, and strive for an education. While I never had the opportunity to be nurtured by him or had the chance to learn from him, I believe that inheriting certain parts of him was his gift to me.

Not long ago, I was in line at a Walgreens in Glendale and a short, scrubby man with a ponytail was paying for a red Gatorade at the checkout counter. He was fidgety, his shirt loose and bedraggled, and his worn shoes were coming apart at the seams. I assumed he was homeless.

The cashier scanned the Gatorade, and the man swiped his card.

"Declined," the cashier said.

The man swiped his card again. Declined. And again. Declined. He threw a skittish tantrum with every rejection, grunting and murmuring to himself. After he was declined yet again, I stepped toward the counter. "Here, sir," I said, raising my credit card. "Allow me—"

When the man turned to me, my heart stopped. I instantly recognized those fragile brown eyes, except now they looked glassy, tired, and bloodshot. His face was thinner and bonier than when I'd seen him last, nearly four years before at Amá's funeral.

The way his face lit up, I knew he recognized me too. Little Sammy.

"Güera! Oh, I can't believe this. It's you!" he shrieked, wrapping me in a big hug.

"Sammy! It's been too long."

"Too long, Güera. Years too long." He pulled back and smiled.

As I was about to ask him what he had been up to, his face changed from animated and surprised to serious. He put his hands on my shoulders and pulled me toward his face. His breath reeked of cigarettes and alcohol.

"I need your help," he whispered, our foreheads almost touching. He swayed from side to side frantically, like he couldn't keep his balance. "I-I-I need you to take me back to your house. I'm being hunted by t-two women." He held up two fingers. "Two women, Minu. They're out to kill me."

The cashier eyed me suspiciously. I excused us and led my little brother away from the checkout.

"Sammy, what're you talking about?" I saw a quick glimpse of Apá on his face.

"No, no. You don't understand," he said, his voice now raised. "Th-th-they're trying to kill me, Güera. I-I need your help! Please!"

The cashier snapped her head in our direction. "Everything all right over there?" she asked.

I squeezed his arm. "Shh, Sammy, you need to keep your voice down. I'll help you."

As much as I wanted to take my youngest brother home with me that day, I wasn't equipped to give him the proper care he needed. But he was my brother, for better or worse.

"Wait here." I stepped a few feet away and dialed my sister's number. She would know what had been going on with our youngest brother.

"Praise God! I'm glad you found him," Esméralda said. "He ran away from the damn rehab center. They've been looking for him since last week!"

I looked at my brother, who was watching me with wide eyes. He twiddled his hands, shifting from one foot to the other, his drained face stiff and uncomfortable.

"He's saying two women are trying to kill him," I whispered.

"He's probably hallucinating, Minu. Get him back pronto."

My heart sank as I watched a police car drive Sammy away from the Walgreens and back to the rehab center.

As for the rest of my siblings, Esméralda inherited our childhood home when my mother died. She ended up selling it and splitting the proceeds four ways with our remaining brothers, Ruben, Danny, and Sammy. With her share, Esméralda bought a teardrop trailer, parked permanently on her youngest son's yard in Phoenix.

Sadly, Sammy used the money to feed his drug and alcohol addiction. He is never out of rehab long enough to hold a steady job. Ruben has had his own struggles, but now lives in Cashion with his wife of twenty years.

Dolores moved to Mexico, and Irma lives on the outskirts of Cashion. Amá had been right about Danny being sick like Apá, but with medication, his condition is stable. He lives with Irma and her family, and I help manage his health and disability.

Out of my siblings, I stay in touch with Irma and Danny the most, talking on the phone most weeks and sometimes eating at our favorite Mexican restaurant in Tolleson. We often get together to celebrate our birthdays, making up for all the cake we didn't have when we were kids.

Every weekday morning, I call Jacqueline on her way to work, and we usually chat about her two young sons. Over the years, she and I have developed a strong bond, something I never had with my own mother. Blessed with a generous spirit, Jacqueline always asks me if I need anything. More than my daughter, she has become my best friend.

Her ongoing love and support have helped me resolve any lingering bitterness, heal my heart, and see the world through a different lens, like a black-and-white movie turned into color—more magical and wondrous in the end.

For the first time in my life, I can fully accept myself. I am a white girl, I am a Mexican, and I have a story.

I am Minu Cash, a grown woman who now knows where she came from and who, at last, has found peace.

Maurice Cash. 1960.

Uncle Chalio and me. 2012.

Acknowledgments

I am deeply grateful to Courtney Schrauben Haik. Without you, this book would never have been possible. You not only assisted in the creation but also provided a safe space for me to revisit a lifetime of buried memories. Your expertise, writing talents, and creativity have left an ingrained mark on this memoir for which I will be forever grateful. Thank you for believing in me.

To Sandra Jonas Publishing, I extend my heartfelt gratitude for taking a chance on my story and providing a platform for it to be shared with the world. Your belief in the power of my story has made all the difference.

To the remarkable women who served as beta-readers: Darlene Ziebell, Kristin Travis, Patricia L. Brooks, and Rose Garlasco. Your invaluable feedback and insights played a pivotal role in shaping the manuscript.

A special thank-you to Maurice's daughter for graciously opening her home and heart to me, sharing cherished memories and photographs of Maurice. Your support means the world, and I am deeply grateful for the opportunity to honor his legacy through these pages.

Finally, to my sister-in-law Ruth, for her encouragement and steadfast presence throughout this journey. Your grounding influence carried me through the most challenging times.

About the Author

Minu Cash is an Arizona native born in 1958. She received her dental hygiene degree from Rio Salado College. When she's not immersed in a good book, Minu enjoys traveling and delighting her loved ones with her culinary creations—her spicy salsa is a crowd pleaser.

But her heart truly belongs to her family, especially her grandchildren, who bring endless joy to her life. She lives in Glendale, Arizona, just north of her childhood neighborhood. *The Painted Pink Dress* is her first book.

For more information, visit MinuCash.com.

Printed in the USA
CPSIA information can be obtained
at www.ICGtesting.com
LVHW041319140624
783120LV00007B/592

9 781954 861190